MW00780921

Arminius and Thusnelda
Versus Rome

Michael Kramer at Australian Base Camp, Nui Dat, Vietnam October 1968

Michael G Kramer OMIEAust.

ISBN 978-0-6488219-5-3

COPYRIGHT © 2021

Book Titles by Michael G Kramer OMIEAust.

Arminius & Thusnelda Versus Rome

A Castle of Doomsday

A Gracious Enemy

Anglo-Saxon Invasion

Now What?!!

For the Love of Armin

Full Circle for Mick

Table of Contents

Origins of the Germanic People

I am the ghost of Adalhard, an ancient Germanic warrior. Adalhard is an ancient Germanic name with two parts, with Adal meaning brave and hard meaning hardy. While I was alive, I was a noble of the clan called Amandid of the Germanic tribe called Cherusci. My people were extremely independent in both nature and outlook. This perhaps making a future clash between the Romans and us at some point in the future inevitable. I will now tell you of the goings-on that took place and finally resulted in the Roman army leaving Germania forever. The events that proceeded this and the events after my people's great victory over the cruel and arrogant Roman invaders.

Tracing the roots of the Germanic tribes of the Teutonic branch of the present European population before the first conflicts with the Romans has proved to be complicated. The only thing to be accomplished is the confirmation of historians' opinions that the ancestors of the Germanic tribes had much in common with the Cimmerian, Celtic and Slavic Clans. They migrated originally from the Caspian Sea areas, extending from the Caucasian and median alps' foothills through Transoxiana to the Ural and Volga steppes.

All these nations were known to Greek historians and geographers by the name of *Scythians.* That name was never used by these races of people themselves. In general, we can say that *Scythians* was a name used to describe the many people who had the characteristics of being tall, robust, fair-haired, and blue-eyed. These people continued to occupy the vast plains of the Oxus and Iaxartes, and they were nomads right up to the birth of Christ. They migrated and spread themselves from the Caspian to the Great Wall

1

of China before eventually settling in areas of Finland and Sweden.

The origin of the aboriginal Germanic tribes (Aboriginal – the word is of Latin origin and means original inhabitant) living in ancient Germania is unknown. During the Bronze age, Germanic people lived in Finland, Southern Sweden, and all the Jutland peninsular. Including northern Germania between the Ems and Oder rivers and their territory covered all land through to the Harz mountains.

The tribes known as Gepideans, Goths and Vandals lived in areas between the Oder and Vistula rivers near the Baltic coast. The Germanic tribes also migrated southwards and westwards, driving out the Celtic people who were at the time living in large areas of Germania. The Roman historian Tacitus thought of the Germanic tribes as an indigenous race with pure blood that was unmingled with either conquerors or colonialists' foreign stock. (Greenwood, 1836)

The Germanic tribes were all fiercely independent in both nature and outlook. Given that the Romans intended to make conquests and subjugate everyone with whom they made contact, future clashes between my people and the arrogant, exceedingly cruel Romans were inevitable. I will now tell you of the goings-on that took place in many different areas and different countries.

I must tell you of these events so that you will understand why and how my people were able to wipe out the Roman invaders of Germania. Something that made it very difficult for the Romans to subjugate my people is that ancient Germanic people did not live in towns and cities. They preferred to live in tiny clusters of homes that could not even be called hamlets. They would assemble in large formations for joint defensive or offensive operations against an enemy.

Cherusci Nation and the Romans

When the first Roman traders contacted the Cherusci people, it was found that the Cherusci women placed a high value upon the Roman red cloth, which was obtainable from the traders who were after the amber and feathers of the eider goose held by Germanic tribes. So it was that slowly, over time, a trading and business relationship developed between the Cherusci tribe and the Romans.

That was further developed to the point where many of the nobles of the Cherusci liked to send their sons to Rome for Roman education and training, which they felt would be for the good of their people.

Some of the most important of the tribes were the Chatti, who lived at the mouth of the Weser. To their south lived the Cherusci. These were the people of Arminius or Armin, if you prefer his Germanic name. The Suebi lived near present-day areas of Mecklenburg, Brandenburg, Saxony and Thuringia.

Suebic people such as the Lombards were in the coastal regions between the Havel and Ems Rivers. Some of the other tribes were the Hermunderuri, Marcomanni and Bastarne People. These made up some of the primary original or aboriginal Germanic tribes. Other tribes followed at later dates through the process of amalgamation of two or more tribes. Two examples of these were the Franks and the Saxons, who became dominant at later dates.

So that you can readily understand that many of the people in this story were first active in other places, we must return to the earlier historical times. So, we will look at events of Gaul, Germania, Judea, Rome, and Syria so that the significant events that caused follow-on effects at later dates are adequately covered.

To have a complete understanding of how and why a few hundred of my people's warriors were able to annihilate the Roman army in Germania, we must study the armour, weapons and minor infantry tactics of both the Germanic warriors and the Roman legions. We shall also see the use of ancient forms of artillery and Roman war machines in general.

Roman Army Ranks

Consul	– a military commander who was also an elected official with military and civic duties, he usually commanded several Legions
Praetor	- appointed military commander of a legion or grouping of legions
Legatus Legionis	- the legate or overall legion commander
Tribune	- second in command of a legion
Prefect	- Third in command of Roman legions
Primus pilus	- commanding Centurian for the first cohort – senior centurion of the legion

Centurian	- basic commander of the century. Prestige depended upon which cohort the Centurian was part of
Decurio	- commander of the cavalry sub-unit or *turma*
Aquilifier	- standard bearer of a legion – a position of great prestige
Signifier	- one for each century, handled the financial matters and decorations
Optio	- equivalent to a sergeant of modern armies, second in command to the centurion
Cornicen	- horn blower or signaller
Imaginifer	- carried the standard bearing the emperor's image
Decanus	- equivalent to a corporal, commanded seven men

Roman Army Force Organisation

Ala – Latin for "Wing" or in its plural form, *alae* was the term used to name military formations of cavalry. From Emperor Augustus's time, the term ala was used to name smaller units of the Imperial Army consisting of up to five hundred and twelve (512) men. It was a pure cavalry unit of the non-citizen auxilia corps. The Ala was made up of sixteen sub-units called Turma, which had thirty-two (32) men each.

Auxilia and Velites - were allied contingents, providing light infantry and specialist fighting services like archers, slingers, or javelin-men.

Contubernium – smallest unit of the Roman heavy infantry was eight men commanded by a Decanus.

Centuria - eighty men commanded by a centurion. Unless it was the first century with one hundred men, they were the legion's best soldiers.

Cohort - the cohort consisted of six centuries or a total of four hundred and eighty to six hundred fighting men. Added to these were the officers, as well as the supporting units. Such as the cavalry serving in the wings and other specialist units.

Legion – was made up of ten (10) cohorts and generally numbered five thousand men.

Field Army – a grouping of several legions and auxiliary cohorts.

Equites – Each Legion was supported by five hundred and twelve cavalrymen (equites). That gave the legion an additional five hundred and twelve troopers plus their officers.

Entering the Roman Training System

It was the custom of the Cherusci Tribe to send the sons of the nobility for training to Rome so that they would become better leaders. That meant that the boys who were fortunate enough to receive the Roman training were schooled in mathematics, Latin literature, basic engineering, and military subjects. The boys quickly learned to become highly disciplined and highly organised. In return for this valuable training, the boys would routinely enter service with the Roman army in various Roman Empire parts outside of Germania.

In 13 B.C., three young boys from the Cherusci tribe entered the Roman schooling and military training systems. The three boys were Armin, his brother Flavus and me. When we entered the Roman education and military structure in 13 B.C., Armin was five, and I was six years old. We found that the Romans changed various people's names to make their names sound more -Latin-like.

For that reason, they changed Armin's name to Arminius; they also changed his brother's name, which they changed to Flavius. After completing the educational and military training, we were all put into service with the Roman army as auxiliary cavalry officers.

We had all travelled in the company of an escort of twenty-five Cherusci warriors from the north-west of Germania. When we all finally arrived at the military academy barracks in Rome, we were met and greeted by an old ex-officer of the Roman army. He was a tall and erect man who carried himself with dignity and appeared to be highly self-disciplined. He spoke to Leofric, who was in command of the Germanic warrior escort of us three Cherusci boys.

He said, *"Warriors, my name is Julius Septimius, and I am the chief instructor at this Roman Officer Academy and Training Barracks. The three boys you have bought with you shall live and learn by Roman rules, and by the time they return to your homeland in Germania, they will be Roman army veterans. First, they have to prove themselves, after which they will be granted both Roman citizenship and the* status of officers in the Republic of Rome's army by the Senate of Rome[1]!"

He then spoke to each boy in turn. He began by talking to me and then Flavus and followed that with speaking to Armin. Speaking to Armin, he said, *"What is your name, boy?"* Armin was defiant from the start, and he spoke to the Roman. He said, *"Julius Septimius, I am a Cherusci Prince, and my name is Armin. I fully realise that you are just a Roman and that you are not of the nobility. I realise that you may not like to do so, but when you speak to me, remember your place and address me as 'Your Royal Highness! I am five years old'"*

That was, I thought, the first of the mistakes made by Armin. The Roman did not like being spoken to in such a manner by a boy who was five years old. Now enraged, Julius Septimius yelled, *"That is more than enough of your bullshit, boy! Get it into your head that you are here to learn and obey! Although I like your fiery spirit, I will not tolerate any disrespect from you or anyone else! While you are here and you will be here for the next ten years, you will obey my staff members and me!*

I am now going to give you your Roman name. After all, we cannot have a Roman serving cavalry officer who has a Germanic name! That will not do at all! From this day onwards, your name shall be Arminius!" Having said that, Julius Septimius turned his attention to me. He said, *"And you, boy, what is your name and age?"* I answered with, *"I am Adalhard, six years old, and I am a Cherusci noble in the service of Prince Armin. Although I see that you are in*

---

[1] During the times of B.C., and before the emperors, Rome was a republic.

charge here. I believe that you should be more polite to Prince Armin. That you have changed his name to Arminius is both the wrong thing to do, and it is an insult to us!"

If he was angry before when speaking to Armin, he now became enraged and shouted at me. He said, *"You impertinent Germanic upstart! The name of the Cherusci Prince shall remain as Arminius as I have already stated! As for you, your name shall now be Adalhardius. That way, you shall have a Latinised name, as does your prince! As for the third member of this group, the brother of Arminius shall have his name changed from Flavus to Flavius! Get used to being called by your new Roman names, and make sure that you all answer to them! I can see that Flavius is some years older than you two boys. What age is he?"* Flavius called out, *"Julius Septimius, I am Flavius, and I am ten years old!"* Julius Septimius said, *"Very well then, it seems strange that you Flavius are five years older than your brother, but we shall carry on and complete your training!"*

He then left, and for a while, the three of us were left alone. When he returned two hours later, he was in the company of two very hard and tough-looking non-commissioned officers. One of them approached Arminius and started talking to him. He said, *"The Roman Commandant of this Officer Academy has told me that you are a Germanic prince and that you think that you somehow have the right to challenge what he said to you! That is not good enough! While you are here, you shall always address the Commandant as Sir, or Commandant or else by his name of Julius Septimius after you have his permission to do so! As for myself and the other instructors in this academy, you shall address us as Optio in my case!"* He then hit Arminius

9

in the face with his clenched fist. His next act was to spank Arminius using a stick.

Having finished, he said, *"Get it through your thick Germanic heads that you are here to learn and obey all Romans at all times! Arminius has suffered a small example of what will be done to all of you if you are not obedient and completely loyal!*

With that, he grabbed me and began punching me. He said, *"Adalhardius, you are now going to be punished in the same way as your Cherusci prince has been."* He suddenly hit me right in the stomach area, which made me double up. He then spanked me with a stick until it broke.

Meanwhile, all of this was seen by Flavius, who reacted by yelling at the Optio. He yelled, *"That will do, Optio. I am disgusted by what you have done to my brother and his companion!* That resulted in the Optio grabbing hold of Flavius and hitting him repeatedly. So it was that on our first day at the Officer Academy, we had messed up badly, and we were at odds with the instructional staff. Not a good beginning!

Later that day, as we passed a classroom while on our way towards the weapons training areas, we overheard the commandant speaking with his non-commissioned officers. He talked to the Optios.

He said, *"Gentlemen, in the three new arrivals, we have excellent prospects of making very effective Roman Cavalry Officers of all three of them. I am impressed with the fighting spirit that these boys have. That spirit must become organised and channelled into disciplined action on behalf of Rome! See to it that it is done and that the boys become outstanding Roman Cavalry Officers!"* Our training commenced and continued until we were all officers in the cavalry units serving Rome. We were taught how to make mathematics a lot easier by learning things like the time's table. An example of this is, $(9 \times 9) = 81$.

Status of Ancient Germanic Women

The ancient Germanic tribes thought that their women had many prophetic powers, so their influence was such that it resulted in them having a greater status than that held by women in other societies. It was usual for the Germanic woman to share the dangers of the battlefield with her husband, and so, she had the right not only to love and cherish but also to take part in battles if necessary. That resulted in her having the right to advise upon military matters.

Firstly, she would cheer her husband onwards to battle, and she, along with her children, was the most valued applauder of the Germanic warrior's deeds. With the children being taken to safe areas under the supervision of elder women, the other women and girls would get closer to where their men were engaging the enemy. They would have with them their battle axes and other weapons. They would enter the fight if their men did badly against the enemy. Often, the women would be scornful of their male partners and scold them.

Moral and Funereal Customs of Germanic Tribes

Hospitality was strictly observed; both friends and strangers had the security of a welcome under the Germanic people's roofs. My people had a great fondness of feasting and binge drinking, often to excess, compared to other people's drinking habits. All public assemblies, private meetings and family gatherings were used as excuses for this feasting and drinking. That included the time after funerals.

The Germanic tribes cremated their dead, with the warrior's weapons always being burnt with his body and sometimes, his war-horse as well. The only monument to him was a mound of soil or stones heaped over his remains by his relatives and friends.

No tears were shed over his ashes, but each family member deeply felt the grief over the loss of the warrior, which continued for a long time. The women were left to mourn the dead while the men believed it to be their duty to enshrine the memory of the dead warrior by trying to equal or surpass his feats.

Military Habits

As war was the only way of gaining riches or distinction, Germanic youth were eager for war so that they could plunder their enemies and obtain military fame. If a long period of peace came about, they offered their services as warriors to neighbouring tribes who were at war.

Their chiefs would provide them with arms, dress, and decorations while entertaining them with feasts and banquets. The cost of which was paid from plunder taken from enemies. At all times, they preferred fighting enemies and the possibility of getting severe wounds or death to cultivating the ground and then waiting for a resulting crop.

The offensive weapons of the Germanic tribes were spears, and the most favoured weapon was a long two-edged sword. The tribes who specialised in cavalry operations also liked to use a lance they called 'framea'. A long-curved shield was their only defensive equipment.

The Germanic warriors were scantily dressed at most times, and they often went into battle naked. The warrior would decorate his shield with colours and items. The loss of a shield was punished with the forfeiture of civil rights and exclusion from the warrior's communities' religious practices. (Greenwood, 1836)

Order of Battle – Infantry and Cavalry – Germanic Tribesmen

The usual order of battle for the Germanic infantry was a wedge-shaped phalanx which had the best soldiers placed into the front ranks. The movements of the cavalry were simple and effective. It was usual to mix the cavalry with the infantry forces.

That was the reason for having numbers of the ablest and most active young men trained to run alongside the cavalry, and they kept pace with them. In this way, using both infantry and cavalry preserved the Germanic attack's impetus, resulting in the enemies being confronted with combined infantry and cavalry attacks. The effect of these combined attacks often resulted in a shock to the enemy.

Due to the fact that the ancient Germanic people did not have a written language of their own at the time of Augustus, everything I heard was either legend, or it came from Roman historians like Tacitus. It was known among the Cherusci that *"The numbers of infantry assisting the cavalry were fixed at one hundred men per cavalry unit."* These one hundred men were selected as the infantry assistants of the cavalry from every canton or gau. (Local government area)

The Germanic people called them Centeni or one hundred men. (Greenwood, 1836). What was originally just a number soon became the name for elite shock troops. The members of every "One Hundred" went into the field as one body or unit. They increased each other's confidence through blood or family association, resulting in all men fighting within the eyesight of their kinfolk and friends.

Moral Habits and Religion – Ancient Germanic Tribes

My people did not erect temples or make images of their gods. They used certain places, mainly in the darkest areas of their forests, for religious worship. These sacred places were given the names of their gods, and my people approached them with awe as the gods' visible dwelling places. At those places, all sacrifices were performed, and all religious rites were celebrated. The great god or divinity of most Germanic tribes was Woden, also known as Odin, Tuisto and Teut. Another name associated with him is his son, Thor, the Thunder God.

Seven tribes of the Suevic Nation worshipped the Goddess Hertha or Mother Earth. The worship of whom had a rite which always left a great impression upon all who saw it. In the Baltic Ocean, there was an island with a grove that had a consecrated wagon. It was covered with a robe that no-one except a single priest was allowed to touch. In the wagon, the Goddess was supposed to reside.

When her wagon, drawn by cows, was bought out by her priest, it caused great joy among her believers. Her arrival always resulted in festivities lasting for many days after her arrival. During that time, there was no war or conflict.

The Naharvali did not have images for the gods worshipped by them and called their gods Alces, the twin Gods. The Aestyii had a goddess who was the mother of all gods. Her worshipers wore the figure of a boar as a talisman of the Goddess. (Greenwood, 1836)

Ancient Germanic Distribution of Land

My people (all Germanic tribes) had an adventurous spirit and combined it with warlike outlooks that produced attitudes that made them more interested in pastoral than agricultural activities. The Germanic tribes divided the productive lands according to the needs of communities, and the land was then allocated according to fixed rules and customs. No people were allowed to settle upon these allotments, and no-one could take more than one crop from it. After that, the land was to become fallow, or else it was transferred to a different set of cultivators.

They did not organise labour in proportion to the soil's fertility, and they had no gardens or orchards. They did not enclose their lands, and they did not irrigate them. They confined themselves to only growing enough grain to supply their needs for the following year. That resulted in famine when it came, being severe.

No Germanic warrior could possess property or own any specific portion of land. Caesar had the wrong idea about them from the start. He thought that Germanic tribesmen thought that fixed possessions could tempt them to exchange their lives of warlike adventure for the soft town life of city dwellers such as Romans and Gauls. The fact is simply that my people did not want it to become possible for large scale acquisition of land by individuals who would then become land owners oppressing the majority of my people and end up being a landed aristocracy.

Such things were contrary to the outlook of the free Germanic warrior's code of life and behaviour. He would not willingly go down to using a spade or plough, and he had no interest in what the soil could produce as long as he had enough barley to make his beer and enough grain for his bread, along with his cattle and venison from the forests.

For his luxuries, he got them as plunder from his enemies. So, the land was communal and tended to by individuals who could use it correctly.

Suevi, Marcomanni, and Alemanni Tribal Nations

The Romans just used the first name they encountered to describe my people, without attempting to find out the exact significance or how the name was applied to the people concerned. That is one reason Roman writers such as *Plutarch* used the name *"Teutones"* to apply to a single sector of the Cimbric confederacy.

Julius Caesar recorded the Suevi as being in the territory of the Chatti. In their writings about the Germanic tribes, the Roman historians of Pliny, Strabo, and Ptolemy contradict each other about the tribal names and confuse them with the names of tribal nations and various confederations.

These historians thought the names of *Suevi, Marcomanni and Alemanni* were single tribes like the *Chatti or Tenchteri.* They were, however, a cluster of nations that were spread over the greater parts of Germania. They were distinguished from each other by several different tribal names but were collectively known as the **Suevi**. Their territory extended from the upper Rhine River towards the Elbe and the Baltic Coast, extending towards present-day Scandinavia. The *Suevic* nations were also on the Saale, the Oder, and Vistula Rivers, extending along another line from the Danube to the North Sea.

What is surprising is that the *Suevi* are not written about by the Romans using that name. In Julius Caesar's writings about the Belgic Germanic tribes, we can read much about them, but always as if they were written about from a great distance. They gave the *Ubii* a hard time and expelled the *Tenchteri* and *Usipetes*. *Julius Caesar* wrote, *"The power of the Suebi is regarded with superstitious awe, and the gods themselves are thought to be incapable of coping with them"*. (Greenwood, 1836)

Marcomanni – these people attacked the *Bojenhaim* people in the year A.D.9 by using many warriors who called themselves *Mark-Mannen,* meaning men of the marshes. Under the leadership of their king, called Marobod, they established a formidable monarchy that became as dangerous to Rome as to Marobod's Germanic countrymen's independence.

The *Mark-Mannen* used great masses of border dwelling warriors sent forth on an annual basis to attack and safeguard the Suevi's frontiers. The name they adopted stated their fighting speciality, which was fighting in swampy and marshy areas. Due to Roman historians, they became known by the group name of *Marcomanni*.

Alle-Mannen – the name became Latinised to **Alemanni** by ancient Roman historians. The *Alle-Mannen* occupied territory between the Rhine, Maine and Danube rivers in areas formerly occupied by the Mark-Mannen who left those areas to follow the orders of Marobod, who led his people to the east of Germania.

Alle-Mannen was their name for themselves and the name by which they became known to the Romans. The name is a compound of the old Germanic names of Alle, meaning all or universal and Mann, thus implying that this was a union of warriors from all clans and tribes. Because of the above, some people think it is fair to say that the Suevi, Marcomanni and Alemanni are the same warrior people.

The Alle-Mannen did not immediately succeed the Mark-Mannen after Marobod displaced them. The Mattiaci, a tribe that was in alliance with the Romans, firstly replaced the Mark-Mannen. To the north of these people, the **Usipetes** or **Usipii**, living in the Weser and Elms Rivers areas. Their military allies, the Tenchteri, lived in areas to the southwest of them. In the country from Düsseldorf to the mouth of the Lippe River and easterly towards Arensberg and Paderborn.

In what we now call the modern state of Hessia, live the Chatti. Tacitus described them as a warrior nation that combined the native courage and daring of all Germanic tribes with deliberation and prudence. They achieved advances in military science greater than that of other Germanic tribes. They also paid attention to military discipline.

They would rely on the talents of their generals rather than just the brute strength of their warriors. They provided for warfare by carrying the necessary stores and supplies with them as they moved towards the battle. By doing that, the Chatti would wage organised war against their enemies.

Some Other Germanic Tribes

To the north of the **Chatti** were the **Chamavi**, Angriarii and **Marsi** people. The area was formerly occupied by the **Bructeri**, who had left it. In the flat and the swampy regions between the lower Rhine and the Ems

18

Rivers were the Friscii, while on islands between the Rhine and the Meuse's mouths, the **Batavi** and **Caninefates** lived on swampy ground.

To the east of the **Friscii** were the **Chauci**. That powerful nation of people had expelled the **Ansibarii** and become the neighbours of the **Chatti**. The Chauci tribe tended to remain neutral in the war between the Romans and other Germanic tribes.

The **Cimbri** (Latinised name) or **Kimbern** (Germanic name) were initially located on the Jutland Peninsular but spread to the north of the Danube and Franconia and Saxon duchies. So, the Kimbern (Cimbri) were also living in the tribal areas of the Heremunduri.

Cherusci Tribal Nation

To the south-east of the Chauci were the lands of my tribe. The Cherusa (Germanic name) were renamed Cherusci (Latin name) by Roman historians. The Cherusci proudly maintained the honour and independence of their homeland. Their territory was between the Weser and upper Elbe rivers to the Saale's beginnings, where they shared borders with the **Hermunduri**. Towards the southwest were the Chatti.

The Cherusci nobility were from six different families or clans. These were Marodid, Gelimmerid, Dagaricid, Amandid and Anicidid. Some of the people in these clans were closely related. Among those were Armin, and his father, Segimer and his uncle Inguionerus and his brother Flavus.

As has already been discussed, the Cherusci nobles like to send some of their sons to Rome for training. To repay Rome for this training, it was necessary for the Cherusci men who had been trained in this way to spend time in the direct service of the Roman army as auxiliary officers.

The Cherusci tribe's benefit of having some of their sons trained in this way was continuing contact with the more highly developed Roman culture and the men bringing needed Roman money into their communities. That resulted in the future young leaders being experienced military commanders when they took their places as the leaders of the tribal nation. Various Germanic tribes specialised in different military applications. In the case of the Cherusci, their speciality was in the offensive and defensive use of cavalry. It was customary for Roman legions to have large cavalry units (often Cherusci) located on the legion's wings.

After our initial schooling and proving ourselves at various things, we began our military training at later dates. After satisfactorily completing it, we were sent to our Roman Army units. That resulted in our losing contact with Flavus for a long time. Because he was sent to a different unit than both Armin and me. We stayed together in the same Roman unit.

We learned Roman cavalry and infantry tactics with a great deal of instruction in minor infantry tactics being of great importance during our training. While it was of great benefit for us to learn these things, it was a very costly mistake for Rome to teach them. Armin used his knowledge with devasting effect against the Roman invaders of Germania at later dates when he led the Germanic tribes against Rome.

First Meetings of Germanic Tribes with the Romans

By about 100 B.C., the Roman army's military effectiveness had beaten all of the Roman Empire's enemies, and Rome was still functioning as a republic. The strongest threat came from Carthage, and that city-state had been destroyed. The Greeks had also been conquered, thanks to the power expansionary policies of the Roman Republic and the efficiency of the Roman armies. The Romans established provinces in most of Gaul, the Rhone River, all of Spain, all of north Africa, other than the desert, and Asia minor, leaving only Syria and Egypt to be conquered and turned into Roman provinces.

It was from 100 B.C. onwards that new enemies endangered Rome and the way of life of its citizens, resulting in Romans hearing for the first time the names of Germania, Teutones and Cimbri. These two Germanic tribes appeared in huge numbers at the Italian frontiers. The warriors' appearance was very tall and muscular and had either red or blond hair and blue eyes. They were also reported as appearing to be very fierce warriors.

Their weapons were said to be a long double-edged sword, a short spear, and a club. Their order of battle was a wedge-shaped column that would quickly become a phalanx when needed. They had no armour, their only protection being a large shield made of raw hides and stretched over a wooden frame. They used a terrifying war-cry, which, when combined with their great strength and contempt of danger, filled their enemies with fear.

Both the Boii and Taurisci Norican nations lived in the land of Bavaria, and the area of Tyrol was attacked by the barbarians. That led to the Taurisci claiming the protection of the Romans as allies of the republic.

Having been informed of that, the Consul known as Papyrius Carbo exploded in rage! He yelled, *"Summon all available Roman legions! I have received word that the barbarian terrors from Germania called Cimbri have entered our allies' territory, that of the Taurisci. We shall march at speed into the territory of the barbarians, and we will closely watch them!"*

The Cimbri noticed the Roman movements, and after setting up a meeting with the Consul, they spoke directly to him. A *Cimbri* warrior known as Achim said, *"I am told that your funny name is Papyrius Carbo, and you do not impress me! Now look here, you stupid Roman arsehole, your allies of the Taurisci are weak and therefore, it is correct for us, the Cimbri people, to attack them and use their property as our own. You and your Romans now have until sundown today to leave here, or you shall be put to death by me and my army! Do you understand that you exceedingly stupid and arrogant Roman?"*

Consul Carbo said, *"The reason for advancing my army into your territory is to watch you people and what you are doing. The Taurisci are Roman allies and are therefore under the protection of Rome. The Cimbri must immediately stop interfering with them and leave their territories! You must never interfere with them again! I can see that your people are ignorant of hospitality rights in existence between Rome and the Taurisci. I thank you for your moderation, and I point out that I have assigned the men whom you can see before you to act as guides to take you back to your areas in safety!"*

Achim looked upon the cohort of Romans before him and decided to play along with the Roman Consul before making him and Romans in general pay for the mistake of interfering in the business of Germanic tribes such as the Cimbri. (The Germanic name for the tribe was Kimbern) He said, *"Very well, Roman, I need to consult my staff so that a most suitable decision is implemented."* The Consul said, *"Very well, Cimbri warrior, it is now midday, and I expect you to be here before late afternoon today with your decision."*

Achim departed and re-joined his Cimbri comrades. Upon returning to his encampment, Achim spoke to his warriors, one of whom was Baudran. He said, *"Baudran, I have just returned from a meeting with the arrogant Roman upstart, Consul Papyrius Carbo. He demanded that all of us Kimbern warriors leave this area, and he thinks that we should leave the Taurisci alone.*

He has threatened us with the Roman cohort you see before us. It has a strength of six hundred men. I know that because I checked the number of Roman soldiers in that unit. It seems to me that the Roman fool thinks that his unit of Romans will somehow stop us. All the same, the six hundred Romans are an impediment to our progress. We must get rid of them!"

Baudran answered, *"I will ride ahead of you and get our warriors ready. Ensure that you come back towards our encampment using the track over the mountains through the forested area! The other warriors and I shall be waiting in ambush positions for you and the rest of our unit and for the Romans to arrive. When they do so, they shall face attacks from my warriors and me. As well as that, you and your men will turn on the Romans as soon as you have heard the sound of our horns. I also suggest that we send warriors to our camp to help defend it against this Roman bully and his other units!"*

Meanwhile, Consul Papyrius Carbo was speaking to his cohort, which was to accompany the Cimbri. He said, *"When you assume your new duties of being guides to the Cimbri, I want you to lead them in a circular route, while the rest of us make a forced march in a direct line towards the Cimbri camp. The cohort will slay their warriors, and we will wipe out their women and children in their camp area! That way, a message of "Do not interfere with things, Roman" will be forcibly engraved upon the barbarian minds! When you are sure that you have the Germans at your mercy, wipe them out!"*

He and his army arrived at the Kimbern or Cimbri camp, expecting an easy victory. That backfired on him because he failed to surprise the Cimbri, who had managed to wipe out the cohort he sent to kill them. And they had managed to alert their comrades. The Cimbri were flush with the recent victories over Romans, now engaged the Consul Carbo's units in battle. The battle took place at Noreia, close to Aquileia, the most vulnerable part of the Italian frontier.

The Cimbri and Teutones, together with Toygenes and Tigurini, crossed the Rhine and defeated the Gallic locals. The Germanic warriors then supplanted the locals with their own people. The result was that Gaul was depopulated over a great area, which drew Romans' attention, such as Julius Caesar. The latter saw the danger of permitting these new neighbours to settle on Roman Gaul's borders and become strong, resulting in a threat to Rome's security.

The Roman Senate debated the apparent danger of the Germanic tribes in Gaul. That resulted in the Consul Silanus being sent to Gaul with a large army to take on the Germanic warriors and defeat them if the right situations presented themselves. It was fortunate for Rome that the Germanic warriors did not want to conquer the Italian peninsular. They only wanted to consolidate their new settlements.

At an orders group (a meeting of warriors of various ranks at which information is exchanged, and orders are given.) The Council of Elders of the Kimbern spoke with Achim and Baudran. They said, *"Achim and Baudran, we need you to draw upon your experience of dealing with the Romans! We want you to tell the Roman Consul Silanus that we are not going to invade the Italian Peninsula, and we just want to be left in peace in our new territories."*

That resulted in both men going to the Roman Consul's encampment with an armed escort of six hundred warriors. Arriving at the Roman camp, they were quickly introduced to Silanus. Achin was the first to speak. He said, *"Consul Silanus, I am Achin of the Kimbern tribe whom you Romans call Cimbri. We shall not be invading your Italian Peninsula homeland, and therefore, we are not a security threat to Rome. We only want to be left in peace in our new territorial acquisitions in Gaul, where we will consolidate our new settlements! I am to take your answer to my leaders!"*

Silanus answered, *"Achin and Baudran, I am just a Consul, and I do not have the authority to grant you and your people your wishes! The best thing I can do is refer your desires to the Senate in Rome, where the senators will decide! It will take time for that to happen and for the decision to be relayed back here. Therefore, expect a delay of about a month before you can have an answer!"*

Achim said, *"Both I and Baudran have authority to make treaties and enter into them. For now, we shall take your answer back to the Council of Elders, and we shall be back to see you in one month from now. In the meantime, do not try any treachery because if you do so, we shall wipe out everything Roman in all places!"*

The time passed quickly, and both Achim and Baudran again met with Silanus. Achim spoke. He said, *"Silanus, what is the answer from Rome?"* Silanus answered, *"The Senate of Rome has stated that no deals shall be done with any Germanic tribe that occupies Roman territory in Gaul! Rome has decreed that the Germanic barbarians occupying Roman territory in Gaul must leave immediately!"*

That did not suit Achim at all! He said, *"You arrogant Roman fool! We came to you in peace, and you have thrown it back into our faces! You have had the hide to demand things from us when you Romans only have one legion and some supporting units in this area! This, I swear to you, Roman! By Wodin and his son Thor, we the Kimbern and other Germanic tribes will throw all Romans out of Gaul, and we shall have it to ourselves! Do not push your luck, or we could march upon Rome itself!"*

With that, Achim and Baudran left in the company of their escort of five hundred warriors. At the next orders group held by the Council of Elders, Achim was asked, *"What is the Roman military strength in this area?"* He replied, *"The Romans have one legion of heavy infantry backed up by two cavalry Turmae!"* Next, an elder spoke. He asked, *"Achim, can you wipe out the Roman legion and make our settlements secure?"* Achim said, *"No problem, Elder, we will teach the Romans not to bother us!"*

The elder now said, *"Achim, go and do it!"* the legion was defeated and ceased to exist as a fighting force. It was scattered all over Gaul. Silanus managed to escape by running away from the location. As a direct result, the whole of Gaul was overrun by the barbarians.

Many of the invading Germanic tribes now left Gaul because they were more interested in securing their land between the Rhine and Saone rather than making new conquests. Meanwhile, many Romans became alarmed at what they thought of as a dangerous peril presented by the Germanic tribes. The Roman Senate became a hive of activity and debate.

A Senator said, *"Friends and fellow Romans, I have it on confidential authority that the Germanic tribe called Tigurini, which is an associated tribe with the dreaded Cimbri, have formed a close alliance with them. The Cimbri defeated Consul Silanus just two years ago, and they are now once again threatening Rome's borders! We must intercept and wipe out the Germans!*

I, therefore, would like the Senate to vote on appointing the Consul Lucius Cassius to lead a Roman Field Army of four legions complete with supporting units to engage the Tigurini at Lake Lehman!" The Senate then discussed and voted to appoint Consul Cassius to save Rome from the Germanic tribesmen. Soon, Consul Lucius Cassius and his four Roman legions of 'Heavy Infantry' supported by cavalry, archer, slinger, engineer, and catapult units were on the way to Lake Lehman. As the Romans approached the lake, the soldiers began to become very uneasy.

Julio spoke to Markus. He said, *"Markus, we have not seen anyone or anything, but I am ill at ease because I think that something is wrong! We are in a Roman Field Army of four legions plus supporting units, and it does not make sense to me that we have not seen or heard the enemy. I can feel unseen eyes watching us, and I am getting the impression that we are marching towards our doom!"* Markus answered, *"I would like to say that you are getting too jumpy, Julio, but I have the same sensation as you! I am also experiencing having unseen eyes, watching everything that we do. I also think that we may not be alive by the end of this day!"*

The four legions were rapidly marching closer to Lake Lehman when it was noticed by the Romans that the road had narrowed and that only two men abreast could move forwards. As well, there was now forest and undergrowth lining the sides of the road. Suddenly, the Romans were subjected to a hail of arrows and spears thrown or shot at them from the as yet unseen enemy forces. The result of the 'Battle of Lake Lehman' was that the *Tigurini* and other Germanic forces wiped out one-third of the Romans near the lake while the remainder fled!

The Fighting and Siege of Tolosa (Gaul)

In the year of 106 B.C., the Roman Senator called Cato Aurelius was speaking during a debate by the Senate. He said, *"Friends and fellow Romans, we have a severe security problem in that the Gallic nation called Tectosages has joined into a confederation by the dreaded Cimbri! The capital of the Tectosages is known to be Tolosa. The simple fact is that by joining forces with the invading Germanic tribes, the Gauls in those areas are a clear and present danger to Rome!*

We cannot sit idly by and do nothing about the threat coming from this alliance between the Gauls and the Germans! I, therefore, call upon the Senate to immediately send the Consul Servilius Caepio to lead a large Roman army of at least five legions of heavy infantry, complete with cavalry and all other supporting units to wipe out the threat to Rome; coming from the city of Tolosa!"

The Senate debated the matter and approved Consul Servilius Caepio to lead a Roman expedition to take Tolosa and secure Rome's future by doing so. Caepio sent out scouts ahead of his army, and they reported no significant threats before the army reached that city. Standing on a small hill near the city, Caepio spoke. He said, *"Surround Tolosa immediately! I want that place so tightly encircled that I will know if even a rat tries to get into or out of the place!*

First, we shall make sure that the enemy in Tolosa does not get food or water. We should be able to starve them into submission! Any Gaul or Germanic warrior we can capture, we will be making an example of. We will do so by using the most visual and painful methods of execution available to Romans! Those of either crucifixion or impaling! If no-one ventures outside of Tolosa, I want some Roman units to go to villages and farms close to the city, where they are to take prisoners. I want the prisoners to be brought back to this location.

When we have enough prisoners, the process of crucifying or impaling them shall begin so that the people of Tolosa will see what happens to those who side with the

Germanic tribes and defy Rome!" Soon after that, Caepio had eight hundred prisoners to use.

He ordered, *"Take one hundred of these men to one Roman mile (1,000 paces) from the Tolosa City walls. Select areas which are highly visible to the people of the city! Take one small diameter pole for each of the one hundred male prisoners and then take the men and the impaling poles to the areas of the high visibility of the residents of Tolosa.*

While it is still dark, and before the morning twilight, force one end of the pole into the arsehole of each of the prisoners. Then carry them to where they will be seen by all and embed the free end of the stake into the ground. That way, it will take two days for impaled prisoners to die in agony! Take all of the women prisoners to a similar area near where the men are impaled and crucify them! When you crucify the women, drive nails through their ankles into the crosses' timber they are crucified on!

After we have done those sorts of things for about fifteen days, I will demand the surrender of the city. If the fools do not surrender, we shall keep on doing those things to the people from surrounding areas until Tolosa submits!"

So, fifteen days later, Caepio sent envoys to the people of Tolosa. The envoys returned to him and conferred with him. They said, *"Sir, the people of Tolosa remain defiant, and they will continue to fight you. You may have a long siege on your hands! What are your orders, Sir?"* He replied, *"Keep the siege of the city so tight that nothing can get into or out of the city. We shall impale or crucify up to one hundred and twenty new people per day until those fools surrender!"* After another month of no food or new fresh-water, Tolosa surrendered after having suffered extreme cruelty inflicted by the Romans.

Unknown to Caepio, his actions of impaling people to make the city surrender was quickly becoming common knowledge among the Gauls and the invading Germanic tribes. The warriors spoke to each other. Saying, *"The Romans are a bunch of callous cowards who are forcing thin poles or stakes into the arseholes of men or women to try to beat us! That is because they cannot fight; they have to resort to that sort of thing because of the cowards that the Italians are! We must do something about these cowards!"*

The warriors became so enraged that it resulted in the entire barbaric league joining forces to avenge these wrongs. The Germanic warriors closed with the Roman army under the command of Caepio and destroyed it. Soon afterwards, they also wiped out the Roman army commanded by Manlius. Caepio escaped, but Manlius and his two sons were killed.

Caius Marius is Called Upon to Save Rome

Rome was now approaching a state of near panic. That resulted in the Roman people now calling for Caius Marius to assume the government's leading and take control of the Roman Republic's armies at the threatened frontiers. Soon, Caius Marius was appointed, and he left to fix the situation near the frontier.

Meanwhile, the Cimbri Confederacy had three hundred thousand warriors, with camp followers, women, and children. Marius called for an orders group to be held at his encampment. Present were his legion commanders and other officers. He spoke to those present. He said, *"The Cimbri have confederated with the Gallic Celts and so have formed a powerful alliance which is particularly dangerous to Rome! My scouts have informed me that they have more than three hundred thousand warriors.*

We shall completely fortify our position here and keep a close watch upon the enemy. We shall not strike unless something extraordinary happens which will give us the advantage! We shall remain here and closely watch the enemy, waiting for an opportunity to use against them, even if it means that we must do so for five years before we act!"

So it was that Marius fortified his secure position and watched the Cimbri for three years while always watching his enemies. During that time, he kept his soldiers fit by making them have constant exercise programmes, and he was, therefore, able to restore discipline and morale.

So it was that scouts reported to Marius. They said, *"Sir, there is much movement from the Germanic camp! Some of our scouting units have been closely following the Cimbri and their Allies called the Teutones and the Ambrones. We were able to follow the latter, and we now know that the Teutones and the Ambrones are here facing this encampment while the entire Cimbri force has crossed the Rhine and is approaching the Norican passes. It looks like they may attack Rome itself!"*

Marius was silent for several minutes while he thought over the implications of what he had been told. He said, *"Double the sentries on duty at both the river in front of us and toward our rear! From what you have told me, I can see that we shall soon be under attack from the Teutones and the Ambrones. Ensure that our catapults and Scorpios are serviceable and mainly located toward our rear, where I think the primary attacks upon us will come from. I am sure that the Germanic forces have split their massive army into two parts so that the Cimbri part of it can attack Rome itself. Make sure that our sentries are rotated several times every night and day so that they will always be fresh and alert!"*

The Germanic forces' apparent plan was doomed to failure from the beginning because the distances the two forces had to cover were too unequal. With a typical Germanic eagerness for battle, The Teutones attacked the Roman army under Marius's command without waiting for the Cimbri to take the Norican Passes. Marius was very mindful of the large number of Germanic warriors, and he called an orders group with his officers. He said, *"Gentlemen, Romans mustn't engage the enemy unless we have the advantage! You are all to keep our soldiers within their entrenchments, and all general actions are to be avoided!*

The reason for this is simple! By our avoiding actions against the enemy, he will come to us. The Germanic warriors are unskilled in attacking fortified posts, and they do not have catapults or Scorpios! By our letting them advance close to our positions, we will have the advantage of them being in range-marked locations within the range of the war-machines! The enemy will first encounter burning wood and straw shot into their ranks by using the catapults, which will also throw large rocks at them.

The Scorpios will be firing large arrows and medium-sized spears at them at one projectile rate per minute. That will cut down the number of the enemy! Those who make it through to our defences will find that they come under barrages of arrows and spears when they get close to our lines! Make sure that our men gather up the spears and arrows used so that we have reserves of these weapons for future attacks!"

The Elders of the Germanic warriors called for an orders group. Otto spoke. He said, *"The Romans are avoiding battle with us! The cowards are skulking behind their walls, and that is the strongest proof possible that they are gutless and are too scared to fight us! I have experienced the way the Romans like to use their war machines! If you get close to their encampment, you will notice that all vegetation has been removed for a considerable distance. You will also find that ranging pegs have been placed every fifty paces.*

The ranging pegs all have the distance from the Roman perimeter marked on a disc in code and set upon the peg. All of the pegs are very large and clearly visible to the Roman defenders! That all makes the job of defending the Roman positions much easier for them and much harder to attack it successfully for us! I yearn to battle the Roman cowards!"

A long time passed, and the Germanic warriors were weary from Marius declining battle. At a new orders group, Otto again spoke. He said, *"Comrades, I think that it is time for us to attack the rear of the Romans and take control of the Ligurian Passes! It may take us six says to march past the Romans. While we are going past the Romans, it will be a good time for our men to jeer at them with taunts. Such as, 'Hey, you weak as piss Roman arseholes, do you have any messages for your wife in Italy? We will soon be there raping the bitch and giving her a better time than you can, and she will enjoy it!'"* Marius's position was very secure, and from it, he had a complete picture of his enemy's position. A river was flowing at the foot of the hill his army occupied, but other than this, his army had no available water. The enemy was in full control of all riverbanks other than his own position. That meant that when the Romans wanted to bathe, they had to organise escorts for the bathing men. A delegation of Roman soldiers went to see Marius to express their grievances. They said, *"Sir, we need to bathe; therefore, we ask you to provide armed escorts for our bathing soldiers!"* Marius replied, *"You are Romans and water for bathing can be had by you for the blood of the barbarians you kill!"*

The grooms and camp servants did not wait for his permission. Instead, they went to the riverbank without weapons and carried their water pitchers on their javelins. So eager were the Roman camp followers to bathe that no escort was in place. It was late afternoon, and the twilight of the evening was occurring. Twilight was a time when the enemy would often attack. Sure enough, just as many Romans were in the water, the Teutone and Anbrone warriors who had swum across the river appeared among the Romans and were killing them while maiming others.

Their cries of distress drew other Romans to their assistance, and it aroused the impatience of the Roman soldiers who were worried about the welfare of their servants and their cattle. The fight was now inevitable, and Marius gave orders to his army. He said, *"The time is here for you to close with and kill the barbarian enemy!"* So it was that the Roman catapults and Scorpios rained arrows and short spears upon the attacking warriors. Seeing the carnage in front of him, a Germanic leader called Berard became concerned at the way things were going.

He spoke to those near him. He said, *"Friends and comrades, our warriors are being cut to pieces by the*

Roman war machines and the Roman legions are now attacking. Our warriors are out in the open, which is the strength of the Roman attack! We must retreat and regroup our forces before all is lost!"

Although some of those present wanted to stay and fight the Romans where they were, most of the warriors agreed that they had to withdraw from that battlefield. A warrior called Sigmerge now spoke. He said, *"I fully agree with you, Berard, and I suggest that we immediately go back to where we left our wagons and supplies so that we can safeguard them."* Berard then sounded the retreat!

The warriors went back to where they had left their supplies and wagons, only to meet their women. The women immediately scolded their men. One of the female leaders was Adele. She was very scornful of the warriors and spoke to them. She said, *"Some great warriors and protectors of your families you lot have proved to be! You are running from the Romans, and we girls are rescuing you! Men!!!"*

Adele ordered, *"Girls and women, take up your battle-axes! It is high time to show both our own men and the Romans that Germanic women are the equal of all males and that we are much better than any Roman, be it a Roman woman or man!"* Next, she ordered, *"All women, we now attack the Romans where they are feeling very secure; namely, we attack them at their camp!"*

So it was that the Germanic women attacked the Roman camp and, again, established the reputation of the Germanic woman being at least as fierce as her male counterpart. During their attack upon the Romans, the women suffered many casualties themselves, but they also inflicted many casualties among the Romans, who now regarded all Germanic people with dread.

That night, both parties spent the time preparing for the fight, which would resume in the morning. It was during the night that Marius held an orders group with his officers. He said, *"Gentlemen, our side has lost many Roman soldiers, and many more of them are wounded. I want you to take about three thousand of our most able and fit soldiers to quietly leave here and go to the rear of the Germanic force. It is critical that we do this. By so doing, we shall attack the enemy from in front of them and behind them at the same time! It is therefore likely that the enemy formations will scatter, and we will be victorious!"*

The Romans did as Marius had ordered, and the result was a complete Roman victory. Consequently, most Germanic warriors were killed or made prisoner to be sold later as slaves. At the Germanic camp, the women, children, and baggage handlers fell into Roman soldiers' hands. Many of the women were found to have killed their children and then themselves, rather than let them suffer the dishonour of being the sexual play-things of the Romans and slavery.

While all of that was happening, the second part of the Germanic force, consisting of the Cimbri, reached the Norican Alps' slopes. They crossed the mountains and attacked the outposts of the Roman army stationed there under the Consul Catulus because they opposed the way of the Germanic warriors into Italy.

Destruction of the Cimbri by Marius and Catulus at Vercellae.

Leading a large unit of Cimbri was the warrior leader called Clothildis. He spoke to those around him. He said, *"I* want immediate information about the Romans before us! I need to know their strengths, weaknesses, and their location. I also want to know about things like their proximity to rivers and the state of the ground surrounding their positions on the banks of the Adige River."

Eadric answered him. He said, *"My scouts have returned from assessing the enemy. They report that the enemy has some large numbers, to be sure. They also note that the Romans are spread all over the Adige Riverbank and that many of them will be trapped if we launch a surprise attack upon them.*

The Romans have mainly located themselves in an area where the river bends and forms a horseshoe shape. By us firstly taking the riverbank opposite the Romans, we could have many of our warriors swim over to where the Romans are and attack them from directly in front of them. At the same time, I would like masses of warriors to attack the Romans from all of the territory on all sides of them.

Because the Romans have taken up position in the bend of the river, they will find it almost impossible to escape because the river will be a barrier to them. Our warriors will attack by coming across land and those who will be swimming towards them!"

These things were put into place by the Cimbri warriors, who now started swimming toward the Roman position. The Romans were completely unprepared for them and quickly gave ground. News of this was immediately taken to Catulus.

He said, *"So, the Cimbri are attacking our front, and also they are coming at us from our rear and sides! The river currently traps us! I want our engineers to construct bridges across the Adige immediately. When that has been done, some Roman cohorts shall act as our rear-guard while the rest of my units escape from here!"* However, that is not what happened because the Romans fled without waiting for orders. They fled in a confused and quick retreat which only finished when they had put the broad River Po between themselves and the pursuing Germanic warriors.

The Cimbri were satisfied with having beaten the Romans now sank into inactivity and were ignorant of their allies' progress in Gaul. They had conquered northern Italy between the Alps and the Po, and they were finding the productiveness of the soil and the climate there was agreeable with them. That gave them a desire to settle where they were rather than continue to Rome itself.

There were angry debates in the Roman Senate resulting from the news of the defeat of Catulus on the Adige. The Roman Senator Cassius Titus was speaking during a debate. He said, *"Fellow Romans and countrymen, our forces under the command of Catulus have been wiped out by the Cimbri, and their Germanic warriors are yet again a threat to Rome! Rome has barely had time to be joyful over the deliverance from one danger when the city finds itself threatened by a second danger which is more terrible than the first one, and it is much closer to us all! I praise the gods that Catulus managed to escape!*

I call upon Marius to immediately stop preparing for his triumphant procession of victory over the Teutones and go to our rescue! So it was that Marius and his men immediately marched towards the hard-pressed and dispirited Roman army on the Po. Having arrived, he joined the two forces together and then with united Roman forces, he crossed the river and began action against the barbarians.

After having been treated contemptuously by the Romans, the Cimbri were eager for battle. A Cimbri prince rode out in person to take the challenge to the Romans.

The challenge stated, *"We of the Kimbern nation, whom you arrogant Romans call Cimbri, challenge you and all cowardly Roman skulkers who like to hide behind walls to battle tomorrow morning on the plains of Vercellae. We will defeat you, you Roman arseholes!"* Marius agreed, and both parties prepared for the final battle.

The next morning started with the barbarians bringing out their entire army. The Germanic warriors were in two groups of equal length to the primary battle. Other groups known as wings were held back to allow space for their cavalry to intervene freely. The horsemen who the Romans feared were at the strength of fifteen thousand warriors.

Their great strength and agility were legendary among Romans who feared them. Their helmets were in the shape of the heads of savage beasts, which had open jaws, and the heads of which were surmounted with groupings of feathers in the form of wings. They wore iron breastplates, and their weapons were a javelin for the beginning of the fight and a heavy broadsword for close combat.

The Romans were deployed into a semi-circle that followed the contours of the ground. Catulus commanded the centre, and Marius ordered his soldiers to positions on the two wings. The Germanic tribesmen attacked in their usual wedge-shaped formation, still full of contempt for all Romans. With the soldiers of Catulus receiving the first formidable attack, the Germanic cavalry attacked the flanks of Marius and tried to surround him. They also tried to trap him between their cavalry squadrons and the right-wing of their infantry, but that failed. Catulus repelled their attack.

The Germanic column was unprepared for negative movements like a retreat and withdrew from the battle in confusion. The Germanic cavalry left the field, while their infantry became outflanked and surrounded by Roman wings. The barbarians were forced back to their camp at Vercellae, where many of them were butchered by Roman heavy infantry resulting in Rome being saved.

Julius Caesar - Early Life & Career

In the mid-seventh century B.C., following Alba Longa's destruction, the Julia family was granted patrician status and joined with some other Alban families. These Julii were also at Bovillae, where there is an ancient inscription on an altar of the town, which tells of their sacrifices.

When Gaius Julius was born, his mother suffered complications, and the attending physician suddenly decided to remove the baby from the mother surgically. The Latin name for this operation was caes - meaning to cut. So it was that his name became Gaius Julius Caesar. In time, he married Aurelia, and on 12/July/100 B.C., they had a son whom they also named Gaius Julius Caesar.

Relationship with Powerful Romans.

As has already been covered, Rome was saved from the attentions of the Germanic tribes by Gaius Marius. The uncle of Rome's future general and dictator, Gaius Julius Caesar, was the Roman governor of the Roman province of Asia (Syria, etc.) His father's sister was married to Gaius Marius, one of Rome's most influential people. The mother of the future general was Aurelia Cotta, and she was part of a very powerful Roman family. When he was five years old, Julius spoke to his mother. He said, *"Mother, I understand that my uncle is Caius Marius and that his wife is my aunt called Julia. They are influential people in the Roman republic. They are from my father's side of this family. Please tell me about your side of my family."* Aurelia answered, *"My mother is Rutilia, and my father is Aurelius Cotta. He became a Consul fifty-nine years ago. Three of my brothers are or will become Consuls."*

Julius Caesar as Head of His Family When Aged Sixteen

In 85 B.C., Aurelia Caesar spoke to her son. She said, *"I have bad news for you, my son, your father, the governor of Asia Minor, has died suddenly. Caius, your father, Caius Julius Caesar, wanted you named in precisely the same way as he was named.*

That has been done, resulting in people becoming confused as to whom other people mean when they talk about Caius Julius Caesar. Because of your father's death, you are now the head of the family, even though you are only sixteen!" Caius Julius Caesar junior answered, *"Rest assured my mother, that I shall always do what is right by you and that I shall strive to make you and my father' proud of me!"*

Next, Caius said, *"As you already know, Mother, I was undergoing training as a priest in the Temple of Jupiter. My training has been completed. I am now going to be nominated by you as the new Flamen Dialis, which means that I shall be the High Priest of Jupiter, which is in line with our family traditions!"* Aurelia said, *"I shall support you, my son, and you can rest assured that in me, you have not only your mother but a potent and able ally who will do everything to make sure that you will always triumph! The new Flamen Dialis you wish to become, and you shall do so!"*

However, problems were coming in the form of a civil war between Caesar's uncle, Gaius Marius, and Lucius Cornelius Sulla. That prompted Aurelia to say, *"My son, I do not know how it will play out, but there is now the real possibility of civil war between your uncle Gaius Marius and his rival Lucius Cornelius Sulla. So let us quickly have you consecrated into the Priesthood of Jupiter!"*

That was done, and during his duties as High Priest of Jupiter, the young Julius Caesar met and courted the daughter of Lucius Cornelius Cinna named Cornelia. Pleased with both himself and Cornelia, Julius bought her to meet his mother. As both he and his girlfriend were entering the house, Aurelia called out. She said, *"Is that you, Julius?"*

Julius answered, *"Yes, mother, and I have with me my girlfriend, who would very much like to meet you!"* Aurelia answered, *"Wait a little while, and I will be with you both."* Sure enough, she came to meet the two young lovers in the courtyard of her Roman villa.

As she approached them, she spoke. She said, *"I am glad to see that you are taking an interest in fine-looking young ladies, Julius. I like the looks of your friend; please introduce us."* Caesar said, *"Mother, this is Cornelia; she is the daughter of Lucius Cornelius Cinna. Her father is one of the best allies of my uncle, Gaius Marius!"*

So it was that some time passed, allowing Julius Caesar and Cornelia to wed. During that time, Caius Julius

Caesar was fulfilling his duties as the high priest of Jupiter with enthusiasm. He became dismayed to hear that Sulla had been victorious in a final battle against his uncle. He found that he wanted to take up arms himself against Sulla and discussed the situation with his mother. Aurelia quickly thought the matter through and advised her son, who was present in her house with his wife, Cornelia.

She said, *"Gaius Julius Caesar, my son, you are the serving high Priest of Jupiter! That being the case, you may not even touch a weapon, or ride a horse or even get within a long distance from a horse. You are at the highest level of the Priesthood, and as such, your future is assured!"*

Cornelia said, *"Mother Caesar, The oppressive Sulla has won the civil war, and he is putting in a programme of revenge against all who were somehow connected to Gaius Marius and my father! Sulla has decreed that your son Julius is to be stripped of his inheritance and also my dowry to him. Sulla has also taken the Priesthood of Jupiter off your son. Therefore Julius should be able to both ride horses and make war upon his enemies!"*

Aurelia said, *"Thank you for this valuable information, my Daughter-in-Law. I will always be there for both you and Julius. Now then, let us discuss the things that are of the utmost importance. These are the safety of both of you, my children! Sulla will never dare attack this villa because of the fact that I am connected to the most powerful leaders and senators of Rome! Julius, your wife Cornelia must live here in this villa with me. That leaves us with organising the safety of yourself, Julius!*

I think it is best if you were to join the army and campaign far away from here where Sulla cannot reach you if the dictator changes his mind and tries to kill you! Marcus Mininius Thermus has told me that he has a vacancy for a Centurian in his legions in Asia Minor.

If it turns out that he has already filled the position when you apply for it, try being appointed as a Centurian with the legions of Servilius Isauicus in Cilicia. Julius said, *"Thank you for your gracious assistance: my mother. That is what both Cornelia and I shall do! Thank you for saving us both. After some time, I shall return to Rome, and Sulla will pay for his crimes against this family!"*

So it was that Caius Julius Caesar (junior) entered the army of the Roman Republic and served with great distinction, even winning the Civic Crown for his outstanding service during the siege of Mytilene.

In 78 B.C., Caesar was talking to some of his associates in the legion. Marcus Aurelius said, *"Julius, my friend, it has come to my attention that Sulla has died and that it should be safe for you to return to Rome now!"* Caesar answered, *"Marcus, dear boy, that is the best news that I have heard for many a year! The problem is that I have had my inheritance confiscated, so I shall have to use the money accumulated during my service with the army in Asia Minor.*

Although my money reserves are not at the level of my confiscated inheritance, I still have enough money to buy a modest house in the Roman suburb of Subura, and I shall live there. While I am so doing, I shall become a legal advocate!"

He quickly became well known for his exceptional skills as an orator. He combined a high-pitched voice with impassioned gestures of his hands and became ruthless in the prosecution of former governors who were notorious for extortion and corruption.

Caesar and the Pirates

He was in a meeting with some friends when he spoke to them. He said, *"I am going to cross the Aegean Sea, and then, I shall return to Rome. I know full well that the Aegean Sea hides many pirates. Some people think that I shall be putting myself into harm's way by using sea travel; however, I cannot think of a better way to wipe out the pirates than letting them capture me and demand a ransom for my return!"*

He went to see a cohort of Roman soldiers with whom he had served in Syria. Seeing his old comrades, he said, *"Gentlemen, I lay an adventure before you that will both make you famous and rich when you complete it! I am going to cross the Aegean Sea soon, and I think the pirates will intercept my ship and take me hostage.*

I want you all to be ready to board the ships in front of you. You will come to my aid as soon as the pirates deliver their ransom demands to you through the help of Crassus. They will not know that the older man organising the ransom demands for them is my friend! Just be ready to move on the pirates when the time comes; we must wipe out all such criminals!"

And so, Gaius Julius Caesar boarded his ship and sailed into the Aegean Sea. After the ship had been sailing for two hours, Caesar could see the oars and the sail of an approaching ship that had the appearance of a Greek trireme. Caesar noted that it was not a Roman ship, and he correctly assumed it to be the pirates he was expecting.

He thought, *"Good, it appears that the pirates have heard that I am on board this ship, and they are coming after me to get a ransom! Keep on coming, you greedy pigs, soon enough, you will rue the day you became criminals and enemies of Rome!"*

The pirate ship closed the gap between the two vessels and attached ropes with grappling hooks at their ends between the ships. After making the ropes fast and thereby locking the two ships together, a group often pirates boarded Caesar's ship. A dirty man who also had a foul smell about him went to Caesar's ship's crew and started talking. He said, *"I am looking for the Legal Advocate called Gaius Julius Caesar!"* Caesar said, *"look no further, for I am he!"*

The pirate said, *"Good! You are coming with us to our base in Asia Minor, where you shall be held captive until Rome pays a ransom of twenty talents of silver for you!"* Caesar thought, *"Good! Your base is close to the Roman Naval Fleet's base in Asia Minor, and soon after you have delivered your ransom demands to my friend, you will pay the price of being criminal pirates! I will now make sure that you more than double the ransom demand, which will annoy Rome! That will be easy because you pirates are extremely stupid people,"*

He said, *"What?!! You are so cheap and stupid that you are only asking for twenty talents of silver for me? I am Gaius Julius Caesar, and you only wanting such a small amount of money for me is insulting to me! It would be best if you told Rome that you want a ransom of five hundred and fifty talents of gold for my safe return.*

It would be best if you delivered the message and ransom demand to Crassus in Asia Minor, where you have a port close to the Roman Naval Fleet. After I am safely returned to Roman territory, I shall begin to track you down. When that has been done, I will crucify all of you!"

That made the pirate leader laugh! He said, *"Very funny joke Caesar! You are in no position to threaten us pirates or anyone else, yet here you are saying that you will hunt us down and crucify us! You are a very funny Roman!"*

So it was that the ransom demand was paid, resulting in the release of Caesar. He set about raising a fleet and, together with his cohort of soldiers, pursued the pirates. After bringing his four ships into the harbour where the Pirates were anchored, Caesar ordered the arrest of all of the pirates. They were all arrested and jailed. He went to the jail and spoke to the leader of the pirates.

He said, *"Hey Pirate, when I was in your captivity, I made you the promise that I would track all of you down and crucify the lot of you! You thought that I was joking, and you dismissed everything I told you! The fact is that I do not joke!*

In the early hours of tomorrow morning, about twilight, all of you shall be taken to the small hill just out of town, and all of you will be crucified! Because of the fact that you pirates treated me well when I was in your captivity, I shall be merciful to you, and I am ordering that all of you are to have your throats cut after you have been placed on your crosses and tied to them. The reason that you shall not be nailed to the crosses is that nails are in short supply, so you will be attached to your crosses by rope!"

Soon after the pirates had been crucified and had their throats cut, Caesar was recalled to the cohort so that he could deal with an incursion from the east. Then he returned to Rome during the year 68 B.C... Soon after his return to

Rome, he was discussing his situation with his friend, Crassus.

He said, *"Crassus, my friend, I am at a bit of a loss of what I should do now. Can you advise me?"* Crassus answered, *"Certainly, Julius, my friend, you could return to the Priesthood of Jupiter now that Sulla who stripped you of that position no longer exists, or you could do something more suited to your personality. I think that you should stand for election as a military tribune, which will become your first step into a political career. After you have built up your reputation as a tribune, you could try standing for election as quaestor* (governor) *next year!"*

Caesar Becomes Tribune

Caesar said, *"Thank you for the advice, Crassus; that is what I shall do!"* Soon after that, he was elected as Tribune, and he continued to serve Rome with distinction. A year later, again, he was discussing his future with Crassus. He said, *"Thank you for advising me to stand for election as Tribune. It turned out that my standing in the army was such that my peers voted me into that position as soon as I announced my candidacy! I shall now stand for election as quaestor* (governor) *of Spain."*

For Gaius Julius Caesar (junior), this was a tumultuous time. His aunt Julia had died, and he was called upon to deliver the funeral eulogy. He did that and organised the funeral procession to include paintings of her husband and his uncle, Marius.

As well, his wife Cornelia had died during this time, and he organised her funeral. Soon after that, he went to Spain to serve his governorship in Hispania (Spain) in the early summer of 69 B.C... While he was serving as the

Roman governor there, he saw a statue of Alexander the Great. Seeing the statue of Alexander made Caesar feel insignificant.

He was speaking to one of his serving centurions. He said, *"Here I am at the age when Alexander the Great was the master of the world, and I have done nothing compared to that great man! I am insignificant at the moment! I must do something spectacular and noteworthy so that people will always remember me!"* During a visit from Crassus in the same year, he discussed his prospects with his friend and benefactor.

Crassus said, *"Julius, it seems to me that you should use your experience as the High Priest of Jupiter. And your past standings as a Roman military Tribune and your current duties as the Roman Governor of Spain. To stand for election to the post of "Pontifex Maximus." which is the position of the main priest of the Roman State religion. However, please be aware that you shall be facing two powerful adversaries. They are the Senators of Catiline and possibly Cicero!"*

Caesar did so, and during his investigations, he found that Catiline was plotting against him. Catiline had the help of others, such as Cicero. He discussed the situation with Marcus Licinius Crassus. Crassus told him, *"Julius, be warned, that several senators who are friends of Cataline are saying that you were actually behind the plot to seize control of the Republic which you have proved against him! Make sure that you serve Rome well in your post as governor of Hispania* (Spain). *I know that soon, you shall be promoted to propraetor and that you will govern all of Spain known as Hispania Ulterior. I shall continue to back you."*

So it was that in 60 B.C., Crassus paid some of Caesar's debts and acted as his guarantor for others, in return for Caesar's political support for Crassus against Pompey. While in Spain, Caesar and his army conquered two local tribes. That resulted in Gaius Julius Caesar being hailed as *imperator. (During the time of the republic, this meant "Commander in Chief". After that, the name applied to the emperors)* by his soldiers. He reformed the law regarding debts and completed his governorship in high esteem.

He was discussing his options with Crassus, who now spoke. He said, *"Julius, my friend, I fully realise that you wish to have an official triumph. For that, you must first have approval from the Senate. Now then, Julius, I know that you also want to stand for election to the position of Consul. Either way, you must have the approval of the Senate. Under Roman law, if you are to celebrate a Triumph, you must stay outside the city of Rome until the ceremony.*

To stand for election to Consul, you must resign from your command and then enter Rome as a private citizen. However, there is a possible way around all of that. You could address the senate yourself and ask for permission to stand for election in absentia while you and your legions are waiting outside of Rome. (Legions were only allowed into Rome to have parades such as a Triumph.)

Caesar replied, *"Thank you, Marcus. I shall put this before the Senate at the meeting today."* He did so and was shocked to hear Cato speak out. He said, *"There is no way in which I can support anyone having a Triumph in Rome and at the same time stand for election to the position of consul! What Caesar is proposing is downright dangerous to the Republic! Caesar, you now must make the choice of becoming Consul or of celebrating your triumph over the*

Spanish tribal nations. You cannot have both, so make up your mind which of the two options you want!" So it was that Caius Julius Caesar became a consul and took command of four legions. He won the election along with Marcus Bibulus.

Although Caesar was in debt to Crassus, he was also his friend. Caesar was thinking of how to obtain more power for himself, and he knew that he could not challenge those in authority. He spoke to Crassus. He said, *"Marcus, I have an idea which will make both of us a lot more powerful. However, we need to have Pompey with us, or we will not completely control the Republic. Therefore, I suggest that you let me attempt to get Pompey to join us in an informal alliance that I call the "First Triumvirate" (Rule of the three men).*

Crassus answered, *"By Jupiter, Julius, I like the way that you think! Yes, please see Pompey and have him join us in governing Rome for ourselves!"* After that, Caesar saw Pompey and the "First Triumvirate" became a reality. By now, Caesar had married again; this time, his wife was Calpurnia, a powerful Roman Senator's daughter. The relationship with Pompey was sealed by Pompey marrying the daughter of Caesar, called Julia.

A meeting was held between Crassus, Caesar, and Pompey. Crassus said, *"Gentlemen, as the First Triumvirate, the three of us hold great powers! However, we also have dangerous opponents. One of these is the rival to Julius, and he is Marcus Bibulus! I think that we must somehow enlist the support of the ordinary poor people of Rome. That could be the best way for us to remain in power. So, please, the pair of you, let's discuss what we can do to ensure that we somehow remain as the supreme rulers of Rome!"*

There was complete silence for a short time while the three men considered the implications of what they were discussing. Caesar said, *"It seems to me that the lower-class citizens of Rome do not have much going for them! They have very little in the way of property rights, no matter if the property is the home, they either rent or own, and their prospects are very far from what is acceptable to men like us! Therefore, to obtain support from the populous lower classes of people, I will introduce into the Senate a law that will redistribute all public land to the poor.*

Such an act will be opposed with vigour by Rome's wealthier citizens, and you can bet that to make it come about, we shall have to be willing to enforce the new law by the force of arms! If both of you support me this, I shall place the new law before the Senate in the next morning!"

After a short period of silence, Crassus spoke. He said, *"Julius, thank you for yet again coming up with a workable solution to the problems facing us! I agree with you that we should introduce the new law you speak of to allow the poor people to have property rights comparable with the more prosperous ruling cases! Therefore, you have my full support!'*

Pompey now spoke. He said, *"Thank you, Julius, I shall also support you. I am sure that our enemies such as Marcus Bibulus will make a lot of trouble, and the only way to control that will be for me to see to it that my army is placed on duty in Rome itself, even though Roman law forbids the permanent presence of the legions within Rome!*

My soldiers will be placed on duty in Rome despite the law in order to enforce the rights of the lower classes. Therefore, go ahead in the morning and introduce the new law. You have my backing and that of Crassus. Together, we are the First Triumvirate. My soldiers will enter the city tonight, and they shall stay within it and make sure that no physical action by our opponents is possible!"

At mid-morning of the following day, Caesar was speaking in the Senate. He said, *"Fellow Romans, in order for Rome to always be invincible, we must have the full loyal support of all citizens. The lower classes of Roman society and the poor Romans do not have any property rights! I am introducing new laws which will make the withholding of property rights for the lower classes and the poor against Roman law!"*

He had barely uttered those words when he was rudely interrupted by Marcus Bibulus. He angrily shouted, *"There are nothing but bad omens regarding the stupid laws such as this! The underclass and the poor are necessary for the rich to stay rich, and unless we can exploit the poor, the Roman ruling classes will end up being poor themselves!"*

Despite his actions of saying that there were only bad omens surrounding Caesar's new laws, the Senate passed the laws. That resulted in Markus Bibulus being in fear of losing his life, and he retired to his house, and he was only seen on rare occasions after that.

One year later, with his political allies' help, Caesar secured the passage of the *lex Vatinia,* which gave him the governorship of northern Italy and *Illyricum* (south-eastern Europe). He completed his Consulship and left to take up his new provinces' governorship in the north of Italy and Gaul.

Settlements of Germanic Nations in Gaul

Although the Romans regarded the Rhine as the boundary between Gaul and Germania, both Gallic and Germanic nations overstepped it and obtained settlements within each other's territories. The tribes of Germania regarded Gaul, its people and wealth as their own and continued to invade Gaul whenever they chose to do so. The Romans wanted Gaul for themselves. Julius Caesar exploited the enmity between the Gauls and the Germanic tribespeople in order to subdue them both.

There is much evidence of Germanic take-overs of Gaul. For example, while invading Gaul, the Cimbri and Teutones left behind them on the Rhine their bulkier stores and baggage. They were left under the guard of six thousand of their own people. After the destruction of their fellow Germanic tribesmen, this group of people became involved in constant clashes with neighbouring nations until they settled the district between the Meuse and Scheldt Rivers. (Greenwood, 1836)

There can be no argument that the Balgae people, although Caesar mentions them as being among the nations that made up Gaul, were of Germanic origin. In order to find answers to various questions, he set off with his army on foot to find out the strength of the Belgic league which had been formed against him.

He had been speaking to some members of the local tribes who informed him. He was told, *"The Belgic tribes in Gaul are made up of a union between the local Celtic tribes and the invading Germanic tribes. When the Germans came here, they intermarried with the original Celts and, to a large extent, even took up the language and the customs of the people whom they had conquered.*

They did, however, pass on their Germanic outlook and love of warlike adventure. The result is that the descendants of these Germanic warriors are the only people who were able to withstand successfully the Cimbri and Teutones nations' invasions!" The facts about this are that Germanic tribesmen's invasions into Gaul were so numerous that there were many parts of the country that had settlements of Germanic tribespeople.

The main ones being, *Bellovaci, Nervii, Aduatici* and *Treviri*. It is known that the Bellovaci occupied the area around Beauvais, while the Nervii settled in Brabant, Flanders and Hainault. The Aduatici in the area of modern Tiers, on the banks of the Mosel. Their wars with their Celtic neighbours were frequent until they had intermarried with the Celts to form the people of Belgium and parts of France.

Two powerful Gallic nations, the *Aedui* and the *Sequani,* were engaged in a struggle for supremacy. The Sequani occupied the district between the eastern banks of the Arar and the Jura. The Aedui stayed on the western banks of the Arar. The Aedui applied for and were granted an alliance with Rome. The Sequani sought and were successful in obtaining an alliance with their Germanic neighbours. (Greenwood, 1836)

The Helvetii, Boii and Gallic Tribes

The Roman historian Tacitus regarded both the Helvetii and Boii as nations that occupied Germania's southern regions between the Mayne and the Alps as being of Gallic origin, without any evidence to support that theory. The fact remains that both tribes occupied land in Germania through to Switzerland. On the other hand, there is a great deal of evidence supporting the theory that the aboriginal Germanic tribes overstepped the Rhine and made the territory of the Celtic Gauls their own whenever they wanted to do so.

The **Helvetii** were a huge Germanic tribe comprising many people. They had settled the land between the Mayne River, and the Alps were present along the eastern banks of the Upper Rhine River. The Mayne separated them from the *Suevi,* and many of the *Helvetii* people at the time were living in Switzerland.

At a meeting of elders called to discuss how best to manage their crowded areas, Chlodochar spoke. He said, *"My brethren, we are experiencing over-crowding at the moment! Much of our territory is in mountainous areas, and we are seeing many of our cattle die from a lack of good grass to eat!*

That can not be allowed to continue, for if our cattle all die, so will the Helevii tribe! I propose that the entire Helvetii tribe migrates to better pastures areas! In order to not have to make war upon other people, we should approach the people of all areas through which we will have to pass and get their approval for us to do so!"

The next man to speak was Egino. He said, *"Fellow members of the Helvetii, I fully agree with Chodochar that we must migrate with our herds of cattle in order not to starve to death. I also agree that we must avoid conflict if possible, by asking the people who hold the land that we must cross for their permission to do so! In fact, my group of warriors and I have already asked for the Governing Celtic Gaul's approval for us to cross Gaul without any problems coming from the Gauls. We now also need to obtain permission to cross Gaul from the Roman Governor called Gaius Julius Caesar!"*

An older woman named Alodia now spoke. She said, *"I am most pleased to hear that the male members of this society are now calling for negotiations with the people who own the land which we must cross. I have always thought that we should have a consensus with these people, and that way, we will not have to fight everyone all of the time! Therefore, I give approval and blessings to obtaining authorisation from the Gauls to cross their lands on our way to other places.*

We shall take anything from them that is not already ours, and if we need something they have, we shall pay for it! However, be warned that we are very likely to have trouble with Gaul's new Roman Governor, called Caesar! That is because the Romans want Gaul for themselves, and this Caesar wishes to enrich himself at our expense! So, my people, be ready to have Caesar reject our application to cross Gaul with our herds of cattle and people! It is highly likely that we will have to fight him."

So it was that the envoys of the Helvetii had an audience with Caesar. He said, *"Who are you, and what is it that you want?"* The leader of the diplomatic party of the Helvetii was called Filibert. He said, *"We are from the Helvetii tribes, and we are asking for your permission to cross Gaul on our way to better grasslands for our herds of cattle.*

We shall not take anything that is not ours, and we will pay for everything we may need along the way. By doing this, there should be no complaints, and everyone will be happy with the result. We must take up some new areas, and we must cross some territory that you control to be successful at this!"

Caius Julius Caesar did not even consider what the Helvetii wanted. He said, *"No, you may not cross my territory, and I will regard any attempt to do so as an act of war! I remind you that I have four legions compete with supporting units on hand, and I will march against you people if you attempt to cross my territory!"*

At another meeting of the elders of the *Helvetii* tribe, a woman called Bodil spoke. She said, *"Comrades, think back upon what has happened. We have obtained permission to cross Gaul from the Gauls themselves. Only the arrogant Romans have acted against us. Caesar has made it plain that he has four legions and supporting units to use against us, and he will do so!*

No matter what the Romans say or think, we have to cross Gaul to get to our new grazing pastures, or we will die! The Romans stand between us and what we must have. War is now almost inevitable! I call upon this council of elders to go into a joint defence pact with Ariovistus because of the threat coming from Caesar and his Roman legions!" The matter was further debated, and it was agreed to form a defence pact with Ariovistus.

Ariovistus (Battle Chieftan of the Suebi) in Gaul

The powerful Gallic tribe called Aedui were involved in a bitter power struggle for supremacy with the Sequani tribe, and that resulted in the Aedui being allied to Rome. Due to the Aedui being allied to Rome, the Sequani sent envoys to their Germanic neighbours across the Rhine. That resulted in fifteen thousand Germanic warriors crossing the Rhine to provide immediate assistance to their Gallic allies. The leader of the Germanic warriors was known as Ariovistus. (Latinised name)

The first groups of Germanic warriors were followed by many others resulting in the numerical strength of them being one hundred and twenty thousand fighting men. All of them were within Sequani territory. These warriors were collectively called Suevii by the Romans, even if their tribes were Helevatii or Boii. When it came, military action resulted in the Aedui being defeated in every battle and losing their chiefs and nobles on the battlefield. Not only that, but their Roman allies deserted them. Meetings of the various councils of elders of the various tribes agreed that they should trust the Germanic warrior called Ariovistus.

At a meeting of the Elders of his tribe, the warrior leader called Ariovistus spoke. He said, *"Our allies, the Sequani are now victorious due to our recent help infighting their enemies! The victory was obtained due to our male warriors with great help of our Germanic women!*

We shall now bring forth many more of our warriors to settle the lands of the Aedui and establish permanent Germanic settlements in Gaul! Many of our warriors shall intermarry with the Gauls whom we have defeated. We must do that because it will not be long before the news of the Aedui being defeated by us reaches Rome. The Romans are sure to attempt to stop our progress in Gaul because the greedy little southerners want to have Gaul for themselves!

By intermarrying with the Gauls, our tribes of Helvetii and Boii will become part of Gaul, and that will act as a fortified border protecting our original homeland against the Romans. You can all be sure that the Romans will attack us soon!" As Ariovistus had said, it was not long before Caesar appeared.

Meanwhile, due to having the same problem of being ruled by the Germanic warriors, envoys were exchanged between the Aedui and the Sequani. A chief of the Aedui called Andecombos was in conference with a leader of the Sequani called Carillius.

He said, *your Germanic allies have conquered us of the Aedui, and I would like it if we can both work together to get rid of these Germanic upstarts who have taken over our country. I know that they are your allies, but you must also be paying the price of being allies with them!"*

The chief of the Sequani, called Carillius, spoke. He said, *"Yes, Andecombos, there are many strings attached to our joint victory with the German warriors. However, the burden we have to bear is nothing compared to what you are experiencing.*

Because your people attacked the Germans, they have waged war upon you. Your people lost the fight with them when you were attacking us. As a result, of your people being conquered by the Germans, you now have to provide them with hostages on an on-going basis. Your alliance with Rome is at an end. Due to your actions of ending the alliance to please your conquerors. They will do the same to us if my people are not careful."

Andecombos of the Aedui now spoke. He said, *"Carillius, I think that it will not be long before the greedy Romans under the command of Julius Caesar comes here to see why the goods usually sent from Gaul to Rome have stopped coming. If we now set up a confederacy of Gallic Chiefs opposed to the Germanic invaders, we should be able to begin actions against them and hopefully drive them out of Gaul."*

Andecombos of the Aedui said, *"I like the way you think, Carillius, but the fact is that the Germans are intermarrying with the Celtic Gauls, and they are taking up the ways of the original people of Gaul.*

Their language and ours are slowly changing to become a mixture of the Celtic tongue spoken by many Gauls and German. So, unless we can come up with a way of defeating Ariovistus and his Germanic warriors, we shall have to wait for Caesar to arrive and to put things right!"

Spies were everywhere among the Gauls, and news of the newly set-up confederacy between the Gallic chiefs was taken to Ariovistus. After he had been informed of the Gallic Chiefs' activities, he became enraged. He shouted, *"So, both our allies, the Sequani and our defeated enemies, the Aedui, are combining their men to try to make war upon us! Very well then, let them try to do that!*

We will now immediately march upon both the Sequani who have turned 'Dog' on us, and we shall teach the Aedui a lesson that they will never forget! They shall pay more tribute and hostages directly to me! The Sequani shall, as of now, give up two-thirds of their land to us. We shall settle that new territory!"

While Ariovistus was subjugating both tribes, Caius Julius Caesar had taken up command of the Gallic province in the name of "The Republic of Rome" on behalf of the Roman Senate. He took up his consulate and set up his government, which allowed him to use his military and political talents to the full. The reasons for this were Rome's greed and the memories of Romans that Rome was under threat by Germanic forces on previous occasions. Therefore, the movement of such a large number of people and their capabilities under leader Ariovistus were of concern. Having the recent successes of Ariovistus fresh in their minds, combined with the earlier perils of Cimbric and Teutonic invasions, the Germanic migrations were seen as alarming proof of Rome's dangers so recently escaped were now as present as ever before.

Battle of Bibracte

At a meeting between the representatives of the Helvetii and Dumnorix of the Sequani, approval was given for the Helvetii to cross Gaul. Just as the meeting between Helvetii and Dumnorix was concluding, a spy left for the camp of Julius Caesar.

Being ushered in to see Caesar, he said, *"My liege, I have urgent news for your ears alone!"* Caesar said, *"Very well then, what is the news? Hurry up, man, and I do have all day!"* The spy said, *"Mighty Caesar, do you know where the city of Bricrate is and do you know who the leader of the Gauls is?"*

Caesar was becoming rather impatient. He said, *"Of course I know where Bibracte is, and I know who Dumnorix is. Are you trying to provoke me?!"* The spy was now concerned that he might be getting into difficulties with Caesar, so he decided to tell him everything without trying for a reward for himself.

He said, *"Mighty Caesar, I have just come from a meeting between Dumnorix and the Helvetii. They asked him for safe passage across Gaul for their people and their herds of cattle. Dumnorix has given the Helvetii approval to cross Gaul.* Caesar shouted, *"Hades and damnation! I told the*

Helvetii that if they came to Gaul with their herds and people, that I would regard it as a declaration of war! But they appear not to be taking any notice! Very well, then! War they want, and they shall have it! Do you know the name of their leader?" The spy said, *"I heard them call their new leader, who has come to aid them from the Suebi Tribe in Germania, by the name of Ariovistus! Apparently, he is a mighty warrior!"*

Caesar was alarmed by the news. He said, *"I find your information very worrying! So, the Germanic tribes are in Gaul and becoming a lot stronger! To make sure that the Germanic enemy is held in check, I am going to Gallia Crisalpina. There, I shall take five entire legions of heavy infantry and support cavalry turmae and specialist support turmae. Then we will march across the Rhone River into the lands of the Sequani who are already under attack from Ariovistus backed by both Helvetii and Suebi warriors!"*

Hearing of this resulted in the *Aedui* trying to renew their previous alliance with Rome. Caesar received their envoys. He said, *"Before when Ariovistus invaded your territory, you did not fight, and you lost your lands and hostages. I should throw you to the wolves and make you take on the Germans on your own! However, this time, I will be merciful and let you have your previous alliance with Rome back!"*

In the meantime, the Germanic enemy had overrun the entire country between the Jura and Saone Rivers. Caesar wanted to stop the invading warriors before they had time to make use of Gaul's resources. He now crossed to the left bank of the Saone. The Helvetii moved three large parts of their army to the opposite bank. Also, they sent a large detachment of Tigurini warriors to aid those already in place.

Caesar called for a "Council of War" with the officers of his forces. When this conference began, Caius Julius Caesar spoke. He said, *"You will immediately get all soldiers of your various cohorts and their sub-units together. We are conducting a forced night march to the Tigurini camp, and when our forces arrive there, we will immediately attack.*

No-one is to make any noise of any kind during our forced march to the Tigurini Camp, and we will have no mercy for the enemy! We will wipe them out! Right now, we have five full legions of heavy infantry and all necessary supporting units, including cavalry! Ensure that you kill all of the enemy warriors and if there happen to be some survivors, see to it that they are taken away and sold as slaves. By doing those things, we will protect Roman interests in Gaul, and by the selling of prisoners as slaves, we will recover some of the costs of these campaigns in Gaul!"

Caesar's forces did as he ordered and closed with the enemy, killing them as he wanted. Having accomplished his aim of wiping out the Tigurini warriors, Caesar ordered a bridge to be built over the Saone River.

At an Orders Group, he said, *"Gentlemen, we are going to use the highly increased mobility of being able to have all five of our legions; plus all of their supporting units, including cavalry, to both cross and recross the river at any time we decide to do so! That will enable Roman forces to at all times be familiar with the movements of the Germanic forces facing us. That will give us the edge over the enemy*

, who will be surprised at the speed of the movement of Roman army units!"

As Caesar had predicted, the barbarian warriors were surprised at the speed of the Roman army's movements, and they sent an older chief named Divico to negotiate with Caesar. He said, *"Caesar, I am Divico and a chief of the Helvetii Tribe. I am authorized to offer Rome some concessions which are to the advantage of Rome to have. Take note that we shall not be the first to attack even though we are rightfully defending ourselves! The only thing that we want is for Rome to leave us alone during our migration to the pastures in the north. In order to get there, we must go through your territory. We will not take what is not ours, and we will pay for everything that we may need, so there is no need for you to harass us. On the other hand, if Rome continues to act against us, we will make a war upon you!"*

Caesar laughed as he said, *"You Germanic warriors do not worry me! I have five full strength legions of Roman heavy infantry, all of which are supported by cavalry and specialist units. As I told you lot the last time you asked for my permission to cross Gaul with your herds and people, the answer is no! Just as before, you are officially being warned that if you do cross Gaul, your actions will be regarded by me as an act of war, and I will mobilise my Roman army units against you immediately!*

That also means that we shall kill all women and children that may be with you warriors. As well, we shall take your cattle and sell them to the highest bidder. Get it through your thick Germanic heads that Rome rules!" As he was departing, Divico yelled, *"Caesar, you have just made the first of several mistakes which shall cost you dearly, you arrogant Roman pig!"* He and his escort of two hundred Helvetii warriors then departed for the Germanic held areas.

Caesar and the Influence of Dumnorix

At an 'Officers' Dining in Night', Caesar was in discussion with many of his officers of various ranks. The main subject under discussion was that of Ariovistus and how his Suebi warriors were becoming a major problem to Rome. A Centurion was speaking to a Tribune.

The Tribune said, *Centurion, what do you know about the situation with the Sequani and their Helvetii allies?"* Centurion Maximus said, *"Tribune, the word from the Germanic tribes that are settled in Gaul is that Rome is a bully and our leader, Gaius Julius Caesar is a plunderer who is little better than the worst pirates or other criminals.*

The Germanic tribes are openly saying that they asked for permission to cross Gaul peacefully and offered to pay for anything that they required. However, that was thrown back into their faces by Caesar, who will now reap a bitter harvest.

As a result of Caesar not permitting the tribes to cross Gaul, they have confederated, and now the Helvetii are having their ranks swelled by the addition of Suebic warriors coming directly across the Rhine from Germania. Things have become worse because the leader of the Sequani called Dumnorix has granted the Helvetii permission to cross the Sequani territory.

My informants tell me that because Dumnorix gave the Helvetii permission to cross his territory, they have been able to go as far as the interior of Gaul." Caesar overheard the conversation, and he then spoke to both the centurion and the tribune in turn. He said, *"Centurion, how reliable is your information that Dumnorix has defied Rome and me by letting the Helvetii pass through his territory and that they are already in Roman-occupied Gaul?"*

The Centurion answered, *"Sir, I have complete faith in the intelligence about the Germanic enemy from my sources. Not only that but do I have some spies working for me in the Sequani city of Bibracte. When I was told of the actions of Dumnorix, I organised a reconnoitre patrol, and my soldiers have backed up the information that the Helvetii are now in the parts of Gaul, which you regard as a Roman Province!"*

Caesar was indignant. He said, *"Centurion Maximus, I am promoting you to the position of Senior Centurion, and your century of soldiers is going to be increased from the current eighty men to one hundred men. That will give your century the highest amount of prestige in the 'VIII Legion'. Make sure that you serve it well, for it is one of my favourite legions!*

I am sending you to arrest Dumnorix and then bring him before me for a show trial. While you are arresting Dumnorix, I am sending Labienus and his legions to attack the Helvetii. He and his units are to seize the high ground and the crest of hills behind the Helvetii.

This army is now approaching the Aedan city of Bibracte. There, we should be able to obtain all needed resupplies because the Aedui are Roman allies!" Unfortunately for Caesar, the tactics of Labienus were anticipated by the enemy. That resulted in the Romans failing to take the high ground. Labeinus and his men were now being hard-pressed. Meanwhile, the Helvetii took the high ground themselves and positioned themselves into the path of Julius Caesar. Battle was now unavoidable!

A Centurion reported to Caesar. He said, *"Sir, we currently do not know the where-abouts of Labeinus and his legion. Our own situation is that the three legions and their supporting units, which are with us, are under constant attack by the Helvetii. They are attacking our positions with fury, and they have driven the first line of Roman soldiers back upon the second line, which they continue to attack with great fury! Having formed into a deep wedge-shaped column, the Germanic warriors are charging up the hill with their customary contempt for both danger and Romans!"*

Caesar said, *"Keep on defending Roman lines against the Helvetii advances. We currently hold some uneven high ground. Return to your cohort and hold your ground! Other soldiers are bringing our Scorpios and Ballistae to that area. When the siege weapons (Scorpios and Ballistae) are in place, use your weapons to continue raining arrows and spears upon the Germans.*

When the Scorpios and Ballistae in position, use them to throw large rocks and burning material at the enemy. Use the Scorpios to shoot large arrows and spears at them. (a Scorpio could launch a large arrow or spear every minute and have a range of up to three hundred metres depending upon the experience of its crew.) The result was that the Romans used skill and took advantage of holding the uneven high ground. The Helvetii found that they could not take the Roman positions. Ariovistus said, *"We have shown the arrogant Romans that we are a force to be reckoned with! We have been fighting the cowardly Romans for a very long time in this battle, and our warriors are tiring. As well, many of our warriors have wounds. For those reasons, we will retire to the next hill, which is about one thousand paces to our rear. When we arrive at the hill, we will take up defensive positions, which will give us the advantage of holding the high ground once again."*

A Roman soldier yelled. He said, *"Look at that! The enemy is withdrawing from here! Let's go and get the bastards!"* Many Romans now chased after the retreating Helvetii warriors. As they were chasing after the Helvetii, a Roman soldier called out in alarm. He said, *"Look over there in the south-west; there are two vast masses of Germanic warriors! Unless the God of War called Mars is with us, we will all die now!"*

The Roman had seen the arrival of the Boii and Tulingi bringing new units into the battle. The day was saved for Rome by the sudden arrival of Caesar with his reserve legions. Caesar attacked while also bringing up his second grouping of soldiers, which immediately wheeled into line to assist the first Roman units. Simultaneously, a third mass of Roman soldiers attacked the Boii and Tulingi to their front.

The well-directed Roman military tactics finally beat the Germanic tribesmen after a long and bloody fight. The Helvetii were capable warriors of great strength who had immense capabilities and combined that with their utter contempt toward danger and their probable deaths. At the same time, they were contemptuous of the Romans, whom they regarded as cowards who liked to skulk behind walls and avoid battle.

On the other hand, the Romans had a high degree of discipline and were skilled in minor infantry tactics. Also, they had both chainmail and plate armour and superior weapons compared to their Germanic foes. Their superior amour, weapons, and tactics gave the Romans the edge over their enemies.

The ruling 'Council of Elders' held a meeting to discuss the tactical situation. Baldwin addressed the gathering. He said, *"My brethren, Caesar and his Romans have been successful in occupying some uneven high ground which they can use to press down upon us! It is of critical importance that we move out of this area in an orderly manner and without confusion.*

I would much like to see some of our warriors covering our retreat. For that, I think it best to have our ally from the Suebi speak about how he and some of our warriors can cover our retreat while inflicting severe damage to the Romans. Ariovistus, please address this meeting of the Elders of the Helvetii!"

Ariovistus strode into the centre of the debating area and spoke. He said, *"My dear comrades, the Helvetii, you are Germanic warriors as are the Suebi! At times such as these, the Germanic tribes will join together for offensive or defensive war! The exceedingly arrogant Romans have refused Helvetii requests to cross Gaul to reach the pastures in the north. That means they want you all to die!*

As Baldwin has just said, you must all retreat to better and more easily defended areas. I have five hundred Suebi warriors with me, and I will take three hundred of your Helvetii warriors to help me. Together, we shall attack the Romans where they are currently feeling very safe, in the uneven high ground that they are holding. Late tonight, when it is very dark, and the Romans will no longer have the advantage of being able to see over long distances, most Helvetii will move out in an orderly fashion.

Your retreat to other more easily defended high ground shall take place now. While the main body of the tribe moves out, my Suebi and Helvetii warriors will slowly advance up the Roman held high ground. We will use cover from view afforded by the terrain to get close to the Romans, and then we will slay them!"

Adalhard now spoke. He said, *"Thank you, Ariovistus! I am most glad that you are here aiding us. It is said that you have had fifteen battles and that you have won all of them! Our people shall now move out of here to the other more easily defended areas which we have selected. Ariovistus and his men will secure our rears and inflict much pain onto the Romans while we depart."*

While Ariovistus and his men were covering the Helvetii rear, the tribe moved out of the area. Meanwhile, Ariovistus and those he commanded went to the uneven high ground. They annoyed the Romans by launching probing attacks along the entire Roman perimeter and the shooting of arrows and darts into the Roman position until the next morning's very early hours.

A Centurion of the First Cohort of the X Legion was holding an 'Orders Group' with his men. He said, *"Men, our legion commander, has ordered that we find out what the enemy is doing, and if the right circumstances present themselves, we are to wipe them out! Decanus Aloysius, take your seven other men and scout towards our immediate front. Move-in a south-easterly direction. Do not engage the enemy in combat. Make notes of everything you see about the enemy, and be sure to report what you have seen to me by mid-morning. You and your men will move out now!*

Decanus Dominic, you and your men will move forwards in a southerly direction. Your job is to observe any enemy activity that may be present. You and your men are not to engage the enemy in combat; you are only to observe and report your findings directly to me at mid-morning. You move out now!

Next, he called out. He said, *"Decanus Petran, you and your men will move in a south-westerly direction. Just like the other two units, you are not to engage the enemy. Your job is to observe the enemy and come back here to report your findings about the enemy to me by mid-morning. You will move out now towards your objective. All of our units and sub-units are to go no further than six Roman miles (Roman mile = 1,000 paces) from this location. If you reach that limit without seeing the enemy, just return to this position!"*

Decanus Aloysius and his other seven men were carefully and silently moving through some undergrowth when they saw many wagon and supply vehicles. These were acting as a bulwark between the Romans and the Helvetii. Aloysius said, *"By Jupiter and Mars! Just look at that! Before us must be almost the entire rear-echelon of the Helvetii! This information must be taken back to our Centurion immediately! We are returning to camp now!"*

Having returned to the position of the legion, Aloysius reported to his centurion. He said, *"Sir, we have found that the rear-echelon of the entire Helvetii column is within two Roman miles of this position. The column of wagons, rear-echelon workers, and camp follower is acting as a bulwark between the Helvetii warriors and us. What are your orders, sir?"*

Centurion Marcus Titus said, *"Decanus Aloysius, go and join the rest of the men in this Cohort! We shall now take this fight to the column of wagons that you have told me about. Your Century shall form the main one of the main parts of the cohort attack upon the Helvetii wagons. That should be a comfortable victory for us because the only warriors with the wagons will be the old and infirm. Other than that, there should only be women with the wagons!"*

So it was that Centurion Marcus Titus spoke to his commanding officer, and they agreed to attack the Helvetii supply train of wagons. Marcus was with two of his forward men's scouts and was peering through some bushes when he became satisfied that it was the best time to attack.

He went to his Optio (equivalent to a sergeant in modern armies) and conferred with him. He said, *"Optio, this is the First Century of the Cohort. As such, we have a total of one hundred men, not counting the officers, because we have more prestige than the other centuries. They also happen to be the best soldiers in the Cohort. You can see the Helvetii column before us out there on the plain just beyond the river crossing.*

One of our scouts has reported that among the people with the column, there are some persons who are holding high ranks. We can see the general direction they are going, and it is to our advantage to go ahead of the column so that we can find suitable sites to ambush the column and then to storm it!"

Like most sergeants before and after him, the Optio immediately took charge of things. He said, *"No problem, sir; let's immediately move out of here, get ahead of the Germanic warriors and place the ambush of their supply wagon train."* The Romans left their area and moved to a point ahead of the Helvetii. They then placed their ambush in an area of forest where the track through it was bending.

Centurion Marcus Titus saw the leading wagon of the approaching Helvetii coming, and he went to his men lining the side of the track. He said, *"Men, you are to let the wagons through until the leading wagon is directly opposite the last Roman in this ambush site. You will know that our when Cornicen (trumpeter) makes loud trumpet calls! When you hear the trumpet, you are all to storm the wagons and kill all of the Germans who are present!"*

The Romans were in a good ambush position which was totally hidden from the view of the approaching enemy wagon train. After almost thirty minutes had passed, there was the expected loud trumpet call. The Romans rushed forth and expected to have an easy victory. What they found was that the wagons were accompanied by other supply vehicles and pack animals. The Roman soldiers were not expecting to find fierce resistance to them, which the Helvetii women offered. In keeping with their Germanic traditions, they did much to slow the advance of the attacking Romans.

After a day and a night had passed, the Romans were finally successful and found that they had killed many enemy. They were surprised to find that they had lost many Romans due to the Helvetii women's intense fighting. Centurion Marcus Titus was happy with having secured the supply train of the Helvetii. He said, *"Today is a good day because we have captured the supplies of the Helvetii. As well, we have made prisoners of several people of high rank among them.*

It is most unfortunate that the main body of the enemies of Rome managed to escape. Our informants tell us that the Helvetii main body has the numerical strength of one hundred and thirty thousand warriors! Within the next few days, they should become tired, hungry and discouraged by our success! I am going to see the legion commander for further orders now!"

Caesar was aware of the things troubling the Helvetii. When the Helvetii finally reached Lingones, they accepted Caesar's terms to return to their own territory, and they became passive subjects of Rome.

Julius Caesar was discussing the security situation in Gaul with some of his officers. He said, *"Gentlemen, I have allowed the Helvetii to return to their newly conquered lands in Gaul. If that is not done, then other Germanic nations from across the Rhine will come in and take all of Gaul away from Rome! This way, we shall have a strong Germanic tribe who are Roman allies in Gaul's parts closest to the Germans. I only want nations that are known not to be dangerous to Rome to have territory in Gaul. Much of Gaul has been depopulated by the activities of both the Germanic tribes and the Romans."*

By the time the Battle of Bibracte was over, the rumour mills among the majority of Gauls had flourished. That resulted in most of the Gallic states' leaders hearing about it and hurrying to meet with Caesar and become allies with and congratulate him. Caesar was now being regarded with a sense of awe as well as admiration and fear; the Gallic leaders aligned themselves with Rome.

Julius Caesar and Ariovistus

The Sequani rejoiced at the news of Julius Caesar's victory over the Helvetii, knowing that Caesar's victory had delivered them from the enemy and they were determined to shake off the yoke of Ariovistus and his Germanic warriors.

At a conference between Caesar and the Sequani, Caesar was listening to the Sequani complaints. The Sequani called Ducarius spoke. He said, *"Mighty Caesar, We, the Sequani, will now once again take up our alliance with Rome that we were forced to renounce by Ariovistus and his Germanic warriors. He thinks that we have been dishonourable and even that we double-crossed him, but that is not true. We have only been trying to live our lives as best we can. Now that Ariovistus has conquered our lands, we have to submit everything to him. We have to pay him vast amounts of riches in tribute, and we even have to supply him with hostages and slaves constantly. We welcome your Victory over the Helvetii because he is on their side and against both you and Rome!*

We beg you mighty Caesar to liberate us from the Helvetii and their Suebi allies." Around Ducarius, several other Sequani (Celtic tribe of Gaul) men were crying. That sight amused Caesar, who now spoke. He said, *"You are men, but here you are in front of me, crying your eyes out like a bunch of old women! I can see why the Germanic warriors have beaten you. Instead of fighting them and throwing the invaders out of your country, you just weep and act like a bunch of soft women!*

I have no love for Ariovistus and his German warriors, but I deeply respect that man because at least he is courageous and honourable, which is so very unlike you, the cringing Sequani! So, Ducarius, what else is there about this matter that I should be informed of?"

Ducarius said, *"Mighty Caesar, we implore you and your Roman army to rid us of Ariovistus. We also implore you not to let anyone know that we have come to you for help in getting rid of the Germanic occupiers of our territory. We ask that of you because if Ariovistus hears that we have gone out to get Roman help to wipe out the German invaders, he will return, resulting in us suffering badly."*

Caesar said, *"You Sequani people do not impress me at all! I shall give you the help you want, but only because it will benefit Rome! I would rather be friends and allies with the Germanic warriors because at least they have both courage and honour, which you Sequani do not! No matter what the Helvetii and their allies such as Ariovistus may think, Rome has possession of Gaul, and I regard it as a prize well worth fighting for!"*

Next, Caesar spoke to the Roman officers near him. He said, *"Gentlemen, I need you to send your most able messengers to me, in particular, if they happen to be able to speak a Germanic language! I have important work for them!"*

The Roman officers conferred, and then the Tribune called Vitus Titus Magnus spoke. He said, *"Sir, one of my men, called Sergius Petran, was bought up in the household of a member of the Cherusci tribe. I think that you should consider using this man because he is fluent in Germanic languages!"* Caesar replied, *"Apparently, your man was bought up in a Cherusci household. That is very interesting! What is his rank, and how well does he perform his duties as a member of my X Legion?"*

The tribune replied, *"Sir, he has the rank of Optio, and he is perhaps one of the best soldiers of the First Cohort of the X Legion!"* Caesar replied, *"Tribune, I have never met this man, but I like him already! Have him bought before me immediately!"*

Several hours later, Optio Sergius Petran was ushered into the tent of Caesar. Julius saw him approach and stand before him awkwardly. Caesar said, *"Optio Sergius Petran, I need you to take messages from me to Ariovistus, the leader of the current Germanic confederation that has formed against Rome. Your work will be hard, and you may well die in performing it. So, tell me, are you willing to do my bidding, even though the likelihood is that you will die in trying to do your duties to Rome and me?"*

Optio Petran said, *"Sir, I am and will always be there to perform my duties for Rome and yourself! Sir, you can count on me because I will always do whatever is necessary to the best of my ability!"* Caesar replied, *"Petran, I have promoted you to the rank of Centurion. How do you like moving to commissioned rank?"* The new centurion replied, *"Thank you, sir, this will make my mother proud of me!"*

Caesar replied, *"It is my pleasure that you are now a Roman officer. Just make sure that I never regret promoting you to commissioned rank! Well, Centurion, go out there and take my messages to Ariovistus!"*

That resulted in Centurion Sergius Petran travelling to where the Helvetii were located. Having arrived near Bricrate, he asked people about the location of Ariovistus. Just as he and his escort of eight Roman soldiers were getting ready to have their evening meals, They were attacked by the Germanic warriors.

Soon, all nine men were overwhelmed and taken as prisoners to Ariovistus. It was getting towards the evening twilight when the nine Romans were bought before Ariovistus. He said, *"Do any of you cowardly Romans speak the civilised language of German rather than the uncivilised language called Latin?"*

Centurion Petran answered, *"I am Centurion Petran, and I have orders from Caesar to inform you that Caesar is anxious to consult with you about matters which are of great importance to both the Romans and the Germanic tribes. Caesar wants you to choose a convenient place where both of you can meet in safety and discuss the matters at hand."*

Ariovistus answered, *"Tell that exceedingly arrogant Roman pig that such an interview is very inconvenient, and I can see that such a meeting will place me into a significant risk! As far as I can see, such an arrangement will not lead to any good result for my people or myself because the Romans have already proved themselves to be both cowards and liars! Also, tell Caesar that I do not understand why he or the Roman people should worry about my share of Gaul because I have no plans to interfere with the Roman share of it!"* That resulted in Centurion Petran and his escort returning to Caesar with the answer from Ariovistus. After Petran had delivered the message from Ariovistus, Caesar went into one of his customary periods of silence while he thought over the situation now before him.

He said, *"Centurion Petran, you have done well! Your next assignment is to return to Ariovistus with my demands. You are to tell him that I, Caius Julius Caesar, have on this day decreed that he must not ever again bring more Germanic warriors into Gaul from the other side of the Rhine! Make sure that you tell him that he must immediately restore the hostages of the Aedui whom he is holding and that he must give back to the Sequani all of the land territory that he has taken from them!"*

Armed with this latest message, Centurion Petran and his escort returned to the camp of Ariovistus. Petran told Ariovistus what Caesar had said. That made Ariovistus speak. He said, *"Centurion Petran, return to Caesar and tell him that what he wants and the conditions he has set are entirely intolerable! Ensure that he understands that the hostages and subsidies granted to me by the Aedui are mine by the right of conquest! By that right, I fully intend to hold them. I do not want more enemies whom I have to fight, and I would like to have peace and co-operation.*

Make sure that he knows that although I want both peace and co-operation, I shall never shy away from a fight and that although I have been at war with various enemies for fifteen years, I have never lost a battle! If I am further provoked, Caesar and the Romans will soon find out it is no easy matter for them to take on a nation of warriors who have not lived under any roof for the past fifteen years!"

After his conversation with Ariovistus, Centurion Petran made notes of everything that was said and returned to the encampment of Caesar. Arriving at Caesar's tent, he was escorted into the presence of Caesar. Approaching Caesar, Petran gave the Roman salute and greeted Caesar. The two men then began to discuss what Ariovistus had said.

Now alarmed, Caesar said, *"Thank you, Centurion Petran, for the information. I now know that Rome's danger posed by the Germanic and other Teutonic tribes is real and imminent. If the Germanic warriors led by Ariovistus are allowed to conquer all of Gaul, the Roman Republic's territory will come under direct threat. In particular, now that the Germanic tribes have conquered the Sequani. That only leaves the Rhone River as a barrier between them and Rome."*

A messenger was ushered into the presence of Caesar. Caesar said, *"Well, messenger, what is it?"* The messenger replied, *"Sir, I am Ranulf Atticus. My unit specializes in the gathering of intelligence about the enemy and his movements. I am fluent in the German tongues and therefore know that what we heard is correct because what we heard is backed up by direct observation!*

Ariovistus has sent orders for massive reinforcements from Germania. That has resulted in an enormous force of Suebi warriors already on their way to aid Ariovistus." The reaction of Caesar was like that of a startled animal. He said, *"Great, just great! Things are already bad enough with just the Helvetii now having the help of Ariovistus. To top that off, you have just informed me that there are now massive numbers of Suebi coming here from Germania. Messenger, you have done well, now go and refresh while I attend to the problems at hand."*

An optio was standing near him. Caesar said, *"Optio, move out to all senior Roman officers and bring them here for an information and orders group!"* The optio said, *"Yes, sir!"* and immediately left to fulfil his orders. He returned with the officers as ordered as quickly as he could, and the information and orders group got underway.

Caesar said, *"The Helvetii and the Suebi under Ariovistus are causing many problems, and now an enormous Suebi army is moving out of Germania on the way here. In order to prevent the joining of the Germanic forces, I have ordered Roman legions to make forced marches to the town of Vesontio. It has an excellent natural position and provides a good base capable of supporting future Roman operations. We shall, therefore, make ourselves the masters of the town."*

Meanwhile, Ariovistus and his Germanic warriors were held up by the hereditary enemies of the Suebi, the Ubii. Ariovistus was talking to some of his warriors. He said, *"We must either ignore the Ubii or else we must wipe them out! We must also overcome all other obstacles, and we must get stuck into the Roman bullies! I know that the Romans are at Vesontio!"*

At Vesontio, in the Roman billets, Decanus Sergius was speaking to legionnaire Rufus. He said, *"Rufus, it appears that the Germans may soon be among us, and that does not bode well for us! They are fierce warriors who are exceptionally tall. They have superhuman strength. Their hair is either blond or red, and they have blue eyes! Their war cries are terrifying, and there are reported to be huge masses of them! We may well die when facing these formidable warriors!"*

Caesar was walking through his encampment and listening to what his soldiers were saying and talking to them. Thus, he became aware that many of his men were fearful of the Germans and that fear was threatening to break up his army. He was very aware that he had to impose a delay before attacking Ariovistus to re-establish the Roman army's confidence. For those reasons, he called for an "Orders Group". At the meeting of his subordinates, he spoke. He said, *"We are advancing towards Ariovistus at ordinary paced marches, and therefore, it will take seven days to arrive at our destination, which is twenty-four Roman miles (24,000 paces) from the camp of Ariovistus."*

Meanwhile, Ariovistus had received a messenger. The Messenger said, *"I have just come from where the Romans are setting up their camp area! They are now located twenty-four thousand paces from here. At the moment, there appear to be three Roman legions, and it is possible that more are on the way!"* Ariovistus replied, *"Thank you for this valuable information; now be sure to refresh and eat. After you have rested, I need you to take a message written in Latin to Caesar. While you are refreshing and resting, my scribe shall write the message to Caesar. Later today, you will take it to Caesar".*

The message in Latin read, *"Caesar, I am Ariovistus of the Germanic tribes. Earlier, you proposed to have an interview with me, but what you were proposing would have placed me into great danger. Things have now changed. We are now so near to each other that the interview you originally proposed can now take place without danger or inconvenience. I await your immediate reply." – Ariovistus.*

Caesar agreed, and at a mutually agreed place, the meeting was held. Caesar opened the conference by speaking first. He said, *"Ariovistus, I have the confidence and authority from Rome to do what needs to be done! Rome sees you as someone who is infringing upon the rights of Rome in Gaul! There has been a long connection between the Roman Republic and the Aedui, resulting in the Aedui being allies of Rome! You, Ariovistus and your warriors are to immediately cease your hostilities against the Aedui and their allies. You shall give them back their land territories.*

and hostages, and you will not permit the movement of more Germanic warriors across the Rhine.

Rome will not only aid the Aedui in recovering their territory but will also give whatever military aid is needed by those people to remain part of the Roman province of Gaul and to stay free of the interference of Germanic warriors, no matter who commands them!"

That did not suit Ariovistus. He replied with typical Germanic bluntness, *"My warriors and I crossed the Rhine at the request of the Gallic nations themselves. They promised large amounts of land and many other things, including hostages. The territories that I hold were voluntarily given to my people and me as the fulfilment of the promises made by the Gauls, as are the hostages that you speak of! The conquered Aedui are mine by the laws of war, and if I have fallen out with the Gauls, then they and not myself are the aggressors!*

They have paid the penalty for their former rashness, and if they want another contest of strength, then my warriors and I are ready to meet them in the field. If, on the other hand, they want peace, they must not hold back from paying the subsidies and ransoms that they freely agreed to pay for the services of my warriors and myself!"

Ariovistus went on to say, *"Neither the Romans or the Aedui have ever gone to the military aid of the other. My share of Gaul has come about by conquest, and the other parts of Gaul are Caesar's by conquest. Neither one of us has the right to interfere with the other's right of possession!"*

Julius Caesar did not like what he was hearing, and therefore he broke off negotiations and returned to his camp.

Having arrived back at his encampment, Caesar said, *"By Jupiter, the hard-nosed German called Ariovistus has behaved with great arrogance! He even agreed with me that all of Gaul belongs to Rome and his cavalry even attacked the Roman escort!"* In fact, Caesar was telling a lot of lies!

Ariovistus fully admitted the right of Romans to the share of Gaul that they had conquered. Also, Caesar broke off the conference, not Ariovistus! By making these false and offensive statements about the demands of Ariovistus, Caesar had excited the vain and arrogant outlook of the Roman soldiers to the point where they became eager for battle. That was something which he had not witnessed before!

Caesar again sent for Centurion Petran to appear before him. When Petran arrived, Caesar said, *"Centurion, your next assignment is to return to the camp of Ariovistus for talks. I am not giving you any power to conclude anything at all, and I just need to know the answer to these talks between the two of you. Waste his time as much as possible without concluding anything at all and let me know what he thinks!"*

Petran said, *"Very good sir, I will do as you have ordered!"* He and his Roman escort then departed for the encampment of Ariovistus. Having arrived there, Petran was escorted in to see Ariovistus. At this meeting, Ariovistus was the first to speak. He said, *"Well, what is it that you have to tell me, Centurion?"*

Petran said, *"My general, Julius Caesar, wants you to leave the areas you have taken from the Sequani and occupied!"* Ariovistus saw that he was being insulted by Caesar having a Centurion hold negotiations for him. The

Centurion had no real power or authority to conduct any meaningful discussions.

Ariovistus said, *"Centurion Petran, by your admission, you do not have authority to enter into any meaningful discussions or treaties. I am grossly insulted that Caesar has seen fit to send men of lower rank and without the power to do anything. I also get the impression that, at best, you and your Roman escort are on an intelligence-gathering mission and that you are both insulting me and wasting my time. Therefore, you and all of your men shall be arrested and put into chains! You are all now, my prisoners!"*

At an orders group held that early afternoon, Ariovistus spoke. He said, *"Warriors and women of the Helvetii and Suebi tribes, the cruel and arrogant Romans are located about six Roman miles (6,000 paces) from us to the South East.*

He then stooped down and began to form a "Mud-map" of the area he was discussing with his people. He said, *"Gather around me and be sure to be able to see this mud-map on the ground.* He pointed to a spot on the map marked with 'X'. He said, *"This is where the Romans are! Over the ridgeline – here, are the Roman supplies! We shall keep them from having access to their supplies! We have six thousand cavalrymen and horses which shall skirmish the Romans daily.*

All Germanic warriors shall be working with the cavalry forces in a joint operation, keeping Romans away from their supplies, which we will use ourselves! Other than that, we will not engage the Roman forces!"

Meanwhile, the Roman legions were hemmed in between the forces of Ariovistus and forested areas. The cavalry of Ariovistus caused havoc with the Romans, who were effectively cut off from their supplies. With the Roman position becoming more critical and embarrassing every day, Caesar called for an "Orders Group" to be held.

It was late afternoon when it began with Caesar saying, *"We must seize some high ground about six hundred paces behind the enemy and then we must fortify the position. That way, it can be used as a strong point to support the operations necessary to defeat the Germans."* The Romans did seize some high ground, and battle was now unavoidable.

Meanwhile, Ariovistus deployed his forces without hurry or confusion. By now, the Germanic tribesmen had formed a coalition of *Harudes, Marcomanni, Tribocci, Sedusii and Suevi*. They were running towards the Romans and had their wagons at their rear to render flight impossible.

Seeing the Germans at a great distance, Caesar ordered, *"Right-wing, attack the Germans!"* That resulted in the Germanic warriors wheeling and running to close with and kill the Romans. That Germanic action deprived the Romans of having the space necessary to use their javelins (pila) and taking up their swords (gladius). The Germans now closed up their ranks and formed a phalanx of spears to counter the Romans' sword attack.

An exceptionally tall Roman called Titus Vistus Tiberius was at the front of the Romans. He had managed to beat down some of the Germanic spears and forced others to give ground.

Meanwhile, on the left-wing, Decanus Florentius Maximus was fighting for his life. All around him, the Germanic warriors were in full control, and the Romans were being slain. He yelled out, *"All men to me! We are being overrun, and unless we can do something to turn things around very quickly, we are all dead men! We are being attacked from every side! Soon, our entire Cohort will no longer exist!"*

While this was happening, Centurion Crassus was looking at the unfolding situation. He thought, *"So, we are being attacked from all sides with great ferocity! There is no time to get orders! I shall have to turn this dire situation around before we are all casualties!"*

Noticing a Roman cavalry unit nearby, he went to it. He said, *"I am now taking command of this cavalry unit! You are all to come with me, and we shall attack those German forces on the left flank which are giving our men such a hard time.* He and the cavalry unit went to the left flank, and he ordered, *"Charge!"*

The advantage now swung back in favour of the Romans, and the wedge-shaped columns of Germanic warriors were beaten back and became broken. After a time of progressing against the Romans, they retreated.

The wedge-shaped column's inferiority had again shown that it was of limited value against the Roman heavy infantry. That was because of its inability to allow quick changes of formation, and that was compounded by it also having poor in-depth defence arrangements. It was also difficult to maintain its shape, allowing the deep phalanx to be broken up.

In physical strength, the Germanic warriors were greatly superior to the Roman soldiers, and they matched them in hardihood, valour and tactics. When the barbarians lost a battle, it was mainly due to their poor military organisation and discipline compared to the Romans.

Siegfried approached Ariovistus and began speaking. He said, *"Ariovistus, your forces have lost the battle against Caesar and his men! Our losses are frightful! It is high time to retreat out of here so that we all live to fight another day when we will be able to wipe out the Romans! Allow me to suggest that you and your family get the hell out of this area and return to our own areas, where we are strong and hold all of the advantages!"*

Ariovistus said, *"Thank you, Siegfried, for bringing this to my attention! For the time being, we shall return to the eastern side of the Rhine until such time as we gain strength, and we can again kill the Romans as you have suggested! Accordingly, my family and I shall escape by using a boat to cross the Rhine."*

Ariovistus was successful in crossing the Rhine, but he lost his wife and two of his daughters. His wife drowned during the crossing, as did one of his daughters. His other daughter fell into the hands of the Romans. Meanwhile, a messenger arrived at the location of the sub-chief of the Suebi nation. He sought out the sub-chief.

Finding him, he said, *"Adalbern, the Roman general called Caesar, and his five legions of heavy infantry have defeated Ariovistus who has barely managed to escape with his life! He has lost two daughters and his wife! Much of his forces have been destroyed."*

Adalbern said, *"Thank you for this valuable information! We, the Suebi nation, have been marching to join the fight against the Romans and to help Ariovistus! Your news changes everything! There is now no point in the Suebi continuing because Ariovistus has been defeated!"* Thus, in a single campaign, Caesar had eradicated the only rival who had any chance of taking Gaul away from him!

Now that Ariovistus had been beaten, Caesar put his legions into winter quarters in the territory of his new allies, the Sequani. In turn, they became alarmed that Caesar and his Roman soldiers showed all the signs of permanently occupying them. Caesar had now conquered all of Gaul. (Greenwood, 1836)

The Germanic Tribes of Ancient Belgium

News of the victory over Ariovistus by Caesar spread all over Gaul rapidly. A resolution resulted in the Germanic tribes of Belgium and the Celtic tribes of Belgium quickly forming a confederacy. The coalition's main tribes against Rome were the *Suessiones, Nervii, Atrebates, Aduatici, Eburones, Paemani,* and *Velocassi.* That is only naming a few of them.

The Scheldt River formed the boundary between the Celts of Belgium and their Germanic neighbours. The southern limit was from the Scheldt, along the Tourney and then the Meuse along the banks of that river and then eastwards towards the Vosges and the Rhine.

All of the Belgic tribes, no matter if they were of Celtic or Germanic origin, were engaged into a great confederacy for their joint defence. There were spies everywhere, and Caesar happily thought, *"The Rhemi, who occupy the area near Champagne, have split from their neighbours, and they are giving us full information of the general uprising of their neighbours, their numbers, strengths, weaknesses, and positions of the confederated lands!"*

The *Bellovaci* had the greatest population of the Belgic tribes and wanted to lead the confederation. However, the majority of tribes wanted Galba, the king of the *Suessiones* as their leader.

Julius Caesar was thinking, *"The Belgians have two hundred and thirty thousand men who are laying siege to the town of Bibrax, which is towards my front. My army at the moment is too small to take on the Belgics successfully. Therefore I need to take up new positions that intelligence has shown as advantageous against these enemies. The map shows that here on the Anise River is a bridge which my legions shall take, occupy and fortify!"* That resulted in Romans taking and occupying the bridge while also doing aggressive patrolling to watch the Anise River fords.

Caesar kept up his besieged men's spirits successfully, having occasional reinforcements and resupplies bought in to them. His enemies, who had been disappointed by their first attempts against the Romans, attacked them as they moved towards the Anise River fords. They were hoping to cut off Caesar's communications and to make him leave his advantageous position.

The enemy movements were reported to Caesar. He said, *"Our heavy infantry legions shall take up new strong positions close to this fortified camp, and we shall keep command of both river banks by using the fortified bridge we captured from the enemy! The reserve heavy infantry cohorts will be watching the enemy forces. If they attempt to cross the river at either the bridge or the fords, they will be attacked by Roman Heavy infantry's joint forces and all cavalry units. It would be a real pleasure to catch them while they are crossing the fords before they can reach the opposite bank!"*

A munifex (The lowest-ranked Roman soldier) approached Caesar. He said, *"Yes, munifex, what is it?"* The soldier said, *"Sir, I have been sent by my Optio to inform you that your orders have been carried out. The Second Cohort of the Ninth Legion engaged some enemy units trying to cross the river at the ford east of here. Many of the enemy have been killed by your soldiers, and many more of them have drowned! We are currently mopping up the enemy survivors and making them prisoners for sale as slaves!"*

That pleased Caesar, who said, *"Very good news indeed, Munifex! Things are getting better and better! I now also have the services of a traitor to the Confederate army. He is one of their leaders called Prince Divitiacus of the Aeduan people, and he is coming here for orders!"*

The Aeduan Prince Divitiacus arrived at Caesar's camp and was ushered into Caesar's command tent. Caesar, who knew the Aeduan prince by sight, called out. He said, *"Divitiacus get yourself over here! Now then, Prince Divitiacus of the Aedui, let's get a few things straight! You and your people have been allies to Rome for many years, and yet, you have done nothing but complain that the Germans have harassed you! You and your people have never seriously tried to attack the Germanic enemy! Yet you cry like hurt women that you need the protection of Rome!*

I and my Roman legions have wiped away the Germanic scourge of your lands called Ariovistus, and you will now serve Rome! You shall invade the land of the Bellovaci, who have deserted the Confederate army and moved off to defend their own country! You must close with and kill the Bellovaci! Do you understand?"

Divitiacus said, *"Do not trouble yourself over my allegiance, mighty Caesar! I am grateful for your assistance against Ariovistus and his German warriors! I shall take what I have in the way of soldiers and attack the Bellovaci as you wish!"*

While Divitiacus was moving through the territory of the Bellovaci at night, the entire Confederate army left their camp in total confusion and disorder. Divitiacus saw that he could win against this disorganized rabble, and he ordered, *"Attack, wipe out the Confederate army!"* With that, his army attacked the confederates!

The Belgic force's rear-guard fought with great valour, which delayed the Roman and Aedui armies' pursuit. However, it was a different story for the confederated Belgic force's main body, which the Romans destroyed almost without Roman casualties.

Having beaten the confederates, Caesar initiated an "Orders Group with senior Roman officers" Opening proceedings; he said, *"Gentlemen, we have beaten the confederates and smashed their main body of fighting men. Our casualties are light, except for those Roman units that took on the Confederates' rear-guard. Now that the Confederated Germanic and Celtic tribes of Gaul are in total disarray, it is high time to strike at the capital city of the Suessiones. Their capital is called Noviodunum, and all of the five Roman legions of heavy infantry under my command shall immediately begin a forced march to Noviodunum now!*

Soon after the arrival of the legions at Noviodunum, the city surrendered much to Caesar's joy. The elders of that city sent envoys to Caesar to negotiate the peace. Caesar spoke to the envoys. He said, *"Return to your Celtic city of Noviodunum and see to it that I receive hostages selected from your elite ruling families! At least two of the hostages have to be the two sons of your King Galba!"* That was done, and Caesar soon had the two sons of King Galba as hostages.

Caesar spoke to his senior commanders during an "Information and Orders Group" he was holding to discuss the success at Noviodunum and plan the next step in conquering all of Belgic Gaul, regardless of if it was settled by the Celtic Gauls or the offspring of the Germanic warriors. They had settled in Gaul and became Belgic.

Caesar said, *"Today, we have taken a major Celtic Gaul city! Noviodunum is now ours! At first light of the morning, we force march into the territory of the Bellovaci, and we shall occupy their capital city of Bratispantium. After that, we take over the territory of the Ambiani."* The Ambriani also did not resist the Romans, and they were pardoned on similar terms to the Suessiones by Caesar. That meant that Caesar had beaten the three prominent Celtic Members of the confederacy.

He initiated and "Information and Orders Group", with strict instructions that all Roman officers of the ranks of Tribune and higher had to attend immediately without exception. Caesar had been thinking of how best to take the war to the *Velocasses* and *Caleti,* both of whom were vastly different in temperament to the enemies he had encountered so far. He spoke to his sub-ordinates assembled before him.

He said, *"Gentlemen, so far, we have mainly fought with the Celtic Gauls! We did manage to beat Ariovistus and his Germanic warriors, but we will soon be facing two new enemies known as Velocasses and Caleti tribes. Some of you will remember how difficult it was for us to subdue Ariovistus and his warriors.*

The bad news is that the two tribes that I speak of are apparently, the descendants of the Germanic tribes which settled in Gaul. What is known about these people is that both the Velocasses and the Caleti treat submission with utter disdain. They delight in war, suffer hardship and deprivation with ease, and they do not know fear! So, gentlemen, prepare yourselves for trying times ahead. If any of you have some ideas of how best the Roman infantry can deal with such people, let me hear you speak now!"

Caesar and the Nervii

Conferring with his officers, Caesar spoke. He said, *"Have the reconnaissance of the areas we need to travel through and those which we must attack been completed yet?"* A Tribune answered him with, *"Yes sir, it has, and we have received information from a traitor to the Confederate forces!"*

Cacsar replied, *"Good! While it is still dark during the very early morning, my five legions plus all supporting units shall move out of here and force march towards Scheldt and Sambre Rivers' beginnings. That is where the territory of the Nervii begins.*

Informants have told me that these people will not allow traders or other merchants to enter their country. They do not permit wine or other luxuries to be bought into their territories because they think that these would depress their people's spirit.

The Nervii are a wild warrior race of people who criticise the Celtic Belgics for surrendering to the Romans, thus betraying their Germanic ancestors' honour. They do not send ambassadors or accept conditions of peace! (Greenwood, 1836) *So, gentlemen, before you is the enemy who is unlike the ones with whom you have so far engaged in battle!"*

After a march of three days, the Roman army arrived at the banks of the Sambre River. There, they encountered the Nervii and their allies, the *Veromandui* and *Atrebates.* Quickly advancing towards them was the Aduatici to share in the common defence of their territory.

Having been informed of Roman field practices by deserters from the Roman army, the Nervii knew it was the custom of arriving legions at a camp site to take up ground by single units or sub-units separated by long columns of supplies and baggage which were attached to each legion. As soon as they had received this information, the Nervii and their allies planned a bold and skilful attack upon the Romans.

A commander of the Nervii was speaking to the Council of Elders, which governed the Nervii. He said, *"Fellow warriors of the Nervii, if we are to successfully take on Caesar and his five legions of heavy infantry plus supporting units, we must firstly see to the safety of our children. Our children are our future, and therefore, we must ensure their safety!*

Therefore, I propose that all of our old people and our children are moved to safer but habitable places in inaccessible areas of the forests and marshes where the Romans cannot go because of their weight and the width of their columns!

Next, our male warriors shall take up positions along the shallow Sambre River in line with the Roman advance! Our younger women will take up positions a short distance behind our male warriors in case they have to stop the Romans if they happen to break through our lines. In short, our female warriors will provide defence in depth for our male warriors!

We must make use of the gently sloping hills, which has the river and open ground near its base and is densely forested at the summit! At the summit, we should have many warriors who can remain out of sight of the Romans while we are observing them! The Romans appear to be ignorant of our fighting strength, and they have taken up positions for the night on broken ground, which will enable us to get close to them."

The informants of the Nervii were not conversant with Caesar's methods of dealing with approaching enemies. For that reason, they planned the attack upon the Roman position using the ordinary model of Roman encampments when no enemies were close-by. By now, Caesar was fully informed that he had enemies ahead and around him. He managed to obtain reinforcements and additional legions. He now had six full legions of Roman heavy infantry plus supporting units and baggage trains at his command.

An optio approached Caesar and saluted him. Caesar said, *"Well, what is it, optio?"* He replied, *"Sir, your four battle-hardened legions are at the forefront of your army, while the new legion is following and acting as escorts for the baggage trains as you have ordered!"* Caesar answered, *"Good! Take orders to the new legions that they must measure out and fortify this entire camp while the cavalry moves across the river, which is at a depth of three feet!"*

The Nervii and they were closely observing what the Romans were doing. They noticed that the Romans had their order of combat broken up by the uneven ground, so they attacked.

Caesar was constantly informed of progress and impediments in this fight with the Nervii. He thought, *"Oh lovely, in this case, I cannot choose the site of the battle-field myself, and an aggressive and highly capable enemy is confronting my army! The entire position is without any natural defence. There are obstacles containing thick hedges and many other obstacles that can give the enemy cover from sight and even attack by war machines on my flanks. I must recall all Roman soldiers from their work and bring them into line. That way, a front will be presented to the enemy!"*

Caesar did as he was thinking, and then he rapidly rode along the entire line, speaking to his soldiers. He managed to talk to various soldiers in each of the legions, and he encouraged everyone with his presence in the field.

On the left of Caesar, the IX and the X legions drove the Atrebates (allies of the Nervii) across the river and hotly pursued them to the opposite bank. An Atrebate commander saw the Romans in difficulty on his side of the river and shouted, *"Atrebate warriors to me! We have the arrogant Romans at a disadvantage!"*

That resulted in the tables being turned on the Romans, who found difficulty traversing the broken ground and the attack against them. As a result, they retreated to their former positions at the cost of many Roman soldiers' lives.

A Tribune approached Caesar from the XII Legion. After saluting and greeting, the Tribune said, *"Sir, the Nervii have attacked our Right Wing with their entire force! They have penetrated far into the space between the XII and the VII Legions. Also, they have furiously charged up the hill and have taken the partly finished Roman camp area! They have defeated the Roman cavalry, which has retreated to a more secure and distant position. Our terrified grooms and camp-servants have seen the Nervii in possession of the camp, and they have fled or are fleeing towards the rear. A major problem with that is that they are spreading the word of the defeat of our army among the advancing baggage trains and their escorts!"*

Caesar's forces' light infantry fled in every direction, and the Treviran auxiliary cavalry retreated to their homes. They also spread the story to their people of the total defeat of Julius Caesar and the capture of both his camp and baggage trains. So it was that Caius Julius Caesar rode from the X Legion position on the left of his position and went to the scene of activity and danger for the Romans on his right. As he arrived, he was approached by a tribune. The tribune said, *"I am glad to see you here, sir! Our situation is bad, and we have lost many soldiers and officers; the enemy just continues to make simultaneous frontal and flanking attacks which are rendering our cohorts ineffective!"*

Caesar noted that the IV Cohort appeared to be acting without direction and asked why that was so. He was answered by a centurion who said, *Sir, the IV Cohort has lost all of its centurions, either killed or wounded as well as many of its Optios! They have also lost their standard bearer. That has had a very bad effect upon their morale!"*

Many rear-rank soldiers had left the line to shelter from the Barbarians' arrows and darts to make matters even worse. Things were desperate because the Romans had no reserves at hand, and their enemies quickly gained ground on both flanks! Julius Caesar grabbed a shield from a cowering soldier and proceeded to attack the barbarian warriors. Due to his setting the example of personal efforts and leading from in front, he re-established communication with the VII Legion and restored the position of the Romans.

However, they were still in danger, with confusion and dismay being more widely spread in the rear of the Roman army due to the barbarians continuing to take ground from them. The Nervii were confident of victory, and so, they attacked. They were in possession of the Roman Camp but now saw two fresh legions of baggage escort advancing quickly up the hill to their rear.

They were commanded by Labienus, who now issued orders. He said, *"X Legion, attack and disperse the enemy forces to our front immediately!"* Having success in doing so, he moved quickly to the aid of the XII and VII legions. Seeing the re-inforcements arriving caused the Romans to now fight with renewed vigour. The Roman cavalry that had retired from the battle took heart and got stuck into their enemies with the energy born from defeat's shame.

Although Romans now surrounded the Nervii, they fought on and surrendered nothing. They lost no ground, preferring to death to defeat, so they fell bravely on the spot until they thought they had won the battle for a short time. From a rampart made of their comrades' dead bodies, they continued to deal death and destruction to the Romans who came at them. When their own darts did not stop the Romans, they hurled back the Roman javelins onto the Romans, killing many of them with their own weapons.

It was here that their leader, Baduognatus, most of their other chiefs and almost their entire military force died. The extraordinary valour and conduct in general of the Nervii won the admiration of Julius Caesar. After the Roman victory, a tribune and some other officers went to see Caesar. First, to speak was the tribune. He said, *"Sir, we have defeated the Nervii, and all that is left of these people are old men, women and children. The enemy has fought with great courage, and we ask you to spare the survivors! We have spoken to the people, and they implore you to give them clemency and let them return to their own territories and towns and live in peace!"*

Caesar agreed, and he issued a proclamation to both Gauls and Romans. That read, *"I Gaius Julius Caesar proclaim that the Nervii have both my respect and protection. No-one, meaning no Gaul or Roman, shall interfere with these people or molest them in any way. Anyone who does not obey this command shall be crucified!"*

Caesar Reduces the Aduatici and Menapii

Allies of the *Nervii* were the *Aduatici,* and they were moving towards the battle but arrived too late to help their allies. Instead, they returned to one of their most strongly defended cities. After Caesar had attacked it, its local inhabitants sent envoys to Caesar. The leaders of the city had nominated Anubisath to lead the small team of envoys to Caesar. Arriving at the camp of Caesar, the envoys were escorted to his quarters to await his pleasure. Anubisath was the first to speak.

He said, *"Mighty Caesar, I am Anubisath, and I have been sent to negotiate with you as to the future of my city. I fully understand the rules of war and that you have conquered our region. My fellow envoys and I shall do whatever it takes to bring about peace between our city and Rome! So please, mighty Caesar, let us have your terms for the peaceful surrender of our city."*

Caesar replied, *"Anubisath, the people of the city must give up their weapons! I expect your people to throw all swords, axes, bows and arrows, spears and other weapons of every kind over the walls of the city. I am a reasonable man, so I will give your people one night to comply with my demands.*

Unless all weapons have been thrown over your city walls by the twilight of the morning, I will use my army to burn your city to the ground and kill all of its people. The lucky people will die immediately, and the unlucky ones will either be crucified or else they will be impaled. The choice is theirs!"

The envoys returned to their city with Caesar's terms of surrender. The elders of the city held a meeting during which the terms of surrender were discussed. Gryphon said, *"Well, Anubisath, how can we keep the blood-thirsty Romans out of this city?"*

Anubisath replied, *"By meeting the demands of Caesar that all weapons will be thrown over the city walls before sun up tomorrow! Unless we do what he wants, his army will wipe out this city and kill all people within it. The lucky ones will die quickly by being put to the sword, while those who are unlucky will die horrible deaths by crucifixion or by being impaled!"* That caused Gryphon to say, *"Oh, I see! Guard Commander, gather all of your soldiers and use them to gather all weapons and then throw them over the city walls! We shall comply with the terms set by Caesar!"*

As the dawn broke, the Roman army could see that the number of weapons thrown over the city walls was so great that the piles of weapons' height almost reached the Brabant city walls' battlements! The people of the city did, however, manage to keep about a third of their weapons. They now re-armed themselves and also made new weapons.

Next, they threw open the city's gates and freely permitted the Roman soldiers to move about the city. Julius Caesar feared that the love of plunder by his soldiers would make them uncontrollable. He, therefore, summoned the city envoys who had spoken to him about surrender terms.

The envoys arrived, and Caesar said, *"Anubisath and you others, I order you to close the city gates at night, every night or else I will burn your city down and slaughter the people! Roman soldiers shall not enter the city unless I order them to burn the place down! Do I make myself clear?"* Anubisath said, *"Yes, mighty Caesar, you make*

yourself perfectly clear! We shall inform the city leaders."
The envoys then left to return to the city.

Suddenly, at midnight, the gates were thrown open, and the Aduatici stormed out of the city. With all of their forces, they attacked the Roman camp. Caesar moaned, *"Oh, you foolish people!"* He then ordered, *"Legions VII, VIII and X burst open the city gates and take possession of Babrant for Rome!"* that was quickly accomplished. Then the entire city surrendered without offering further resistance.

Caesar now spoke directly to the people of the city. He said, *"People of Brabant, you have broken a treaty of surrender to Rome and me! That is intolerable! Normally, I would crucify every one of you, but this time, I shall be merciful. On this occasion, instead of crucifixion, every man, woman and child in this city shall now be sold as slaves to the slavers who are following my army! I pray to Jupiter that you will now obey Rome!"*

The following year saw Caesar campaigning to complete the conquest of Germanic Belgium as he had already done with Celtic Gaul through the aid of his legate, Crassus. The first to be attacked by the Romans were the *Morini* in Artois and Flanders. These people were fully conscious of their warriors' inferiority when facing the Romans and knew that they had to get away from them. So, during a meeting of elders, Alfbern was speaking. He said, *Fellow Elders of the Morini, since settling in Gaul, we have lost many of our Germanic ancestors' aggressive ways! We have become both farmers and traders and take up the ways of the Celtic Gauls!*

Since we have become farmers and traders, we have largely lost our warrior ancestors' ways, and if we were to now take on the might of the Roman army, we would lose the fight and become vassals to Rome very quickly! It is, therefore, important for our people to be safe! I, therefore, propose that we move into the protection of the dense forests and swamps of our territory."

Chlodochar now spoke. He said, *"Alfbern, I agree that we must flee into the forests and swamps! For I know that Caesar wants to take revenge upon our people for opposing him! If the Romans catch us, we will be crucified or impaled, while our women and children will be sold as slaves! Therefore, I propose that we immediately move out of our homes and leave everything to the incoming Romans. We can always rebuild our homes and rework our farms, but we must remain alive in order to do so!"*

Next to speak was Chlodulf. He said, *"I totally agree with what has been said by both of the former speakers! Therefore let us all immediately flee to safety!"* The Meeting of elders resulted in all of the Morini and even the Manapii leaving their farms and homes. And fleeing as a mass evacuation to the swamps and forests where the Romans could not go.

As Caesar was advancing with his army, he noticed no people everywhere the Romans went. He wanted revenge on these people because they had so far managed to resist him without fighting. He was shaking with fury as he spoke.

He said, *"Destroy everything that is the property of these people! I mean everything, including all gardens, orchards, crops of any kind and kill all farm animals we find! Let it be known to all Roman soldiers that they have my approval to carry off anything that they consider as useful!"*

From their hiding places, the Roman soldiers' activity was being observed by the aggrieved local people. The warrior called Berard spoke to Egkhard. He said, *"Egkhard, look over there, the Romans have broken their formations, and they are performing the actions of foraging for food and cutting wood for fortifying their camp areas. That will allow us to harass them! We must get this information to our leaders! I am sure that Alfbern will be greatly interested in this development!"*

Egkhard replied, *"I am sure that you are correct in what you have said, Berard; we must return to our tribal areas in the swamps and forests to inform Alfbern!"*

The two men returned to where Alfbern was and told him the situation. He replied, *"So the Romans are not currently in their unbeatable formations! They are out and about in small work parties foraging and timber-getting! That is very interesting because it gives us a way of attacking them successfully! Return to your warrior units and proceed to closely observe the enemy!*

When you find Roman soldiers in work situations like the ones discussed earlier, kill them all! In other cases, you may find it more convenient to let them see some of our Aduatici warriors so that they will give chase to them. If the Romans are fool enough to do so, it will be an easy matter for our men to appear to be running away. What they will be doing is leading the Romans into carefully prepared ambush sites! When the Romans give chase, we will kill as many of them as we can! After that, we shall just melt away into the forests and swamps!"

Due to these types of harassing attacks, the Romans were suffering daily losses of men, equipment and horses. Caesar was informed about this and, as a result, went into one of his customary periods of silence before he again spoke.

He finally said, *"As a response to the attacks upon our foragers and timber-getters, we shall respond to the actions of the Aduatici. They are causing much havoc to Romans, and that must be forced to cease! They are attacking our men, who are the life-blood of the Legions. They are striking and then melting away before we can fight them!*

Accordingly, we shall now clear the entire country so that the Aduatici no longer have places to hide after attacking Roman units! The work of clearing all of Gaul shall begin now!" That was implemented, but the work proceeded slowly.

Next, the autumn rains began, and all work ceased, forcing Caesar to stop for the season. That was just as well for the local population because it gave them time to re-organise amid the burned-out ruins of their buildings.

The Romans now thought that the only enemies that they had left in Gaul were the *Menapii*. They did not know that two Germanic tribes whom they called Usipetes and Tenchteri had crossed the Rhine near its mouth and were on their way to join with the *Menapii* in the fight against Rome.

The Romans threw off their mask of being the protectors of Gaul and acted like the autocratic conquerors that they were. They regarded any dissatisfaction as rebellion, which was punishable by crucifixion or impalement. Caesar knew that both the Celtic and Germanic nations of Gaul were looking for a deliverer whom they would receive with great joy, no matter who he was or where he came from.

Gaul's people quickly organised secret messages between them and invited the *Tenchteri* and the *Usipetes* to their country's interior. A messenger appeared before Caesar. Caesar said, *"Well, messenger, what is it?"* The Decanus who was acting as messenger spoke. He said, *"Sir, my orders are to inform you that the large Germanic tribes of the Tenchteri and the Usipetes have crossed the Rhine, and they are on the way to the Menapii, whom they will aid against Romans! We know that the Germanic tribes are presently in the territories of the Eburones and the Condrusi, and it appears that they may be coming here!"*

Caesar was alarmed by the news! He shouted, *"We cannot allow these new Germanic warriors to come into Gaul. If they happen to do so, there is every likelihood that a great general rebellion against Rome will take place immediately! By Jupiter and Mars! I shall not let that happen. We shall take to the field immediately!"* After having marched several days, Caesar and his army were met by envoys of the Germanic warriors. (Greenwood, 1836)

Negotiations with Germanic Warriors

The envoys said to Caesar, *"It is necessity which is compelling us to seek new settlements where we can live in peace and prosper, not just the love of fighting! We respectfully ask you to either assign new territory for us to live in or else to let us settle in the lands we conquer! We are not aggressors, but we will not shrink from any fight!"*

Caesar replied, *"There can be no peace between you people and my forces for as long as you remain on Gallic*

Ground, but if you like, go and live among the Ubii who need assistance in their fight against the Suevi, their mortal enemies. If you like, I will prepare the Ubii for your reception!"

Caesar continued, *"I promise you that I shall not advance more than four miles today. Please return in the morning and bring as many of your leaders as possible with you so that I can have the fullest assurance of their sincerity! That will all wait until our meeting tomorrow morning, now go and return to your various tribal nations!"*

That bought forth an angry reaction from Lothar, who was a Tencherti warrior. He yelled, *"Bullshit! Caesar is treating all of you as fools, and he is setting a trap!"* Indeed, before the envoys left his camp, Caesar sent a message to his cavalry, who were in the advanced guard position. The message read, *"Do not be the first to attack, but if you are attacked yourselves, you can rely upon support coming from the entire Roman army!"*

When the envoys left, Caesar advanced his army for the stated four Roman miles. (four thousand paces). The Germanic tribes' advanced guard was about five thousand men who were from the Germanic cavalry forces. They were closely watching the approaching Roman cavalry because of suspected treachery by the Romans. When the Roman cavalry came into sight, they encircled the envoys and their escorting warriors.

Lothar was expecting that, and he shouted, *"Look before you is the Roman cavalry whom Caesar said would not attack us, but they have encircled our envoys and their warrior escort! It is as I said at the meeting! The Romans are cowards and skulkers who will stab you while they smile at you! Germanic warriors charge and kill the Romans for their treachery!"*

That resulted in my people's forces being victorious over the Romans, who were unprepared for the attack and were thrown into total confusion. They fled, leaving a tribune and seventy-four soldiers dead on the battlefield. At a meeting of elders of the Germanic tribes, the possible meeting with Caesar by the leaders of the tribes was discussed. Among those who voiced his opposition to the meeting was Lothar.

He said, *"Please hear me, my people! The Romans are cowards who do not have honour! Caesar has asked all of our leaders to be present at the meeting, which he will use to wipe out the leadership of our tribes! If you allow that to happen, we will be leaderless, and our warriors will be in a state of undirected confusion. Therefore, I and all of my warriors are leaving here now to prevent the Romans from killing us as well!"* He now strode out of the meeting and mounted his horse before riding away with all of his eight hundred warriors. He and his men were the only ones to survive what happened next.

On the next day, at mid-morning, the Germanic Chiefs appeared before Caesar in great numbers. They were immediately taken into custody, after which Caesar joyfully ordered, *"Attack all of the unarmed escorts of the German leaders!". Hence,* it was that the unsuspecting escorts were wiped out to a man.

Caesar now ordered, *"Romans, you are all to form three equal columns! Using the three equal columns, we shall begin a forced march which will take us to within three miles of the Germanic enemy!"* That gap had earlier been eight miles, allowing Caesar to fall among my people! My people had lost their leaders and were totally unprepared for battle. They surrendered after a faint resistance. One hundred and eighty thousand men, women, and children were fleeing as a dense mass, only to be butchered without mercy as they fled towards the Rhine River. There, many of those who escaped the Romans' weapons drowned in the water of the Rhine.

Meanwhile, the cavalry of the Usipetes and the Tenchteri, who had not taken part in the battle, was able to retreat across the river.

Caesar Bridges the Rhine

For those reasons, Caesar sent a message to the Sicambri. Which said, *"You shall immediately get rid of your new allies because they are a danger to Rome. If you choose not to obey this instruction, things will go badly for you. I will not tolerate disobedience!"*

On four occasions, he sent the same message to the Tencherti to ensure that they understood the message. Of course, the Tencherti were a Germanic tribe, and they did not have a written language of their own. As it was unlikely that they would have had someone within their tribe who could read Latin, Caesar realised that he had to send the messages to them using a messenger who spoke the German language of the Tencherti

His messenger was sent to the Tencherti and told them the message. He said, *"My commander, Julius Caesar, is letting you people know that he is coming after you and invading Germania! If you do not submit, he will sell all of you as slaves and more than likely, he will crucify or else impale many of you! So, submit or die!"*

Caesar now called for an 'Orders Group' involving senior commanders to be held. He addressed the meeting. He said, *"I am not waiting for the Tencherti or other Germanic tribes to answer me! This army currently has six entire legions of Roman Heavy Infantry plus all necessary supporting units.*

Within the legions are expert engineers who can use as many soldiers, including officers, as they require to build a bridge across the Rhine, which is strong and wide enough to allow this entire Roman army's movement across the river. As well as enabling us to move across the Rhine into Germania without using boats, the bridge will provide us with a means of retreat if that becomes necessary! All Roman soldiers will be working to build the bridge, other than those who will provide protection to all of the working parties of soldiers!" After only ten days, Caesar bridge across the Rhine was completed! That allowed Caesar and his men to become the first Romans ever to set foot in my country of Germania.

At a dine-in function at the Officers' Mess, a tribune spoke to Caesar. He said, *"Sir, what is the reason for us building a bridge to cross the Rhine when we could have more easily have used boats?"* Caesar arrogantly replied, *"My dear tribune, do you not realise that it is beneath my dignity and that of my legions to stoop so low as to use boats when we can simply build a bridge which will make the barbarians marvel at our skills and power?"*

The Sicambri and Tencherti now abandoned the open country and moved to the forests and swamps' depths. Meanwhile, the Suebi were holding their meetings of Eldoro. It was during one of these meetings that the Suebi sub-chief called Egkhard spoke.

He said, *"Warriors of the Suebi nation, we have a severe problem in that all Germanic tribes are about to be pursued by the strong Roman army commanded by Caesar! Because of the fact that the strength of the Roman army lies in fighting in open areas where the Romans can first hurl their pila (javelins) and follow that up with devasting sword attacks, we must counter their tactics.*

Because of that, we must see to it that the Romans are drawn into the interior of Germania so that they lose their advantage of fighting in the open areas. Making the Romans come after us and make them fight in heavily forested places will also stop them from using their war machines, which they shall have to leave behind because there are only narrow tracks through the extensive forests!

An aid to our cause of defeating the Romans is that they will be expecting to find our towns and cities and then attack them in order to subdue us. That cannot happen because we do not live in towns or cities. As we tend to live in small communities which have only between three and eight long-houses, we can simply melt away from in front of the Romans and then re-appear to hit them from all sides!

When the Romans come to Germanic settlements, they will not find any food they can use because we do not have gardens or orchards, unlike our brothers who have settled in Gaul!"

He was answered by a priestess of Wodin called Adela. She said, *"Thank you for this valuable information, Egkhard! I fully agree with you that the only way for us to be able to fight the Romans is to choose the battlefields ourselves!*

We must never let the Romans do so. Therefore, we shall send out messengers to all of the cantons and other tribal areas of all Germanic people ordering that the older women and children are to be concealed in the safer areas of dense forest and some male and female warriors to protect and help them out.

The main bodies of warriors will watch the Romans and report their movements to our councils on a continuous basis! When things are in our favour, our warriors will assemble at agreed places before taking on the Romans, who will lose!"

Caesar knew that many of his soldiers wanted to chase after the Germanic warriors and kill them. He knew that he had to curb his own ambitions and those of his soldiers with sound reasoning and political views.

Therefore, he began thinking, *"Before me is the endless vast wilderness of Germania. The Germans do not live-in towns or cities, making it much harder to find large groups of them. They live in small, isolated groups in the forests and swamps where the Roman war machines cannot go. At the moment, it is more critical for Rome to consolidate the new Roman conquest of Gaul than trying to conquer the Germanic tribes! It is the strengthening of Rome's influence and the strengthening of the frontiers safe-guarding Rome than it is to try to conquer the Germans! I think that conquering the Germans can wait until later."*

A Centurion went to the tent of Caesar. Entering, he saluted and spoke to Caesar. He said, *"Sir, on your orders, we have been hunting the Sicambri and Seuvi now for three weeks. These Germanic tribes do not have towns or cities, and when we do find them, they are only in small groups of people. We have found a slightly larger than normal cluster of long-houses, and the population of them is one hundred people!"*

Caesar replied, *"The Sicambri just keep on melting away before us, and the Suevi appear to have gone back to their forests. You say that there are one hundred prisoners now. Very well then, take all of the prisoners who are males over the age of twelve years and impale them! Crucify all of the Germanic women and children. By doing that, we will be showing the Roman Eagle to these barbarians! In two days from now, all Romans shall return to Gaul. After we have crossed the Rhine, we shall dismantle the bridge behind us!"*

Having observed the Germanic tribes and shown them the Roman Eagle, Caesar decided that his expedition of observation was accomplished. He and his army retired into the interior of Gaul. Caesar was near the coast looking towards Britain when he started thinking. He thought, *"For the remainder of this season, we shall stay here and prepare for an invasion of the British island that I can see over there!*

I have intelligence reports which say that the British land is much more open than is the land of Germania and that the local British Celtic tribes are much easier prey for Rome than the Germanic tribes. Therefore, Romans shall occupy Britain in the next two years, or my name is not Gaius Julius Caesar!" That resulted in the establishment of Roman power in Britain between Britain between 55 B.C. and 54 B.C...

The Treviri – Cinetorix and Induciomarus

After he returned from visiting Rome, Caesar found that all preparations for invading Britain had been completed. It was just as well for Caesar that those preparations had been completed, for he soon became involved in disagreements between two different chiefs of the Treviri. Their names were *Cingetorix* and *Induciomarus.* Caesar wanted to firmly establish Roman influence among the Treviri, which had not been possible to do before now. He, therefore, decided on direct interference.

Induciomarus was hoping to strengthen his position through Caesar's patronage, so he offered Caesar an alliance with him, which Caesar accepted. Next, Caesar restored the balance of things by giving Cingetorix power and authority, but the rival chief Induciomarus resented that and accordingly became yet another of the many enemies of Rome.

Caesar departed for Britain and set up his camp there. After a season had passed, Caesar was thinking, *"My armies and I have spent the entire season in the British Island without any meaningful victories being had over the British Celts known as Britons! The hostile Britons are engaging my soldiers on a daily basis by attacking small groups of my soldiers with a large number of their warriors! That will not do, and we must return to Gaul for the winter! We shall return in the new season as conquerors of this place!"*

Soon after the return of the Romans to Gaul, a tribune spoke to Caesar. He said, *"Sir, we have some severe supply problems which may cause havoc with your plans to invade the British Island again next season! We have found that the supply and communications line between you, your army and the rest of us in Gaul is too long to be maintained, and that could cause severe problems the next time you invade Britain! Just look at how your forces are spread in Gaul and the north of Europe.*

117

Part of the reason for the lack of supplies is the total failure of crops in the preceding season. Another reason is the distances through sometimes hostile territory between your legions!

The legion commandeered by Fabius is living among the Morini in Flanders. Another legion commanded by Cicero is located in the land of the Nervii in Brabant. At the same time, you have the legion commanded by Roscius situated near the channel between the British island and Gaul!

A fourth legion commanded by Labienus is based with the Rhemi, and it is being used to keep the neighbouring Treviri in check. Also, there are three more legions under the commands of Crassus, Plancus and Trebonius are based among the Celtic Belgians.

To top all of this off, you also have a legion plus another five cohorts (half a legion) commanded by Sabinus and Cotta based forward between the Meuse and the Rhine Rivers. Sir, our lines of communication are too long, and if we manage to get through the winter without a disaster befalling out legions, it will because of good luck rather than good management!"

Caesar replied, *"Thank you, tribune. I totally agree that our lines of communication are too long! But this is what we get for our successes in Gaul and other places! We must keep on applying pressure! It is for these reasons that I and my legions are staying in Gaul for the winter! My legions have started to move into their quarters in Gaul."*

The Celtic Gaul tribal nation called Eburones was governed by two chiefs called Ambiorix and Catavolkus. The

Roman Legion Commanders of Sabinus and Cotta depended on these chiefs for their supplies.

Ambiorix called for an "Orders Group" with his warriors. He addressed his men. He said, *"Warriors of the Eburones, the arrogant Romans are going into quarters within our lands for the winter! Until now, we have had a rather one-sided supply arrangement with the Romans, who continue to pay us very little for the very best of food and wine available!*

They continue to use our women in any way they want without forming permanent relationships with them or getting married to them! They have defiled one of my daughters and insulted my wife! Their behaviour is deplorable, and I want revenge upon them!

In fourteen days from now, we shall approach the Roman camp with large numbers of warriors. That should not cause alarm among the Romans, for they will assume that we are there to bring them more food and wine! When we are close enough to them, I shall sound the attack on my horn. Upon hearing it, you are all to attack the Romans and kill them all!"

So, the fourteen days passed and true to his word, Ambiorix was at the head of a vast gathering of warriors. As he has correctly assumed, the sight of the warriors from the Eburone tribal nation did not alarm the Romans. They continued eating and gambling to pass the time.

Ambiorix pulled his horn out of its sheath and sounded the attack. The barbarians suddenly attacked the Romans and pushed them towards the camp, which they hoped to wipe out. However, that attack failed. Having suffered failure in that attack, Ambiorix sent messengers to the legions. In every case, the message from the messengers to the legions was the same.

They said, *"The leader of the Eburones, Ambiorix wants you to know the following: the attacks upon the Romans are not his fault! His people as much rule him as he rules them! The attack upon the Roman camp is part of a general insurrection for the recovery of all Gallic people's liberty. A very large force of Germanic warriors is on its way to join us in our struggle against Rome!*

These additional forces are already within two days' march from your Roman camps! You are now being given friendly advice to immediately leave your positions here and hurry to the aid of Cicero and Labienus, both of whom are fifty Roman miles away from you. That is the only way that you can prevent the Roman forces from being annihilated as they certainly will be if they remain where they are now!"

Cotta was told what had been said by the messengers. He angrily said, *"What rubbish! There is no way that the Ebrones can get assistance from across the Rhine in time to aid their attack upon my camp; the distance is too great! I hereby order that this camp shall be defended to the last man! We will teach those barbarians a lesson, no matter if they are Gauls or Germans!"*

Meanwhile, Cotta's superior, the legate Sabinus, sent his optio to fetch Cotta for an "Orders Group". Cotta arrived and saluted Sabinus, saying, *"Yes sir, what is it?"*

Sabinus said, *"Cotta, I have been informed that you have doubled the guard on the camp and that you have ordered constant patrols, both by day and night! That will be very tiring for your soldiers! I have also heard what the messengers from the Eburones have said! We must heed their warning and get out of here before we are all dead men!"*

Cotta replied, *"Sir, are you really serious about quitting our positions and walking into an enemy trap? That is what this is! We must not take the bait! I do not know about the Germanic warriors, but the Eburones cannot be trusted!"*

The two men argued all night, often cursing each other. That resulted in the neglection of precautions necessary for Roman bases. To make matters even worse, when the soldiers left their camps, they were burdened by the baggage they were allowed to take with them and saddened by the property they had to leave behind.

As I told you in the beginning, I was a Germanic warrior, and I served as an auxiliary officer of the Roman army. Mainly because of that, it really makes me wonder what the Romans thought they were doing because when they left their fortified camp, they appeared to have little to no apprehension of danger. The fools did not even bother to send out reconnaissance parties or use other means of finding out about the enemy and his positions.

That state of unpreparedness resulted in the Ebrone Gaul warrior called Abrexta seeing the unprepared Romans milling around. He could not believe his eyes or his luck in finding unprepared Romans.

He said, *"My warriors, the gods are smiling upon us today! About two Roman miles (2,000 paces) away from the fortified Roman camp are several unprepared Roman army units in front of us. We shall attack all Romans on both flanks, which will leave them with no room to manoeuvre.*

121

and no chance to escape! Ambiorix should be well please by that!"

The barbarians attacked the Romans by throwing spears and firing arrows at the rear, and flanks of the Romans, at all times, taking care not to engage the Romans in close combat until all of their missiles had been used. After using all of their spears and arrows, the barbarians attacked the Romans using their swords and battle-axes. The combat lasted from dawn to late at night and resulted in all Roman officers either dead or wounded.

The Roman soldiers resisted with courage, and they had no disorder within their ranks. As the evening twilight was setting in, Sabinus saw Ambiorix urging on his warriors and attacking the Romans. Sabinus said to a centurion, *"Centurion, you are to go to Ambiorix and arrange to have a mutually beneficial conference between him and me! It is only by such a conference that we Romans can remain alive now!"*

The Deaths of Cotta and Sabinus

Cotta was wounded and bleeding, but he refused to leave his post. While he was defending the Roman camp, his legate, Sabinus and many of his men threw away their weapons to participate in the conference.

While Sabinus and his men were going towards the area where the talks were to be held, Ambiorix was preparing their destruction. He spoke to several gallic warriors.

He said, *"Adietumarus, take Bilius and Caturix as well as any other warriors you may need to make life difficult for the Roman envoy party when they arrive here! I shall keep the discussions going until I can see that you and the rest of our warriors have completely surrounded the Roman legate and his personal attendants and their escort! The signal for you and your men to kill the Romans is me sounding my horn, which I have with me! When you hear the horn sound, you will kill the Romans immediately!"*

With Cotta and other Romans seated before him, Ambiorix said, *"Well, Legate Sabinus, what is it that you can do for the Eburones?"* Sabinus replied, *"If you and your people recognise that Rome rules all of Gaul and pledge your allegiance to Rome and Caesar, all will be well, and you will find that Romans will look after you!*

On the other hand, if you chose to defy Rome and rebel against her, then you and your people shall be branded as outlaws and hunted down! After we have you, you and most males of your tribal nation will be ether crucified or impaled! By the way, I cannot help but notice that horn you have hanging from your neck. Does it have an excellent deep sound?"

Ambiorix could hardly believe his luck! He had been wondering how to sound his horn without alarming the Romans. He said, *"Legate Sabinus, yes, it does have an excellent deep sound. Would you like to hear it?"* By now, the Eburone warriors had surrounded the Romans. Sabinus said, *"Please do so. I like the sound of horns!* Ambiorix sounded his horn, resulting in all of the Romans in the envoy group being killed within sight of their own soldiers.

The Eburones renewed their attack with shouts and war cries, resulting in order ceasing among the Romans. Cotta fought well and gallantly while at the head of his men, whereas other Romans retreated to the camp that they had just left and then committed suicide by falling onto their swords!

Decanus Dominic Linus and Munifex Paule Marcus, and four other members of their eight-man unit were running along forest paths towards the camp of Labienus. They were challenged by an alert sentry and bought before Labienus.

He said, *"Well, Decanus, what do you have to report?"* Decanus Dominic Linus said, *"Sir, we have narrowly escaped from being slaughtered by the Eburones! They have taken our camp, and through treachery, they managed to slay our Legate, Sabinus! They are commanded by Ambiorix, who has vowed to wipe all things, Roman, from the map of Gaul!"*

He went on to say, *"Rumour has it that Ambiorix has moved to the territories of the Nervii and the Aduatici, where he is boasting that he has killed Roman generals and destroyed Roman legions, including your Eburone Legion, sir!"*

The two tribal nations eagerly decided to take part in clearing Romans out of Gaul and sent instructions to their cantons to assemble warriors. That was accomplished with such a speed that Cicero and his legion were under attack before the news of the disaster that befell Cotta and Sabinus could reach him.

His messengers were killed and sent back to the Roman camp tied to their horses. His outposts and foraging soldiers were attacked and resulted in his communications with other Roman units being cut off. The enemies of the Romans began their first assaults, but they were beaten off!

Ambiorix proposed a conference which was agreed to by Cicero. Ambiorix opened the conference. He said, *"All of Gaul is in arms and rising you, arrogant invaders! Our allies, the tribesmen of Germania, have now crossed the Rhine, and they are helping our task of ridding your legions from Gaul!*

The Eburone Legion is already destroyed, and Caesar's winter camp as well as of the other legions are either under attack or they soon will be! It will be a gross error by you to expect assistance from other Roman units that are no better off than yourself. Still, since the Gallic Confederation only wants to get rid of the Roman soldiers who are quartered among us, and to prevent that abuse from recurring, we shall freely permit your legion to quit its base and withdraw from our lands without being attacked!"

Cicero replied, *"It is not the custom of the Roman people to take the advice of an enemy who is armed and threatening to use these arms against us! If you wish to be able to redress the grievance that you complain of, you only have to lay down your arms and trust to Caesar's justice, to which I will intercede on your behalf so that you can have a favourable answer to your petition!"*

Ariovistus became enraged and stopped the conference. He said, *"To Hades (hell) with you, Roman bully! I have come here in peace trying to bring about a peaceful and beneficial settlement of benefit to both sides, but you have thrown it back into my face! You Roman bullies will now pay for your arrogance and your rashness! The Gallic and Germanic attacks on your positions and your units shall now be continued with renewed vigour!"* After the failure of the conference, the attacks upon the Roman camps were resumed with good judgement, courage, and renewed vigour!

At an "Orders Group" called to discuss the Roman war machines and their use, Ariovistus spoke. He said, *"Friends and comrades, our joint experience in fighting Romans has taught us many things which we must do in order to wipe the Romans away from Gaul forever!*

We have noticed the Roman use of towers and their war machines such as catapults and scorpios! My engineers have been able to construct our own version of Scorpios and catapults, which we shall now use against Romans! We have successfully designed and built several siege towers around Cicero's camp, and we have in them to be a tremendous aid in observing the Romans!

They have commanding views of the Roman camp, and catapults are close to them. The warriors in the towers observing what the Romans do in their camp can give directions to launch burning material and rocks to the catapult crews! The scorpios shall throw many long arrows and short spears into the Roman entrenchments!

It will give me great pleasure to watch the Romans being battered by rocks and burning material falling onto the thatch of the Roman buildings and even their entrenchments! While the war machines are attacking the Roman camp, our warriors shall storm it from several directions at once!"

Due to the attackers being too eager to close with and kill the Romans, they became disorganised. As their masses moved towards the Roman camp's boundaries, their front ranks became crowded and wedged between the walls and their own warriors' approach. That deprived them of the use of their weapons and the means of escaping from the area. The result was that the assault was driven back on all sides with a great loss of life among the barbarians!

The siege went on for several more days with obstinacy by the barbarians and equal resistance by the Romans. However, time was a big enemy of the Romans, with every hour bringing greater casualties and weakening the garrison. Finally, Vertico, a devoted Nervian slave, left the area to make contact with Julius Caesar's Legions. He reached the Roman general's quarters in safety. He told Caesar about the situation and received his answer. Delivery of the response to the besieged Roman camp was a different matter.

He had to dodge enemy vigilance and found that he could not get back into the camp. Therefore, he attached the answer from Caesar to an arrow and fired it into the Roman camp.

For two days, the Romans remained ignorant of approaching help until Munifex (equivalent to a private soldier of modern armies) Rufus Septimus Floentinus discovered the arrow with the message tied to it, sticking out of the woodwork of the wall of the Roman camp. He called out, *"Decanus Aloysious come to me! I have discovered something of great importance!"*

The Decanus (equivalent to a corporal of modern armies) went to him, and so, the message of relief by Julius Caesar became common knowledge among the Romans. So it was that hope, confidence and courage were restored among the Roman soldiers. The problem was that Caesar was not yet able to assemble a force large enough to lift the siege of the threatened Roman camp.

Labienus was under threat from Induciomarus and the Treviri. A large force was required to provide security for the Roman stores, weapons cache, and treasury at Samarobriva on the Somme. After providing the necessary detachments of soldiers, Caesar's forces were reduced to seven thousand heavy infantry soldiers and six hundred cavalry troopers. The enemy fielded an army of sixty thousand warriors.

Caesar approached the enemy forces slowly and cautiously. The Treviri watched the Roman relief force when suddenly, the confederate force raised their siege of Cicero's forces and attacked Caesar!

At an "Orders Group" called to discuss the current situation, Caesar spoke. He said, *"Gentlemen, we have accomplished the main goal of lifting the siege of Cicero's camp! You must now see to it that only a minimum of sentries are visible from any point at any time.*

We are changing our tactics and awaiting the barbarian attacks. We know that the barbarians will consider Romans to be easy meat for them! With any luck, they will attack our fortified positions with great numbers of their warriors, and that will result in their defeat!"

Meanwhile, the barbarians thought that the Romans were dismayed by vast numbers of barbarians and their wild war cries! Suddenly, all gates in the Roman camp were thrown open. The Roman cavalry charged the disorderly rabble of barbarians with great effect, resulting in their dispersal and killing many of them.

There were now no enemies between Caesar and the quarters of Cicero. After he had relieved the damaged legion, he went to Celtic Belgium, where the reports of his successes against the *Nervii* and *Aduatici* had put an end to insurrection there.

Induciomarus left the position he had taken up in front of Labienus and dismissed his army. Caesar spent the rest of the winter watching and intimidating the Gallic Celts. Induciomarus had a vast military reputation and was highly thought of by the population. Resulting in exiles and discontented people flocking to his banner to seek his friendship and alliances.

The Death of Induciomarus

The existence of the Belgic-Germanic confederacy depended upon Induciomarus. Because he wanted to harass the Romans within their quarters, he called for an "Orders Group" to take place. He said, *"My fellow warriors, as you already know, I wish to harass the Romans while they are within their own camps and quarters for the winter! I want to begin by firstly attacking the winter quarters of Labienus again!*

We shall make frequent harassing attacks and skirmishes upon the Romans by using small units of warriors to taunt Labienus and his soldiers by carrying out these attacks right up to the boundaries of the camps and entrenchments of the Romans!"

Meanwhile, Labienus allowed the barbarians to taunt his soldiers and annoy them with showers of spears and arrows, not retaliating until he saw an apparent lack of order among the barbarians. Having seen that, he spoke to a tribune. He said, *"Tribune, it is high time to teach the barbarians a lesson that they very badly need to learn. You and all of the men in this command must make the complete destruction of Induciomarus and all of his warriors your only objective!"* Induciomarus and his Treviran staff were returning to his home base. A scout of a Roman cavalry units rode to his commander. He said, *"Sir, I have encountered a heavily armed escort of the barbarian Induciomarus; now is our chance to finally kill him!"* That resulted in the entire cavalry alae moving out. The scout was told, *"You know where Induciomarus and his escort are; therefore, you lead the way!"*

So it was that the Treviran chief was located and killed. His head was cut off and returned to the Roman camp in triumph. The formidable confederacy he had been able to form between the Nervii, Eburones and Treviri broke up, and all of Gaul became peaceful before the summer. During the winter, Caesar made inroads into the Nervii lands, resulting in some of the clans giving hostages and Caesar returning to central Gaul to subdue the *Senones* and *Carnutes.* They were again rising in the north in order to obtain more independence for their people. During that time, the Treviri again rose against the Romans, spurred on by the memory of the fighting spirit of Induciomarus and his unbeaten outlook.

The Nervii obtained a promise of help from the warriors of Germania. Although Labienus had obtained two fresh legions, the Romans still appeared to be an easy target for rebels. The two armies were close to each other on opposite banks of the Meuse, near where Verdun now is. At first, neither the Romans nor the barbarians wanted to risk a passage through the area in the other side's presence.

Labienus Defeats the Treviri

Labienus was in conference with his officers. He said, *"See to it, that all of the soldiers of each legion, sub-*

unit and all supporting units are assembled for a major reviewing and information parade at first light of tomorrow morning!" The tribunes and centurions near him said, *"Yes, sir, it shall be done as you have ordered!"*

It was during the twilight hours of the following morning that Labienus spoke to the assembled soldiers. He said, *"Soldiers of Rome! In Gaul, we are to vanquish the Gauls for-ever and stop and more Germanic warriors from crossing the Rhine and giving assistance to the Gauls!*

I am assigning five cohorts to conduct 'Search and Destroy Patrols' from now until all of my legions have moved to other areas. Other than the cohorts[2] which shall be providing security for our movements away from here. You shall now all break camp unless you are in the cohorts providing our security!"

As he had hoped, the news reached the enemy, carried to them by their many spies at the Roman camp. The Treviri chased after their Roman enemies without waiting for the arrival of their Germanic warrior allies, who were not far away from them. Their tactics were always poorly adapted to such operations, and in this case, they had to cross difficult and broken ground on the opposite side of the Meuse.

Labienus was speaking during an "Orders and Information Group" among officers. He said, *"Gentlemen, let the barbarians come close to the camp walls! Then rain burning materials, arrows and spears fired from scorpios and catapults, and the javelins and arrows from our soldiers*

---

[2] A cohort had between 500 and 740 men not counting officers.

at them. After you have wiped out many enemies in this way, charge the enemy!"

That resulted in the Treviri becoming startled by the charging Romans. The Treviri turned and ran into the forest without striking a blow against the Romans. As the Treviri retreated, they were pursued by the cavalry of Labienus.

A tribune spoke to Labienus. He said, *"Sir, our cavalry forces have pursued the Treviri into the forest and killed many of them. In fact, the wholesale slaughter of the Treviri has taken place, with many prisoners being taken by our soldiers. Following our legions, the slavers have bought the captured Treviri as slaves whom they can sell at Rome's slave markets. The Germanic allies of the Treviri are still on the Eastern side of the Rhine!"* Those actions resulted in the Treviri becoming the vassals of Rome, and their civil authority was entrusted to the now Romanised Cingetorix.

Caesar had been informed that there was trouble brewing among the Eburones and the Menapii. At an 'Orders and Information Group' called to discuss the situation, Caesar spoke. He said, *"I have been informed that trouble is again brewing with both the Eburones and the Menapii. Both of these people are making contact with the Germans and the Trans-Rhenane Germans in particular!*

Our first objective is to beat the Eburones by depriving them of the resources which their connection with the Menapii gives them! Our next issue is to cut the communications of the Eburoones with Germanic warriors across the Rhine! In order to achieve these goals, we shall march five legions into the territory of the Menapii!"

The local inhabitants fled to the forests at his approach. That left their homes, crops and livestock defenceless, and the Romans were able to destroy them, which forced the people to sue for peace. The Trans-Rhenane tribes, from whom Ambiorix and Induciomarus obtained most of their supplies, and the most frequent helpers were called *"The Suevi"* by Caesar.

Caesar Bridges the Rhine, Again

After the surrender of the Menapii, Caesar again prepared to cross the Rhine River. Having called an 'Orders Group', he spoke to his assembled officers. He said, *"Gentlemen, while three of my legions shall be obtaining food and other necessities of life for the rest of us, my other two legions shall be building a strong bridge across the Rhine!*

The bridge shall have strongly fortified bridge-heads at each end of it. It shall be located a short distance from where we built the first bridge across the Rhine! After that, we shall move my army into the territory of the Ubii and then we shall make them gather their wives and children as well as all of their moveable property into towns.

This army shall build the towns which the Ubii must live in from today onwards! That will make controlling these people a lot easier. The Suevi shall also find themselves at a disadvantage because they shall no longer have their needs supplied by the Ubii!" However, Caesar was to find that the Suevi were very different from other people he had encountered so far!

Unlike the large armies of Ariovistus, or the armies of the Usipetes and Tenchteri, they were not either immigrants or invaders, and they knew their territory well. Their territory and its terrain gave them advantages for long and protracted warfare. When that was combined with the unsettled occupation of their territory and the absence of towns, it took away the terrors of invasion from any possible enemy. That induced them to regard their difficult country's interior as the ideal place to stage battles, when and where they chose to do so.

Several days went by after the Romans had crossed the Rhine for the second time. Caesar had been informed that there was a general gathering of the Suevi clans and that it was to take place in the forest of Bacenis on the borders with the Cherusci. Caesar called for a new *"Orders and Information Group"* to be held with his officers to discuss the situation and to see if better alternatives were available.

Addressing his officers, Caesar spoke. He said, *"Gentlemen, we have some serious problems! I have received information that states that the Suevi clans will be gathering in the forest of Bacenis. While I would just love to go there in haste, I must also look at this problem with caution!*

The Suevi are typical of Germanic tribes. They do not fear Romans and regard us with the greatest of contempt! It is a very long march from here to where the Suevi clans are gathering. As well, there is the added problem of the Germanic tribes not living in towns or cities. They practise too little in the way of agriculture for us to be able to feed this large army, even if we take away everything they have! As well as that, there are no roads, and we shall have to leave all of our war machines behind us if we do invade Germania!

So, Gentlemen, unless you can come up with ideas of how we can have the necessary roads where there are no roads and how we can obtain food for this army from a hostile land where agriculture is not widely practised, we shall have no alternative but to leave Germania and return to Gaul!

While I consider that to be a bitter pill to swallow, I take comfort in the fact that we have again shown the barbarians the strength of Rome and the Roman eagle! Besides, we need to build additional fortifications to our camp, and we shall dismantle the bridge after we have crossed back into Gaul! We will use the summer to hunt down and kill Ambiorix!"

The invasion of Germania had caught the Eburones and Ambiorix off their guard as they were dispersed and at their homes, gathering what little they had in the ways of crop harvests. Caesar was now acquainted with their habits and decided that now was the best time to attack them. He badly wanted to revenge the slaughter of his legions and the deaths of his officers. He realised that he had to do things differently.

In order to do that, he led a large army through the forest of the Ardennes and sent out the cavalry commanded by Minutius Basilus to go into the territory of the Eburones with secrecy and all possible speed.

Basilus said to his officers, *"Get out there in the fields and forests where the Germans are and hunt them down! When you capture the Germans, use whatever means you consider necessary to extract information from them. After you have the information about where Ambiorix may be hiding, either crucify or else impale the man, woman, or child from whom you got the information! Show the Germans no mercy!"*

Adele was working in the field, harvesting with her three children, when they were suddenly surprised by Roman cavalry detachment. They were all immediately tortured, and from Adele and the children, Basilus learned that Ambiorix was at his summer house, located in an area of dense forest.

Basilus and his cavalry forces went directly to that location and approached it carefully. The scouting units of a lead scout and his second scout went ahead to survey the situation at what was thought to be the home of Ambiorix.

Munifex (lowest Roman rank) Titus spoke, he said, *"Look over there, Sextus, around that house there are many horses, chariots and people with weapons! That must be where Ambiorix is right now! It is high time for us to return to our unit and report this to Basilus!"*

When the two scouts returned to their unit, they were taken to see Basilus as they wanted. As they were ushered into the tent of Basilus, he spoke. He said, *"Yes, Munifex Titus, what is it?"* Titus replied, *"Sir, Munifex Sextus and I scouted ahead of the main cavalry force as you have ordered, and we are sure that the man you seek, Ambiorix, is at the house where you suspect him to be.*

We noted that the house has a large gathering of well-armed people and that there are many warriors there as well. We were able to see that the warriors are from several different Germanic tribes. We identified some of the warriors as being from the Suebi, Helvetii, Eubrone, Chatti and Cherusci tribes, but we could not see if Ambiorix himself is there or not, sir!"

Basilus ordered, *"All Roman cavalry, at a gallop, charge towards the home of Ambiorix. Just follow Munifex*

Titus and Sextus; they know the way! This time we will have Ambiorix and his Germanic scum!" The entire Roman cavalry rode very fast towards the home in the forest.

That was a tactical mistake on the part of the Romans. The Germanic tribesmen had alert sentries posted and a very capable rear-guard who were guarding their leader.

As the Roman cavalry got closer, Helmuteige said to his warriors, *"We have ditches dug which are eight paces deep and eight paces wide. We have filled the trenches with straw and dry twigs. We can hear the Roman horsemen approach, and when they arrive, set fire to the material in the trenches, and that, as well as our delaying tactics, will help Ambiorix to escape!"*

Basilus now suffered the indignation of seeing Ambiorix mount a horse and escape from the area. He escaped, but he knew that due to his weakened condition, he could not successfully take on the Romans and that he had to wait until later on to be again able to do so. He now rode over much of the Germanic areas and gave verbal orders (the Germanic people at the time did not have a written language). He said, *"Spread the word to all people of our common Germanic tribal Nations that all people are to move into the swamps and forests or the islands at the mouths of the Scheldt, Waal and Rhine Rivers.*

Everyone is to make sure that all livestock, horses, food and everything of value is taken. Leave nothing for the Romans to be able to use! Everything that the people cannot move themselves easily is to be burned!

To my way of thinking, the sudden disappearance of the entire population with their property and cattle should have prepared Caesar for the kind of warfare that he was now facing.

It was now necessary to have a freely moving and unburdened army because a large one would raise more problems rather than diminishing the issues already at hand. Caesar said, *"I am dividing this army into three corps. Two of the corps will be detached to other duties. I and the third corps shall put an end to Ambiorix, who is in the last of his strongholds on the shores of the ocean."*

The Roman Camp at Atuatica

Having successfully constructed the Roman Camp at Atuatica, Caesar deposited all stores and supplies, including his army's baggage at Atuatica. Atuatica was an outpost in the Eburoean territory, and the camp was protected by the new XIV Legion, commanded by Tullius Cicero. As Caesar left, he assured his soldiers that he would return in person within seven days. He ordered the officers of Labienus and Trebonius to meet him in Atuatica so they could receive orders and changes to plan as these were required.

The enemy was not seen in the field, but the Romans felt the presence of my people's warriors everywhere they went. The region was in keeping with my people's normal practice in that there were no towns, cities or fortified posts.

Wherever there were secluded valleys, woody gens or swampy marshes and places that looked like ideal ambush positions, my people would station themselves.

Caesar Gets an Alliance with Gallic Tribes

Julius Caesar spoke to Cicero. He said, *"Tullius, in order not to have to use so many Roman lives, I am considering forming an alliance with neighbouring Gallic tribes by offering them a share of the booty that I expect to be able to gain after we defeat the Eburones! What is your feeling about that proposed course of action?"*

Cicero replied, *"Yes, Julius, I believe that you are on the right course in doing what you have proposed. When you are successful in obtaining the alliance, we should be able to launch attacks upon those who have taken part in the slaughter of the legions of Sabinus and Cotta!"*

During Caesar's absence from Atuatica, the Sicambri, a large Germanic tribe occupying the Rhine's eastern side, crossed the river thirty miles below where Caesar had built the bridge. The members of that tribe were hoping to share in the plunder of the Eburones, and they had already taken many captives and a large number of cattle. When they heard that Caesar was not at the camp at Atuatica, they also were told that the Roman camp at Atuatica had many riches and was guarded by one legion.

A warrior sub-chief named Aldgrett spoke. He said, *"Eburone warriors, we must hurry forward and surprise the Roman base at Atuatica because the plunder to be had by us in that place will more than offset any value of anything that we have to leave behind in order to wipe out the Romans!* He had barely uttered those words when the entire strength of Eburone warriors, women and children began to chant. They yelled, *"Death to Romans and their allies! Hail Aldgrett! We shall kill the Roman enemy!"*

Until now, the orders from Cicero to the Roman camp had been as Caesar ordered. He had ordered, *"No Roman soldier or camp follower shall go any more than fifteen paces away from the walls of the camp in any direction without an armed escort of at least eight men. No*

Roman is to go more than thirty paces away from the Roman camp walls, even when they have escorts!"

After the absence of Ceasar had grown to seven full days, the camp followers and Roman soldiers' complaints were beginning to wear down Cicero. Finally relenting, Cicero spoke. He said, *"Soldiers and camp followers of the Roman army. I have heard your bellyaching and your complaints!*

Even though I consider you all to be as soft as Roman women, I shall allow a total of five cohorts to leave the camp to gather grain and forage on the plain, which is a short distance from this camp and is separated from the plain; by a low hill! I don't particularly like doing that because it only leaves us with about three hundred men, many of whom are sick or injured to perform the garrison duties."

Cicero must have had physic powers because my people had their Sicambrian cavalry arrive at the camp. Rolf was in command of a large group of Sicambrian cavalry. He said, *"I have scouted all over this area! To our immediate front of this base are the camp followers such as the hawkers and whores. They have established themselves outside the ramparts, and we can easily sneak up and remain unobserved by the Romans. All we need to do is to act naturally, and the stupid Romans will accept our presence. When it is too late for them to resist, we will wipe them out, after which we attack the Porta Decumana!"*

The cohort which was stationed there withstood the first attack, but they were all disheartened by rumours that Caesar had been defeated in the field. It seemed as if the barbarians would overrun the camp and take the treasure, the stores and caches of weapons. While that was happening, a sick centurion was in his bed, recovering when he heard the noise. Sextus Baculus leapt out of his bed and positioned himself at the gates. The example set by him inspired other centurions to do the same thing, which resulted in the barbarians' forces' progress being stopped for the moment.

Meanwhile, the alarm had spread to the other cohorts returning to the camp after completing their foraging. Having seen the cohorts arriving, the barbarians left their objective of attacking the base and turned their attention to the newly arrived cohorts. Before they could recover from the surprise of having been attacked within their own camp, the different cohorts became confused, and they were separated. A cohort (between 500 and 760 men) was surrounded and cut to pieces. However, most cohorts managed to reach their own lines safely.

The barbarians abandoned the hope of obtaining the greater prize. They contented themselves with the booty taken from the camp followers and the Roman army's cattle and those of the Eburones. They then retreated safely back across the Rhine.

Soon afterwards, Caesar returned to the camp and prepared to make the barbarians pay! At an "Orders Group" had called to discuss further action against the barbarians, Julius Caesar spoke. He said, *"We are going to show the barbarians that they cannot get away with annoying Rome!*

We shall lay waste to the homes, fields and farm animals of these barbarians. Unless we can eat them ourselves, we will kill all cattle that we find. I have already arranged for hordes of greedy people to descend upon the lands of the Eburones, and they will destroy those lands as well as all buildings and out-buildings unless the new-

comers immediately occupy them. Also, all land we come across shall be so turned over, spread about and contaminated by salt that it shall be useless for generations to come!"

Ambiorix, who was often within sight of the Romans, continued to elude them. Although my people were suffering from extreme poverty, many of them were killed, which did not stop their quest for independence.

Caesar was not confident of beating or capturing Ambiorix, so he resorted to conquerors' usual ways to utterly ruin the country. The aim was to make the people who may have survived to attribute all of their misfortunes to their leader to stop him from returning and exposing them to more sufferings.

Even though nothing more is known about Ambiorix and his people from history, I know that he died in the same way as he lived, a free man. I know that because, as a spirit, I can move freely in time and space, observing things that people normally cannot.

The Heroine - Thusnelda

The Cherusci had a council of nobles governing them as they did not wish to put up with orders from a king from anywhere. One of the nobles on this council of elders was Segestes, who was the father of Thusnelda. Her mother was called Alruna, and she spoke to her daughter.

She said, *"Tomorrow at about mid-morning, you and I shall be attending the 'Farewell to Battle' of our Cherusci men! They are riding out to battle the Chatti, who have been invading Cherusci territory. The nation must see to it that all incursions of our lands stop immediately! We shall be cheering the men as they ride past us towards the enemy, and there shall also be the unmounted very elite 'One Hundred'.*

They are very fit and able warriors who can actually keep pace with the horses of the cavalry. It always gives the Cherusci the advantage in battle because our enemies find themselves attacked by a combination of infantry and cavalry simultaneously. Every one of our major cavalry units also has one hundred or more of these exceptional warriors.

After the men have gone to battle, the children will be under the charge of the senior women of this tribe, and they will go to safe areas. While you and the other children are in the secure areas, many other younger women and I will be following our men from a close but safe distance behind them. After we have got to a place where we can watch our men, we will intervene in the battle on their behalf if necessary.

All of the women will be armed, and my favourite weapon of choice is the battle-axe. It was given to me as the dowry which all Germanic males must pay to their wives by Germanic custom.

When I married your father, his dowry to me was a bridled charger, a set of battle-axes and a suit of chain-mail armour. All Germanic men are expected to provide dowries such as that to their wives. You are of noble blood and will be a leader; although you cannot yet be called a princess, you are a noble of the Cherusci Nation, and you may jointly lead it in good time."

Thusnelda said, *"Mother, your name is Alruna, is that somehow connected with the Gods?"* Alruna said, *"Yes, my child, it is, but I am flesh and blood as you very well know! How do you feel about your being able to take part in applauding our warriors for the first time in the morning?"*

Thusnelda answered with, *"I am looking forward to it all. Mother, as you have said, I am a Cherusci noblewoman, and I am going to make sure that I can do everything that is expected of a leader of this nation! I think that I will enjoy seeing my father, Segestes, riding off to do battle with our enemies! I am going to learn the arts of offensive and defensive warfare, and I shall make you proud that I am your daughter, or my name is not Thusnelda!"* That made Alruna smile, and she said, *"Get a good night's sleep; we have a big day in the morning!"*

Having been born during the year of 10 B.C., Thusnelda was only five years old at this time. At mid-morning of the next day, she and her mother were applauding the warriors as they were going to battle. First, the cavalry units filed past the applauding women, followed by the 'One Hundred' elite units.

The women noted how young, fit, and able were the elite warriors. Every cavalry regiment had at least one hundred of them, which is the reason for their name. In those times, the cavalry regiment could have between three and eight hundred such warriors.

Thusnelda became wildly excited when she saw Segestes riding towards the enemy in company with the other warriors. She applauded much and shouted, *"The enemy has made war upon us! Go and close with and then kill the enemy, my father, you are my hero!"*

In time, the procession was over, and it was time for Thusnelda to join the other children under the authority of the senior women elders of the tribe in safe and secluded areas. Meanwhile, the younger women gathered their armour and weapons and followed their men until they took up positions a short distance from them.

Alruna automatically assumed the role of leader of the women, and she now gave her orders. She said, *"Eidletrout, take ten other women and get closer to the men and find out what is happening. It is too hard to see things clearly from here. When you know what is happening for sure, come back here, or if time is critical, sound your horns to get aid from the rest of us. If we hear your horn, we will all charge into the enemy and wipe them out!"*

Eidletrout and her companions had only been gone a short time when all clearly heard her horn. Alruna was concerned, so She ordered, *"Girls, we must attack the enemy and save both our other women and our male warriors. Charge! It is time to kill the Chatti!"* That resulted in three hundred Cherusci women taking up their arms and charging the Chatti, who were outnumbering the Cherusci male warriors and already killing some of them.

Alruna yelled to her female companions, *"I can see that we have lost some of our men! Remember girls, we are Cherusci women, and we never run from a fight. All of you are to close with all Chatti warriors you see, and you must kill them. Otherwise, our men are going to all be dead!"* with that said, the Cherusci women attacked the Chatti warriors, and they fled.

Alruna located her husband Segestes and began the typical scornful chastisement of their male partners practised by Germanic women. She said, *"Great providers and protectors of your families, you men have turned out to be! You are rescued by the very women whom you are supposed to be protecting! Men!"*

Now that the fighting was over, the women joined their husbands, and they jointly went to their children. Finding Thusnelda with the other children and the senior women minders, Alruna and Segestes said to their daughter, *"Thusnelda, today, the Cherusci have had a great victory over the Chatti! Our male warriors had been surprised by a huge force of the enemy. The men were outnumbered by five to one. It is only because of the actions of the Cherusci women that our men were not wiped out! Remember to do your military training with enthusiasm so that you will be able to close with and kill the enemy when the time comes for you to do so!"*

The entire tribe followed that with a public meeting. As Segestes was a noble, he spoke to his people. He said, *"Friends and comrades, the emergency of our land being invaded by the Chatti has passed! We have lost warriors and women as a result of the action against the Chatti. Due to a great combined effort of the warriors and our women, we were able to drive the enemy out of our territory! Every military action has the possibility of casualties, and today was no exception!*

We lost eighty warriors and sixteen women who came to our rescue! In the morning, all of these dead heroes will have funerary rites in accordance with Germanic customs. Tonight, we will feast, drink, and give thanks to the God Wodin and his son Thor for our deliverance from the Chatti pest!

Baudran, bring out the supplies of beer so that we can hold our wake for our fallen heroes tonight! Those who have to remain on duty shall not drink anything other than water. After all, our safety depends on a completely sober quick reaction force being able to deal with any attempted incursion into our territory!"

Thusnelda Learns How to Fight

Thusnelda was a quick learner and had speedy reflexes. That made her a formidable warrior in her own right. While she was in her early teenage years, she showed everyone that she was both willing and able to fight whenever that was needed. The Germanic women also were thought to have prophetic power, and the male warriors would consult them whenever they wanted to know about future events.

As she progressed through her teenage years, Thusnelda became an excellent swordswoman, and her use of battle-axes and spears was astounding. She was fearless in battle, and she would not ask for quarter, and indeed, she did not give it either. To top this off, she was a beautiful Cherusci noblewoman. In the year 6 A.D., she was sixteen years old, very fit, self-aware and spoke her mind at all times. Much to the chagrin of her father, Segestes.

Segestes said to her, *"Thusnelda, as you know, I want our people to have complete confidence in all things Roman! Our people stand to learn much from the Roman ways of doing things. Roman architecture and engineering are wonderous things to behold, and I am convinced that the Cherusci should learn from them. There is much opposition to my ideas about incorporating the Cherusci nation into the Roman Empire. I can counter that by having you marry a Roman official, and that is what you shall do!"*

That did not suit Thusnelda at all. She said, *"Pappa, just remember that you can introduce me to whoever you like, but that does not mean that I shall marry that person! I am Thusnelda, and I am a Cherusci, noble-woman. In case you have forgotten, that means that I can make up my own mind about whom I will marry if that is to happen at all!*

I do not and will not have my life dictated to me by someone else, even if the person doing it is you, my father! Until I meet my choice of a husband, I shall remain unattached to any male. It does not matter how you feel about it, this is my life, and it will be lived in my way! So, stop trying to interfere and live your own life, Pappa!"!

That enraged Segestes. He thundered, *"Thusnelda! You are my daughter, and you must do as I say or move out of my home!"* Thusnelda replied, *"Very well, Pappa, I will move out of your home if that is the way it has to be, but I shall always have the say in whom I do or do not marry! You have no say in that, and you never will!"*

All of that was overheard by Thusnelda's mother, Alruna. She said, *"Stop this fighting, the pair of you! Segestes, my daughter Thusnelda is correct! You do not have the right to tell her whom she will or will not marry! She is rapidly gaining appreciation from the other Cherusci women as their leader, and her ability as a warrior is so great that many men envy her! As for your love of all things Roman, I know just how cruel these foreign invaders are!*

I have just returned from visiting the Tungri tribe on the opposite side of the Rhine. The Tungri are a Germanic tribe who invaded Gaul and caused many problems among the Celtic communities in Gaul. The local Gauls called them Wehrmannen. (implying that all of the tribe were warriors,

, including the women. In the Gallic dialect, the name became Germannen.)

That description was applied to the entire Tungri tribe. Just like us, Cherusci, the Tungri women always applaud their male partners as they leave for battle. While so doing, the women implore their men not to lose the battle and let their wives and children become slaves of the enemy!"

As with Cherusci women, the Tungri women follow their men from a distance behind them. Often, they enter the fight if the male warriors do badly. That usually results in insults calling out to the men that they are useless cowards who need to be rescued by the women they are supposed to be keeping safe.

As you know, Segestes, the Germanic women often suffer death in battle and horrific wounds because of entering the fight to help their men and restore the situation! You also know that is one reason why the Germanic male must pay a dowry to his wife. You also know that the dowry can be weapons, such as a set of battle-axes, a bridled charger, chain-mail armour, and anything that the wife will find of use in defending her home and family!

When the Romans, under Julius Caesar's command, went into Gaul intending to conquer that place, the Romans applied a "Scorched Earth" policy. They rendered the land useless for generations to come by peppering the ground with salt so that nothing grows there anymore.

I was told of the Romans' things to the Celtic tribes and the Germanic tribes in Gaul. The Romans came into Gaul, and because they were challenged, they burned down whole villages and towns. They hung up many people on crosses in what the Romans call crucifixion! If the person being crucified is lucky, then she or he will only be tied to the cross.

If the victim is unlucky, he or she will have nails driven through their hands and ankles to inflict more pain upon them! After that, the victim has her/his arms tied to the cross so that the weight of the person does not result in the hand giving way to the downward forces and the crucified person falling off the cross. That is the truth about your Roman friends!"

Thusnelda, Leads the Women

As with most ancient Germanic peoples, the Cherusci did not like the idea of a king or any person telling them what to do! And so, the sixteen-year-old Thusnelda was enthusiastically cheering the men as they were riding to battle. By now, she was the acknowledged leader of the Cherusci women.

She saw her father Segestes among the warriors riding out to battle the enemy! Even though she was very independent and quick to speak her mind, she also deeply loved her father. As Segestes was riding past, she applauded and yelled out, *"Thank you, Pappa, for keeping us safe from the enemy! I hope that you will kill many of them today! Go and wipe out those who threaten us! Go and make us safe again! Way to go, Pappa!"* Soon, her father was no longer visible, but she became interested in the exceptional warriors known as 'The One Hundred'.

She and the rest of the women applauded the Cherusci cavalry and infantry warriors until they had all departed to battle. Then Thusnelda took command of the women.

She said, *"Girls, those of you who have chain-mail armour make sure you have it on and that it is in serviceable condition. Take up your swords, spears and battle-axes and be ready to use them. We are following the men, and I know a short-cut to where they are going to engage the enemy! We will be behind them but close enough to assist them if that has to happen.*

As the Cherusci women got closer to their male counterparts, they observed that their men were being ambushed by a large Chatti unit of male warriors. The Chatti had firstly used arrows to start their ambush and followed it up with a charge of Chatti infantry.

The Chatti were elated that they had wiped out many Cherusci cavalrymen. The cavalrymen were glad to see the sudden arrival of the 'One Hundred' who immediately attacked the Chatti. However, all the Cherusci were outnumbered by four to one, and Thusnelda noted that.

Quickly drawing on her already capable military experience, she set about reversing the situation before her. She spoke to Erminlinde. She said, *"Erminlinde, take thirty women and go towards that little clearing by the creek. Then cross the creek and throw your spears into the Chatti. Then sound a long blast on your horn! When that has been done, attack them with your battle-axes!*

The other women and I will do the same things from the other side of the ambush site. We must all hurry because our men are in trouble at the moment! We are going to engage the enemy in combat from this side of the creek as soon as we hear the blasts of your horn! That way, the Chatti shall be attacked from in front and from behind them at the same time."

Thusnelda now waited until she could see that Erminlinde and her companions were at the shallow creek opposite her. When Erminlinde arrived there, she let out three blasts from her horn. That was the signal for Thusnelda and the other Cherusci tribeswomen to cross the creek and attack the Chatti unit.

The women went into action, and although they suffered wounds and the death of some of them, they killed many Chatti. While they were doing so, they called out to their men. Yelling, *"You bloody cowards and useless men, some great protectors of your women and children you have turned out to be! You are being rescued by the very women whom you are supposed to be protecting!"*

Herod-the-Great

To tell the complete story, it is now necessary to look at Herod Archelaus's father, who was known as *Herod the Great* and who ruled Judea and Galilee on behalf of the Roman overlords from 73 B.C. until he died; in March or April of 4 B.C... He built many public buildings during his lifetime, which included some fortresses, aqueducts, and theatres.

Succession of Herod-the-Great

Herod's land was prosperous, and he became concerned about his succession. He now said to his friend and lawyer, *"Look here, friend, I need you to draft out my will so that there will not be a problem of successions when I die. I want my son named Herod Archelaus to inherit the kingdom of Judea and another son called Antipas to have Galilee."*

The lawyer answered, *"There is no problem with what you want to be done, and I shall have the documentation ready for you within a week, but what about your other son called Philip?"*

Herod-the-Great answered with, *"Forget about him, just make sure that Archelaus gets the main parts of this country and its wealth and that Antipas gets Galilee!"*

Upon the resulting legal will finally becoming public knowledge, it caused much dismay among the brothers of Archelaus, who resented him being awarded the greater part of the kingdom. Archelaus had to go to Rome in order to become the Client King in Judea for the Romans.

Upon the death of his father, Archelaus provided a lavish feast for the people. He even put on a white loose-fitting kaftan-like garment and went to the temple, appreciating the people there receiving him with acclamations like, *"The king is dead, long live the new king, Herod Archelaus!"*

Herod Archelaus

Herod Archelaus now addressed the people from an elevated throne, saying, *"Thank you for your commiserations that you have expressed towards me about my father's death. I really appreciate what you, the wonderful people of my country, have done for me in this, the most trying of times!*

I have been named as the main heir in my father's will. That will make me the king of Judea, at least. And perhaps even more than that, depending on what the Roman Emperor Augustus Caesar says when I see him in Rome.

I hereby thank all people and soldiers who want me to accept the crowning of myself as the king in Jericho, but we must wait for Caesar to confirm my succession to the throne before I can accept it. Still, it should only be a matter of time before this happens. Once I am king, I will treat you all much better than my father ever did, and I will reward richly both the soldiers who want to see me crowned in Jericho and all of the civilian population that supports me!"

The people of Judea were pleased by this speech, and they quickly started making some major requests. Some of the people wanted lower taxes, and others wanted the removal of the purchase tax, and many wanted prisoners to be released.

As he was trying to win his people's goodwill, he simply approved everything and then went out feasting and drinking with his friends after he had made offerings in the temple. While there, he witnessed that many people wanted change as soon as the mourning for Herod-the-Great was over. These people were then in mourning for those who Herod-the-Great had executed for cutting down the golden eagle over the temple gate.

They were grieving using extremely loud lamentations, and their weeping could be heard all over Jerusalem. Many people thought that all who had been installed into high positions by Herod-the-Great should be punished. That included the man who Herod-the-Great had made The High Priest. So, they openly spoke against Herod-the-Great, and a rebellion began. (Josephus, 78 A.D.)

Archelaus did not like this one bit, but he spoke to his advisors because he was in a hurry to get to Rome. He said, *"For now, we shall not act against those who oppose me. That can wait until after I return from Rome! We shall try to reason with them, and I am sending my general to confer with them!"*

When the general arrived at the temple, the rebels threw rocks at him and drove him away from them. That was repeated with everyone whom Archelaus sent. At the feast of unleavened bread called the 'Passover', which used to be celebrated with many sacrifices, large crowds of people came from rural areas to worship.

Many of them remained in the temple and mourned the deceased Rabbis, supporting themselves by imploring and begging so that they could win support for their rebellion.

The rebelling people went about their sacrifices as if they had not committed any crime or done any harm to anyone at all. Archelaus was in conference with his advisors and military leaders. He said, *"I feel that these rebels and traitors are not capable of exercising restraint and that they must be acted against immediately! I have secretly sent a Roman Tribune with a cohort* (about the same numerical strength as a modern battalion) *of Roman Heavy Infantry against them in order to stop this from becoming an organised and popular rebellion!*

The cohort has orders to arrest those who began the riots and to force them all to keep the peace! However, there was little that the cohort could as the populace was stirred up so intensely that many crowd members threw stones at the cohort, killing many of its soldiers!

Therefore, you generals are to take the entire army against the people in the temple and slay them all! I want large numbers of infantry deployed within Jerusalem's walls to keep order or kill the rebels. The cavalry forces will be deployed against the people on the plains in front of the city! The people must obey or die!" Those actions resulted in three thousand people being killed and many of the survivors fleeing to safety among the nearby mountains.

Seated among his aids in 4 B.C., Archelaus spoke. He said, "I am going to Rome to defend my title against the claims to my throne, which are being placed before Emperor Augustus by my brothers!" He then left Judea for Rome.

Arriving at the palace of Augustus, Archelaus was ushered into the presence of the Roman Emperor. He walked to where Augustus was seated and spoke. He said, "Mighty Augustus, I am Herod Archelaus, your faithful servant. I need you to confirm me as the client-king of Judea as soon as you can do so!"

Augustus thought matters over for a time, and then he spoke. He said, "Herod Archelaus, your reputation precedes you! I have received complaints about you from your brothers and your mother. In all of this, it is the security of the empire that is important.

I hereby confirm you as the leader of Judea, but you will not have the title of king! You shall have the title of Ethnarch, although a lesser title, still gives you power, but it will also emphasise your dependence upon Rome!" Archelaus did not like what had happened, but all the same, his position was vastly more comfortable than that of many people in Judea.

Archelaus, his mother and friends of Poplas, Ptolemy and Nicolaus, went to the seaside, leaving his household in the care of his steward, Philip. Salome and her children accompanied him, as did his brothers and sons-in-law. Their reason for them being there was to support Archelaus in securing the succession, but they quickly accused him of unlawful actions in the temple.

Ptolemy spoke to Archelaus. He said, *"Archelaus, it has come to my attention that the procurator (Roman Governor) of Syria, called Sabinus, is coming to Judea to guard Herod's property. We must not let that happen! You have the ear of a greedy Roman consul named Varus, so get him to stop Sabinus from entering the fortresses and treasuries where Herod-the-Great's money is kept!"*

That resulted in Sabinus meeting with Varus. During that meeting, the two men were introduced to each other. Sabinus said, *"Varus, I am the Roman Governor of Syria, and I have been called upon to help out here by Augustus Caesar! The members of my family and those of the Labienus family have always been of Service to Rome.*

My nephew and his friend, who was a son of Labienus, died while serving Julius Caesar in Gaul! I shall be going to where the money of Herod-the-Great is kept, and I shall do what is necessary until this matter has been ruled upon by Caesar!" He, therefore, stayed in Caesarea while Varus left for Antioch and Archelaus left for Rome.

Herod Archelaus Learns of a Rival

During the month that we who live in the twenty-second century A.D., call December, Herod Archelaus was informed of the birth of a dangerous rival. A member of Herod's Guard spoke to Herod Archelaus.

He said, *"Sire, during the evening, between the 18th of the month and the twenty-fifth of the month, a baby boy was born in Bethlehem. It is said by many that he shall be the future king of Judea and Galilee! If you wish to safeguard the throne for yourself and your sons, it may be in your interest to kill the baby boy before he can gain power!"*

Herod was always both pedantic and ambitious and now was no exception. As well as the other two qualities or faults, he was now overcome by both fear and self-doubt.

Accordingly, he said, *"Guard Commander, you are to take all necessary men and travel to Bethlehem immediately! When you get there, you are to find all male children born between the 18ᵗʰ and the 25ᵗʰ of the month. When you find them, kill them all! We must not let this child escape! He is too great a threat to me and my kingdom!"*

Joseph Learns of Danger to His Son

During the evening of the 18ᵗʰ of December of 1 A.D., Joseph Christ was walking past a tavern when he overheard some men discussing King Herod's army's apparent deployment.

The men were saying, *"King Herod has ordered the finding and killing of all boys born in and near Bethlehem between the eighteenth and the twenty-fifth! The word from Herod's palace is that he has heard that a newborn king who has been born in or near Bethlehem will depose him and therefore Herod will act first!"*

That resulted in Joseph going to a horse dealer. He said, *"Horse dealer, I want an animal which can be used to transport my wife for a very long journey. What do you have that I can use?"* The horse-dealer replied, *"Because of the census that is taking place on the orders of Rome, the demand for horses has been great over the past three weeks.*

I no longer have any horses for sale! The best that I can do for you is to sell you a donkey!"

Joseph answered, *"Very well then, a donkey it shall be!"* He then paid for the donkey and took it to where Mary and her baby Jesus were sleeping in the stable in Bethlehem. Approaching Mary, he said, *"Mary, come quickly; we must leave this place if our son is to live! Herod has ordered the killing of all male children born in or near Bethlehem over the past few days, which places our son into great danger! We shall flee to Egypt, which is beyond the reach of Herod Archelaus, and we shall stay there until he is dead! Galilee may probably go to a brother called Antipas due to Herod's family's succession disputes. If he gets Galilee, we will leave Egypt and go to my family's home at Nazareth!"*

Sabinus Goes to Jerusalem and Seizes the Palace

Sabinus grew tired of waiting for Varus to make his move. He called for an "Orders group" with his officers. When they were all within earshot of him, he spoke. He said, *"This army shall march to Jerusalem and seize the palace there! We must summon the fortresses' officers to explain their actions and hand over the accounts and the money held there."* That ended with a problem: the fortresses' officers had written instructions from Archelaus to continue to guard the money. They, therefore, said, *"We shall continue to guard the money, and we are answerable only to Archelaus and Caesar!"*

His Brothers Try to Remove Archelaus

Meanwhile, his brothers were in Rome, seeing Augustus Caesar and trying to get him to remove Archelaus from office and take the kingdom for themselves.

Another brother called Antipas was also in Rome. When he gained an audience with Augustus Caesar, he pleaded his case. He said, *"Mighty Caesar! I am Antipas, and the original will of my father Herod-the-Great is the will that should apply to the succession! In that will, I am named by my father as his successor! So, please, Caesar, make the original will the valid one and dismiss Archelaus from the office of Ethnarch!"*

The Roman Governor of Syria, called Sabinus, supported the brothers of Archelaus in letters he sent to Augustus Caesar. Typically, the text of these letters read, *"Hail mighty Caesar! I am writing to you because I have severe doubts about Herod Archelaus's suitability to hold the office of Ethnarch of Judea!*

According to many people in Jerusalem and its surrounding areas, Archelaus sent armed forces against his people within the city walls and also used his cavalry forces to wipe-out those who were against him outside of the city!

He even is guilty of slaying people within the confines of the temple in Jerusalem! I think that unless you replace him with someone else, there will soon be a popular revolt against Rome, and we must do everything in our power to prevent that from happening! In this regard, I fully support the brother of Archelaus, called Antipas!"

Things were made worse for Archelaus by the arrival of Salome and those who were also giving a list of crimes supposedly committed by Archelaus directly to Augustus Caesar.

After Antipas had made many accusations against Archelaus and produced many witnesses and relatives to prove the accusations against him, he ended his speech. The way was now clear for Nicolaus to stand up and speak on behalf of Archelaus. He said, *"Oh mighty Caesar, the slaughter in the temple was completely unavoidable, and those who were killed were opposed both to the monarchy in Judea and to the rule of Rome itself and Caesar in particular! By bringing the protestors to heel in this way, Archelaus was, in fact, maintaining both his monarchy and Roman rule in Judea!"*

Before Augustus Caesar decided on these matters, Archelaus's mother, called Malthace, became sick and died. Letters were bought from Varus to Augustus about the revolt of the Jews. Varus put down the rebellion and left one of his three legions in Jerusalem to keep order in that city while he attended to Antioch's other problems.

However, no sooner had he left than Sabinus came and gave the Jews more cause for rebellion. He forced the keeper of the fortresses to hand the money and treasure over to himself and then made a thorough search for the money of Herod-the-Great. He then commandeered the soldiers left in place at the Palace of Jerusalem by Varus as his own armed soldiers and used them as his greed instruments.

Some men and women in Jerusalem were discussing Archelaus. Aaron was speaking to Barbaras. He said, *"Herod Archelaus is both of Idumaean and Samarian descent, just like his father, Herod-the-Great! For some time, his actions have shown that he is an alien oppressor like his father before him!"* Barbaras said, *"Yes, but do not fear him because I have lodged complaints about him directly with Augustus Caesar in Rome.*

I have received an answer from the Roman Emperor, which says that Archelaus must go to Rome in 6 A.D. to answer for his crimes against the people of Judea and Rome! Archelaus went to Rome and was put on trial, during which Tiberius defended him. These events finally resulted in the rebellion in which Varus would become the Roman Governor of Syria after successfully putting down the rebellion.

Publius Quintilius Varus - He was descended from an old patrician family; his father, Sextus Quintilius Varus, had been one of the murderers of Julius Caesar. He took part in the Battle of Philippi in 42 B.C. and committed suicide after that event. His son, Publius Quintilius Varus, married into Augustus Caesar's family, which gave him political influence. He became consul in 13 B.C. and proconsul of Africa in 7 to 6 B.C... After that, he became the Roman governor of Syria, where he extorted a great fortune and ruled by repressive means, establishing a reputation for the use of extreme cruelty.

Before he was the governor of Syria, a messenger was ushered in to see Varus. He said, *"Sir, the Roman governor of Syria has commanded that you are to stop what you are doing and immediately proceed to Jerusalem with an army, and you must put down the rebellion there!"*

In answer to that, Varus marched an army consisting of three legions of heavy infantry supported by cavalry and used the army to destroy the rebels with many instances of extreme cruelty.

Like many other Roman commanders, he was very quick to use the excruciating painful Roman methods of execution reserved for non-citizens of Rome, those of impalement and crucifixion.

After finally beating the Jewish rebels, he spoke. He said, *"I am going to make an example of what happens to the enemies of Rome to those stupid Jews! Capture two thousand Jews and make them ready for crucifixion! Make sure that the entire Jewish population watches the scum die!*

See to it that all of them suffer as much as possible, both before and after we put them onto the crosses and make sure that they are all nailed to the crosses. Do not just tie them onto the crosses! That way, things will be vastly more painful for them, and they will suffer much more!"

A centurion was near Varus. He said, *"Sir, think of what you are asking of this small detachment of Roman soldiers! You are ordering us to execute two thousand Jews, and yet you appear not to have considered the very real possibility of the lack of resources such as timber from which to make two thousand crosses! I rather have my doubts that we can gather enough timber to do what you are asking!*

This country is too dry to support the vast number of trees necessary to make two thousand crosses. You have also ordered that the Jews be nailed to the crosses, not just tied to them. We will need three nails per Jew! One nail to be driven through each hand and another longer nail which is to be driven through both ankles and into the wood of the cross! That means that we shall need at least six thousand nails! You shall find that there is nowhere near that number of nails in the entire Roman Empire!

Not only that, but the fact is that there are only eighty men here under my command! That is nowhere near enough labour to harvest such a large number of trees, make the crosses, and then place two thousand Jews onto the crosses! I think that you are asking too much of my men and me!

The only way of executing the whole two thousand Jews is to place about one hundred of them onto the crosses. The remaining nineteen hundred shall have to be impaled by forcing a timber length, which is about the diameter of a broom handle straight up the rectum of each Jew who is not crucified! Coming to think of it, I believe that it would be far more practical to simply use impalement as the means of executing the Jews!

You have ordered that the people of Judea must see justice being done. Very well then, give me the necessary men, and it shall be done! However, bear in mind that the execution of two thousand people on or near the same day will require at least an entire Roman legion or, better still, two legions to perform the executions!"

That resulted in one hundred crosses appearing along the way between Hebron and Jerusalem. Each cross had a rebel tied to it. Between each of the crucified people were nineteen more Jews who had been impaled with small diameter poles. These were roughly forced into the rectums of the victims.

They were then carried with the poles sticking out of them to where the crucifixions were carried out. Next, the pole's free end was embedded into the ground, with the result that the victim began to very slowly slide down the pole while in extreme agony. It usually took as long as forty-eight hours for the victims to die. The distance between each rebel who was either crucified or impaled was about twenty-four paces. The local populations were forced to watch as their friends and relatives slowly died in extreme agony.

That was happening now because Varus had received dispatches from Sabinus and his captains asking for assistance in dealing with the rebels of Judea, so he hurried to their aid. Leaving one legion to execute the rebels near Jerusalem, he and two other legions, complete with supporting cavalry and other specialist units, marched to Ptolemais to meet other Roman allies and Sabinus. At Ptolemais, he received one thousand and five hundred extra infantry soldiers.

Under the command of Gaius were the Arab forces of Aretas. He had a great hatred of Herod. His forces consisted of a mixed force of infantry and cavalry. The force he commanded numbered eight thousand men. The Arab hated all who had served Herod, and accordingly, his enemies fled while he burned the city of Sepphoris. Varus marched his army to Samaria but did not enter the city itself and camped near a village called Arous.

Varus was summoned to Rome to confer with Augustus Caesar. He left his palace in Syria and boarded a ship to Rome. After landing in Rome, he made his way to the lodgings of Augustus. He was ushered into a great hall by a munifex who immediately withdrew once he was settled into conversation with Augustus.

Augustus said to Varus, *"Publius Dear Boy, I have a major job that I am sure only someone with your reaction to threats against Rome can handle. The situation in Germania is out of control! The Germans are not obeying Roman orders, and they remain unconquered! One of the Germanic Kings called Marobod of the Marcomanni is currently building up a vast army. I think of him and his army as probable threats to Rome. In particular if he unites the people of Germania against us!*

Varus was far from impressed by this. He said, *"Sir, I want to remain in Syria, where I have great wealth and where I am very comfortable! I do not want to live among the Germanic barbarians who are not cultured and even smelly because they do not bathe on a daily basis as Romans do!"*

Augustus answered, *"Publius Quintilius Varus, you have amassed a great fortune in Syria by being the Roman Governor of that country! You shall now repay Rome for your great wealth by doing something for Rome against our Germanic enemies!*

I am giving you one month to settle your affairs in Syria and take up command of the Roman forces in Germania. That includes the command of the "Armies of the Rhine." Now stop bellyaching and get to Germania, take up your command of the Roman forces and make sure that the Germans know that Rome is the boss!" That did not suit Varus at all, as he wanted to remain in Syria, but he proceeded to obey the Emperor.

Accordingly, Quintilius Varus was removed from office in Syria a month later and found himself in Germania. He was mild-mannered and had many bodily indulgent habits, including feasting, constant drinking to excess and taking part in sexual orgies. His character was marked by his being cruel, obstinate, pedantic, and over-confident. He also liked to rape those women who would not let him touch them.

Caius Octavius, who Became Augustus

Due to Julius Caesar's insistence and the Roman army's wishes, attempts were made to subjugate Germania's population. This country was considered to be wild and having vast areas of trackless forests. After Octavius changed his name to Augustus, he tried to complete the Germanic people's complete subjugation by trying to conquer them.

When he was twelve years old, he was talking to his mother, named Atia. He said, *"Mother, when I was born, was it during the day or at night?"* Atia answered, *"You were born early in the morning of the third of September.* (63 B.C.) *As you know, your father held high positions within the Roman Republic, which is still functioning. My mother and your Grandmother is named Julia, and she is the sister of Caius Julius Caesar, who is your uncle!"*

That satisfied the young Octavius for the moment. Soon after, his aunt called Julia died, and he was called upon to give the eulogy, which was a triumph for him, and it was his first major public speech. During the year 46 B.C., he was speaking to his uncle Caius Julius Caesar. He said, *"Uncle Julius, many people are saying that the Roman Civil War has ended and that you have won it! Congratulations my uncle!"*

Julius Caesar answered, *"Yes, Octavius, that is correct! Thank you for congratulating me on my victory! Would you like to accompany me in my triumphal procession tomorrow at mid-day? If so, now that you are seventeen years of age, you could stand next to me in my chariot! I think that it will be good for you to be seen in public with me and to let all Romans know that you are the nephew of Caius Julius Caesar!"*

Octavius Rises in Power

While Octavius was in Egypt, his uncle, Julius Caesar, was murdered. Returning to Rome, Octavius was informed that Caius Julius Caesar had named him as his adopted son and his main personal heir. Feeling overwhelmed, he returned to his family home and spoke with his stepfather, who advised him.

His stepfather said, *"My boy, I do not think that it is in your interests to try to take up your inheritance from Julius Caesar because of the perils connected with it! Look out for the other players in the power-grabbing game that is being played out in Rome and which will, in all likelihood, end up as yet another civil war!*

I have it on good authority that Marcus Antonius (Mark Antony), *who was Caesar's main lieutenant, has taken possession of the personal papers and assets of Julius Caesar, and I know that he is expecting that he and not you, will be the main heir to Caesar's fortune and estate. I am sure that you can expect a lot of trouble from Marcus Antonius over the inheritance.*

Not to mention that I am sure that your acceptance of the inheritance may also put you at odds with Caesar's murders, namely Brutus and Cassius. You should also look out for another power-hungry man called Cicero, who may attempt to use you in some way."

Octavius said, *"No, Father! Such actions shall not do! Caesar's fortune and estates are mine by Caesar's legal will, and I shall have what is mine! As, well, I am the legally adopted son of Caius Julius Caesar! Inferior men like Marcus Antonius are no match for me! I shall deal with the likes of him soon enough! As for Brutus and Cassius, they are both just traitors and murderers, and I will deal with them soon enough!"* Mark Antony refused to hand over the funds of Caesar, which he had grabbed for himself.

By putting on many public games, Octavius won over many Caesar's soldiers to his own alliance. Cicero now broke up his relationship with Mark Antony. In the Senate, he said, *"Fellow Romans, we have many problems, and the answer to the problem of some people wanting the power and the fortune of Gaius Julius Caesar lies in us simply carrying out the wishes of Caesar to make his nephew and adopted son called Octavius his main legal heir! As you may recall, Caesar was recognised as a god!* (in 42 B.C.)

Also, it is to our benefit that the Senate now grants Octavius the rank of Senator. Doing that will make this son of the God Caius Julius Caesar, our very powerful ally!" The Senate approved the plan of Cicero for Octavius to become a senator. One of the consuls who commanded the Senate's forces was killed. Octavius spoke in the Senate.

He said, *"Due to our fallen consul, there now exists a vacancy for the position of consul of the Senate's forces! I, the son of the God Gaius Julius Caesar, whereby claim the position! You will very quickly realise that what I am proposing is the best thing to do for Rome because we are in a civil war with Brutus and his friend!"*

That having been done, he went about using the name of Gaius Julius Caesar and obtained official recognition as the son of the murdered dictator of Rome known as Julius Caesar. Together with Markus Antony, he crossed the Adriatic and engaged Brutus and Cassius's armies, defeating them. Their defeat resulted in both men committing suicide by falling onto their swords.

Octavius was at the home of his stepfather when the two men spoke to each other. Octavius said, *"Father, presently, I am at a loss of what to do to gain more power. I fully realise that I must have the backing of Rome's powerful and influential families if I am to become anywhere near as successful as my uncle Caesar!*

His stepfather (on his mother's side of the family) said, *"Octavius, to me, the solution to your problem of obtaining backing from the influential families of Rome is simple! Just marry the right woman from an influential family, and what you want shall be yours! In this regard, I suggest that you court Scribonia, a relative of Pompey the Great!"*

The Wayward Daughter of Augustus

After marrying Scribonia, Octavius gained political advantage because she was related to Sextus Pompeius, a powerful political and military leader whose alliance with Octavius was necessary because of Marcus Antonius's rivalry. He divorced her in the following year on the same day as she gave birth to their daughter Julia, Augustus's only child. She was bought up very strictly with her every move and words being watched.

After being married to Marcus Marcellus for a short time, that marriage ended because of his death in 23 B.C... Julia then married Marcus Vipsanius Agrippa. In 21 B.C... The two sons of Julia and Agrippa were adopted by Augustus and given the names of Gaius and Lucius Caesar.

Augustus was married to Livia, who was the step-mother of Julia. Livia approached Augustus one evening; she was scantily dressed, and she had bathed and was wearing a seductive perfume. Her servants had styled her hair, and she looked both attractive and alluring. She walked to where Augustus was sitting and made sure that he could see one of her well-formed breasts. She made sure of that by completely exposing her left breast while covering the right one. As she came closer to him, she took his right hand and placed it upon her exposed left breast.

She then next lifted her skirt and placed his left hand onto her vagina. She said, *"Come on, Augustus, my love, play with my tits and finger-fuck me and see to it that you work me up until I am entirely sexually aroused! Once that has happened, I want you to make love to me several times, using different positions. Just stop whatever you are doing and dismiss all people from here for the next two to three days while we make love, many times!"*

Her seduction of Augustus worked, and he sent all officials away for the next two days, during which time he made constant love to Livia. After the couple had made love for the third time on the first day, Livia spoke to Augustus. She said, *"Augustus, my passion, I need you to adopt my two sons by a previous marriage, and I would very much like it if you made them your heirs! Do that for me, and you can rest assured that the sexual pleasures you have just enjoyed shall continue forever!"*

Augustus answered, *"Very well, Livia, but I do not even know the names of your boys. So, let us begin by you telling me what their names are."* Livia said, *"Their names are Drusus and Tiberius!"*

After that, Augustus did adopt Livia's sons as his and named them as his successors. A long time passed, and Augustus spoke to Tiberius. He said, *"Tiberius, as you already know, I am the first Emperor of Rome! You have been named my successor, but if you want to rule Rome as a Caesar, you must marry my daughter, Julia! I know that you are already married. Therefore, you must divorce your current wife, and then you must marry Julia if you ever want to rule Rome!"*

Tiberius did as Augustus had told him, and soon, he was divorced from his wife. He did marry Julia, but it was an unhappy marriage for both Julia and Tiberius. Julia quickly developed into a very wilful and licentious woman, causing great embarrassment to Tiberius and her father, Augustus.

Tiberius was so embarrassed that he had an audience with Augustus. Tiberius said, *"Mighty Augustus, you are both my adoptive father and my Father-in-law! The activities of my wife, your daughter Julia, are so vile that they are causing much embarrassment to both yourself and to me.*

In fact, I am so embarrassed by her behaviour that I have no choice but to resign from my position as the commander of all Roman forces in Germania, and then I must go into exile on the Greek island of Rhodes. Until this mess is sorted out and my reputation is restored! My disgust of Julia's behaviour is extreme! Her behaviour is such that I am immediately going into exile on Rhodes. She is continuously dishonouring us both by her disgusting behaviour!

By doing so, I will not have to hear the laughter and snickering of the lower ranks of Roman soldiers who now openly consider me to be a joke, which makes discipline hard to maintain!

Things are so bad that people are openly laughing at me and calling me a cuckold, making me the butt of jokes all over Rome and within my legions! I also believe that you must pull your daughter into line because otherwise, you may lose the Roman patrician families' support. " His Father-in-law Augustus, who was also his adoptive father, was visibly shaken by what Tiberius had told him.

He said, *"Thank you, Tiberius, for bringing this unsavoury situation to my attention! I am disgusted by what you have told me about Julia's behaviour and the likely effect that her excesses will have upon my backing among the patrician families! This situation will not do! I shall clip her wings, and if she continues to embarrass other high-ranking people and me, I shall have to take extreme action against her!*

That brings me to the problem of you resigning from your post as the commander of the Armies of the Rhine. Although I respect your decision, I wish that you will reconsider it. Until you do so, Command of the Army on the Rhine shall pass to Domitius Ahenobarbus!

I am not familiar with the abilities or otherwise of Domitius Ahenobarbus, so I hope that having him replace your command is the right thing to do!"

Augustus Hears About Julia's Excesses

Augustus slowly began to find much more out about his daughter's inexcusable behaviour from various other people. Including when some Roman Senate members began complaining about her behaviour directly to Augustus, and one of these senators said to him, *"Hail mighty Augustus! I must ask You to do something about the behaviour and the excesses of your daughter, Julia! She is initiating both daytime and night-time orgies which are often extreme, to say the least! For example, it is said that two nights ago, she had sex with two men at the same time!*

One man was fucking her mouth while the other man was giving it to her, up her cunt from behind her!"

Augustus was stunned by those words and said, *"Lucius, that is my daughter you are talking about; please make sure that you are telling me the truth! If what you say is true, I must stop this terrible state of affairs before I lose my standing in Roman society! Accordingly, I will speak to Julia and move her onto an island where she will hopefully be forced to stop this nonsense!"*

Augustus Admonishes Julia

Things came to a head one evening when Augustus admonished his daughter. He said, *"You fucking slut and whore! Your behaviour is worse than that of common prostitutes! You are constantly dishonouring me! What is it with you? For fuck's sake, you stupid bitch, I am the most powerful man in the world, yet you keep on dishonouring me!*

You continuously bring great shame to my name and that of the Caesar family by continuing your disgusting behaviour! A new report about you is that you had sex with two men simultaneously, with one of them fucking your mouth, while the other one was fucking you up your cunt from behind you!

Your behaviour is threatening my standing as the Emperor of Rome because the families who are allied to me are talking about withdrawing their support of me because of your inexcusable behaviour! As a result of your actions, I am banishing you to the Island of Pandataria. Also, I must admit that I have been actively considering applying the death penalty to you!

If that happens, you will be beheaded because Roman law forbids the crucifixion of Roman citizens! However, no matter what I do, I cannot erase the fact that you are my daughter and that you a constant source of trouble for me! I hope that when you get to the island, that you will moderate your behaviour and start living as what you are, namely the daughter of the Roman Emperor!"

For some time after residing on the island, Julia appeared to be obeying her father's command. However, she was secretly receiving visitors who would arrive at her island by boat. When these guests arrived, Julia went back to her ways of extreme sexual activity and other perversions.

When he was informed of her continuing sexual practices, Augustus ordered, *"Take Julia and lock her up in a secure location at Rhenium. She is not to have any help from anyone at all, and she shall never have any visitors! She must never leave her new confines for any reason!"*

It is known that Julia died from starvation at this new secure location. She was guilty of everything that people said about her. It is also known that she was a witty and intelligent woman who had a love of the Roman people. Her father showed her no mercy. Augustus said of her, *"Do not talk about my daughter Julia, for she is a disease of my flesh!"*

Campaigns of Drusus in Germania 12 – 5 B.C.

Augustus did not want to expose himself to the worries and problems caused by a war with the aim of the conquest of Germania. It was well known that the driving force behind the idea of subjugating the Germanic people was Julius Caesar and that it was from him that the views of the Roman people and the Roman army were obtained.

175

At his departure from Gaul, Augustus left his younger and favourite stepson, Drusus, in command of the Army of the Rhine, complete with a well-defended frontier and many advanced military posts on the west bank of the Rhine River.

During a joint meeting of the 'Council of Elders' of the Usipete and Tencherti tribes, the Roman extortion of both tribes was discussed. Blanchard spoke to the forum. He said, *"Fellow tribesmen and tribeswomen of the Usipetes and Tencherti. The double effects of Roman taxation of our people and the continuing Roman extortion of us all now leaves us no choice but to cross over to the east side of the Rhine, and we shall take what belongs to others because of what the Romans are doing to us! We are decedents of the Germanic tribes that settled in parts of Gaul, only to be victimised and expelled by the Romans under Caesar! Well, my friends, Caesar is no more, and we shall rise up and defeat the Roman oppressors!"*

The joint 'Meeting of the Elders' of both tribes endorsed military action against the Romans. That, in turn, resulted in both the Usipetes and the Tencherti ravaging lower Germania. Having been informed of these things, Drusus wrote to Augustus.

He wrote, *"Mighty Augustus, I, Drusus, your adopted son and commander of the Armies of the Rhine, have to inform you that two Germanic tribes with whom Caesar had trouble are currently laying waste to large parts of Lower Germania.*

I hereby beg you for permission to deal with the invading Germanic warriors from Gaul as I see fit! I shall drive back the invaders because I have made plans for a permanent Roman presence in Germania!"

In time, an answer arrived from Augustus. He wrote, *"Drusus, my boy, you have my full authority to deal with not only the invaders but also the entire Germanic population as you see fit! I welcome your plan to establish a permanent Roman presence in Germania! It shall be to the greater glory ofRome ifRomans can actually do what has not been possible before and conquer the Germans!"–Augustus.* The effect upon Drusus of that letter was one of pure delight!

Drusus happily began speaking to all those near him. He said, *"Today is a great day! I have in my hand the permission from the Emperor Augustus to go after the Germans and to make them realise that they are conquered by Romans and that they must, from this day, always obey everything that is said to them by Romans! We shall begin expeditions into Germania so that the Germans will know of our presence, and we will conduct raids onto groupings of houses.*

We will take prisoner the Germans who we find at the house groupings. After holding them for a while, we will show everyone the might of Rome and either crucify or else impale all Germanic children, men and women! By doing that, we shall instil fear of Romans among the German population, and that will make the task of conquering those people a lot easier!"

The Batavi were a tribal nation allied with Rome, and as a result, they had great privileges, including not being extorted by the Roman provincial systems. The Romans regarded these people as valuable instruments of war. The

Batavi opened up their country to the Romans and gave service to the Roman army with their young men.

The military efforts of Drusus were directed against the Usipetes, Tenchteri and Sicambri in quick succession. Closely observing the Romans were the Usipete scouts called Emelrich and Folcher.

Emelrich said, *"Look over there, Folcher, the Roman army is displaying its disciplined might and marching about in the tight formations using the cohorts of the legions! We cannot match them out in the open where their superior armour, tactics and weapons mean that we will always lose if we attack them.*

So, all Germanic tribes must somehow draw the Roman invaders into our forests where they will become lost and allow our warriors to get so close to them that their tactics and armour will not save them!

Folcher said, *"Good idea, Emelrich! To get them to follow us into what Romans consider to be vast trackless forests, it should be just a matter of our going to a small hill near the Romans and full view of them!*

When they can easily see us but cannot quickly reach us, we should appear naked and then bend over while calling out to the Romans to attract their attention. Having done so, we can yell out, 'Hey you weak as piss Romans, look over here!'

We should then pat ourselves on our behinds, and although the Romans will not understand what we are saying, they will understand the message that we think that Romans are only fit to wipe our arses!

By doing this sort of thing repeatedly, we can draw them ever further into our forests!" Emilrich said, *"I agree, so, how about we put this idea before the meeting of the 'Council of Elders' being held tonight?"*

While Drusus was in Upper Germania, he sent directions to his Batavi allies to build him a fleet of ships to quickly and safely transport his army. To save distance and transport his forces effectively, he had an access canal dug from the Waal the Rhine, connecting the two rivers.

First and Second Expeditions by Drusus

In the year of 11B.C., Drusus spoke during an 'Orders and Information Group'. He said, *"Gentlemen, we shall embark upon the ships that you see in front of you, and we will use them to transport us to an area that is advantageous for us to attack and destroy the German tribes called Frisii and Chauci! By sailing along the Rhine and some other rivers, we can land within easy striking distance of both tribes. Then we can wipe out both tribes entirely, other than those people whom we wish to make examples of by either impaling crucifying them! Also, against us are the Bructeri who have a strong naval presence."*

After some time had passed, Drusus was able to obtain a treaty with the Frisii by which they piloted fleet into the Ems River, which allowed him to beat the naval power of the Bructeri. He was able to settle a few islands at the mouth of the Ems, where he also built and garrisoned a strong fort. Some Roman watching stations were established near the Lippe, Roer and Rhine Rivers' junctions, but no permanent foothold was established in Germania by Drusus. After a violent storm, the fleet returned to the Rhine, both scattered and damaged, resulting in the army of Drusus taking up its winter quarters.

Drusus's army had been worn out due to being involved in a naval campaign to which it was not accustomed. At the 'Information and Orders Group' called to discuss the situation, Drusus said, *"Gentlemen, due to the fact that our naval operations against the enemy have turned out to be a costly failure, we are entirely reverting to the use of land-based operations in all future military adventures!"*

Third Expedition by Drusus

In the spring of year 10 B.C., Drusus crossed the Rhine River into the territory of the Usipetes. They retreated before him and joined up with their allies, the Bructeri. During that time, most of the country appeared to be vacant because of war between the Sicambri and the Chatti. That was because many people hid in the forests, hills and swamps.

That allowed Drusus to march through the country-side without an apparent challenge. The opposing Germanic warriors were watching his forces and just melting away from in front of the Romans. All of this had cost a great deal of time, resulting in the approach of the cold autumn rains and storms. As well, there was now also a scarcity of provisions being felt by the Romans.

Meanwhile, a sense of impending common danger ended the fighting between the Germanic tribes of the Suevi, Chatti, Cherusci, and Sicambri tribes. They collected their forces and attacked the Romans' flanks and rear, resulting in disrupting the Roman lines of communication and supply on the Rhine!

Drusus was aware of the danger that now threatened him, and he, therefore, ordered a retreat. As the Romans' withdrawal progressed, they were harassed by Germanic warriors who surrounded the Roman army, hemming it in between ravines and forests.

The Germanic warriors were poorly led, and they were over-confident. A Suebi sub-chief named Colberht saw the Romans before him, and he could not resist the temptation to attack, despite the knowledge that the strength of the Roman army was to fight in the open, where they could use their tactics of first hurling their javelins into the enemy ranks before following that up with a sword attack. He ordered, *"Suebi warriors, attack and wipe out all Romans you see!"*

The result was that the Germanic warriors attacked the Romans as a tremendous and disorganised rabble which was defeated by the army of Drusus. That allowed Drusus to continue his march back to the Ems and the Lippe Rivers without further problems. At the junction of the Lippe, Aliso, and Else Rivers, He built a strong fort which he called Aliso after the river near it.

Fourth Campaign of Drusus 9 B.C.

Drusus began his fourth campaign with even more forces, making his army both large and formidable. The Weser had been the limit of all former invasions by the Romans. Drusus pressed on until he was at the banks of the Elbe River.

His enemies, the Germanic warriors and their women, kept to the Germanic plan of avoiding contact with the Romans and just retreated before him and his army. Using these tactics, the Germans were drawing the Roman army ever further into the interior and away from Roman lines of communication and support.

No battle was fought, and no spoils were gained. With the passing of time, Roman soldiers' minds yielded to boredom and lack of contact with the German enemy. These things combined to make melancholy impressions upon Roman soldiers' minds who thought they were in gloomy and lifeless wildernesses in which they were wandering about aimlessly.

Strange things began to happen. My father, whose name was Adalbern (Ancient Germanic name, the elements of Adal meaning noble and bern meaning bear) was riding along with my uncle Alaric, while the two of them were on a scouting mission to ascertain the strengths or otherwise and the positions of Drusus and his army. The Romans were marching along a track when these two Germanic warriors rode their horses straight through the entire Roman column without challenge, and it would appear, without having been seen. That allowed the two men to report back to their superiors about the Romans and what they were doing.

That was most amazing, considering that both my father and uncle were wearing their Germanic helmets with horns protruding from the sides of them and were fully armed with spears, battle axes and long broadswords! The Roman column advanced to a ford in the river where they could cross it.

Just as the Romans were beginning to cross the ford, a statuesque and very nice-looking woman, who had a great deal of dignity and authority about her, suddenly walked across the path of Drusus.

She yelled, *"You disgusting and greedy, insatiable Roman pig! You have been murdering my people! If the people you murdered happened to be high born, you made them Roman citizens, and then you beheaded them! When they were of the lower classes of people, you either impaled or crucified them!*

You shall not see the accomplishment of your designs upon Germania! We hold life as being sacred, so I am telling you to leave this land and get out of Germania forever, for if you stay in this land, your own doom is at hand!"

Her appearance disturbed Drusus, who commenced to retreat using a new line of march. During the retreat, even more strange things began to happen.

Wolves prowled around the Roman camp at night and could be heard howling. Then the night air clearly carried the wailing voices of female lamentations, and to the imaginations of the Roman soldiers, the stars became intermingled in the night sky.

The following morning, Drusus and his army again were on the march. Again, everyone had to cross a river and did so by crossing at a ford. While this was happening, Drusus fell from his horse and became ill. He did not live long after this happened. He died about a month after he fell from his horse.

For Germania, it was good that the country had no towns or cities, which made things very difficult indeed for the invading Romans. It was equally good that the Germanic people so readily adapted themselves to the only system of safe resistance, that of disappearing from in front of the enemy, and in so doing, drawing them ever further into the interior of

Germania, and then choosing the battlefield which would put the Romans at disadvantage. After the death of Drusus, the Armies of the Rhine's command went to his brother, Tiberius.

Treachery of Augustus Year 8 B.C...

With Tiberius now in command of the Armies of the Rhine, Augustus himself went to Germania in the year 8 B.C. with a powerful army resulting in some Germanic tribes asking for peace from Augustus. However, the Sicambri decided not to send envoys along with many of the others. Augustus regarded all tribes who had taken part in the late wars as being one confederate body, therefore refusing to deal with any tribe on a separate basis. The Sicambri then decided to accept the terms, and next, the chiefs of each tribe appeared before the Roman Emperor.

Before the Germanic warriors arrived, Augustus spoke to his soldiers at the site of the proposed negotiations. He said, *"I want you all to remain out of sight of the Germanic warrior chiefs who are coming here to negotiate with me! I am going to draw-out and protract the talks and, in general, waste the time of the German chiefs!*

I will appear to listen to their demands, and as soon as you see me scratching my right ear, I want you to arrest all of the German warrior chiefs! That will leave their tribes leaderless!"

The Germanic chiefs were arrested and imprisoned at various places. Many of the high-spirited chiefs could not bear the tedium of imprisonment or the treachery of the Romans and could not live with the shame of having been duped by Augustus! So, many committed suicide, thus depriving Rome of its hostages.

For the time being, the Sicambri were driven out of their positions on the Rhine's eastern side. Up to forty thousand of them were resettled in the Roman province of Germania Inferior for the time being.

The Hero Gains Experience

The Roman Republican calendar was replaced by the Julian Calendar, the dating system introduced by Julius Caesar during the forties B.C... The older Republican calendar, which it replaced, was found to be three months ahead of the solar calendar.

Caesar was advised by the Alexandrian astronomer, Sosigenes to introduce the Egyptian solar calendar, which had the length of the solar year as three hundred and sixty-five and a quarter ($365^{1}/_{4}$) days and it became known as the Julian Calendar. In turn, many countries replaced this calendar during the early twentieth century (the 1900s) with the Gregorian Calendar.

When the three Cherusci boys called Armin, Flavus and Adalhard were training to become Roman cavalry officers. They had to learn to use both calendars at different times. The republican calendar only had ten months in it compared to the Julian calendar, which replaced it. During the transition between the two calendars, there was a period where both calendars were used, much to the confusion of the people who had to use them!

Armin's month of birth may well have been in what is now called either March or April, but it is not possible to be sure. What is apparent is his temperament, which is typical of those born under the star sign of Aries, and if so, that would fix his date of birth between 21/March/17 B.C. to 19/April/17 B.C... He was virtually fearless, and he proved himself to be a great tactician. As noted earlier, his brother, named Flavus, was also schooled in Roman ways and all three of us served in the Roman army.

To strengthen the Legions' fighting forces, the Roman army recruited soldiers from Roman provinces and even from unconquered territory such as Germania to serve in auxiliary units that were usually between five hundred and one thousand men in number.

Only the apparent nobility status of both Armin and Flavus gave us any advantage at all, and we had to prove ourselves constantly. That was something which resulted in both Armin and myself becoming quite anti-Roman in our outlooks, while Flavus just appeared to accept what the arrogant Romans wanted.

No favour was shown to any of us because of our status as the nobility of the Cherusci. What made it easier for Armin and Flavus was that the auxiliary units were usually placed under their own tribal leaders' command.

All the same, it was known, *"In order to command, a man must firstly know how to fulfil orders when commanded!"* We were posted to our units after our training, with Flavus being posted to a different unit than Armin and myself.

Armin and Adalhard go to Pannonia

The Roman armies conducted a series of operations against the Germanic warriors across the Rhine in the years 6 B.C. to 4 B.C., and some of these were successful, but defeats and rebellions marred others. The Roman armies, which were strengthened by Germanic warriors' addition, had isolated the eastern frontier of Marobod.

These allied Roman armies were about to attack simultaneously from the west and south when a major rebellion broke out in the year of 6 A.D., in what was known as Pannonia. The Roman province of Pannonia was made up of parts of what is called in the Twenty-second century as parts of Austria, Slovenia, and Dalmatia.

Even before this, Armin was serving the Roman army with distinction in Pannonia and other areas that were troublesome for the Romans. He had begun his service at the rank of munifex. That was the lowest rank of the trained rank and file of the legion.

Although he was a prince of the Cherusci, it was necessary for him to learn his soldiering skills by starting at the bottom. In soldiering, Armin found his forte and continuously proved himself in every task assigned to him. As a result, he was promoted to the next rank, that of Decanus.

The rank of Decanus is most easily explained by just saying that it was equivalent to the modern rank of corporal. He was now in command of a Roman army tent unit with eight men, and it was called a Contubernium, meaning tent unit. In terms of modern armies, the smallest Australian unit is the ten-man infantry section.

In June of 6 B.C., Armin and his men discovered a band of Pannonian rebels trying to infiltrate the Roman camp and kill the Praetor (Roman Legion Commander), who was asleep in his tent while this was happening.

Seeing the enemy and realising their intent, Armin shouted orders! He said, *"First contubernium, immediately come here! The camp is under attack from a band of Pannonian rebels, and they are trying to kill our Praetor! Hurry, and we shall use our pila[3] to engage the enemy firstly! If they survive that, we must kill them using our gladii[4]!"*

The Roman javelin or pila had soft iron blades that would bend upon piercing the person's flesh when the weapon was used against them. That, in turn, made it difficult for the wounded man to withdraw the weapon from himself, and he would then become an easy target for the Roman soldiers. They usually followed up an attack using pilas with a charge of heavy infantry using the short gladius.

So it was that after Armin had served as a decanus for two days, he was summoned to the Legion's Praetor tent. Armin entered the Praetor's tent and spoke, saluting as he did so. He said, *"Decanus Arminius reporting as ordered, sir!"* The Praetor said, *"Thank you for saving me from the clutches of those Pannonian rebels, Arminius! I fully realise that you*

---

[3] Pila was the Roman name given to javelins.
[4] Roman sword - pural.

have only been a decanus for two days, but I am now promoting you to the rank of optio! How do you feel about this promotion, optio?" Armin replied, *"Thank you, sir, I am most grateful!"*

Armin again quickly found himself in action again during an attack by Pannonians upon his Tuma[5]. The Pannonians were attacking the Turma with fury, and they managed to wound Olgilhard, the commander. A messenger came running towards Armin. When he got close enough to be heard, he spoke to Armin. He said, *"Arminius, the commander of this turma called Olgilhard, has been seriously wounded, and he has asked for your immediate presence with him!"*

Armin immediately left and went to the location of his commander. As he was getting closer to his commander, Armin saluted him and spoke. He said, *"Olgilhard, sir, I am here as you have ordered. What is it you want me to do?* Olgilhard replied, *"Armin, I am badly wounded, and I may not survive this fighting!*

Therefore, I wrote a dispatch to the Praetor of this legion recommending your promotion to my position of Decurio[6] of this Turma! Try to see to it that you fulfil the role to the best of your considerable abilities. Armin said, *"Yes, sir, I shall do whatever needs to be done! That I swear by the beard of my father and by Wodin and Thor! I shall be worthy of you!"* He was now the undisputed commander of the turma, and he would be continuously called upon to

---

[5] The main cavalry sub-unit. The main cavalry unit was called ala.
[6] Leader of the equite cavalry sub-units called turma.

apply his military skills. In due course, Armin became the commander of the entire ala.

With Armin now in command of up to five hundred and twelve cavalry troopers, he was really beginning to show his military skills and was often in hand-to-hand combat fighting against enemy cavalry units whenever that was called for. His knowledge and ability in tactics against the enemy became very well known to his superior officers.

His ala was attached to various legions according to need. It became fashionable for some Roman legion commanders to say that they had the services of Arminius and his fierce Cherusci cavalry ala.

The XV Legion was being harassed on all sides and in desperate need of relief. A message asking for relief and reinforcements was received by the Legate (commander) of the legion. He immediately sent a decanus[7] to fetch Arminius.

Upon his arrival, the Legate said, *"Arminius, we have a situation that I think would best be handled by you and your superior cavalry. I have also heard that you use light infantry, which can keep pace with the horsemen. Is what I have been hearing about your forces correct?"*

Armin said, *"Sir, I do not know what others are saying about myself or about my Cherusci soldiers. So perhaps I should explain about my men and how they*

---

[7] Equivalent to a corporal in modern armies of the twenty-second century.

are used! As you already know, the Cherusci specialise in having outstanding cavalry forces. As well, we also have up to one hundred very fit young light infantry soldiers per ala who are very lightly armed and who can run alongside their cavalry comrades and actually keep pace with them.

When my combined forces of infantry and cavalry arrive quickly at a battle, we can usually turn the tide of the fight in our favour because the last thing the enemies expect is the sudden arrival of both infantry and cavalry acting as one combined forces!

Legate Titus Caeponius said, *"Gather your men and proceed to the aid of the XV Legion, which has allowed itself to become cut off from other Roman army units, and it is now trapped between the fork of two different rivers! Go and provide relief for our soldiers now!"* Armin answered, *"Yes sir, consider the XV Legion saved if my men and I can get to it quickly enough! Is there anything else about the legion's situation that I should know about?"*

The legate answered, *"Yes, the Praetor[8] of this grouping of legions has ordered the fortification of the position. The work was about two-thirds completed when the rebels' attack started!"* Armin answered, *"Very well sir, my cavalry ala, complete with the light infantry one hundred will move out at a gallop to aid the XV Legion immediately! You say that the fortification was about two-thirds completed when the rebels attacked. With hope, the legion will be able to*

---

[8] Commander of a grouping of several legions.

use the partly completed work to slow the Pannonian attack's advance! We leave now!"

With the horsemen going at a gallop and the light infantry keeping pace with the cavalry, Armin's ala was finally in position on the wing of the legion facing the open plain, which was the only access to the legion without having to cross deep and fast-flowing rivers on the other three sides.

Before Armin and his ala arrived, the Pannonians attacked in strength, and they found that their way was blocked on three sides by the forking rivers. They also found that many of the fortifications of the Roman camp had been completed.

Armin immediately went into action at full gallop and closed with the enemy with his ala coming behind him. The first enemy to die by Armin's hand that day perished by Armin swinging his long broadsword and cutting off the head of the enemy closest to him. Next, the Roman Heavy Infantry poured out from their positions and fell about the rebels.

My job was to access the situation and to report as quickly as possible to Armin, to let him know things such as the positions of both enemy and friendly forces, the speed and strengths or weaknesses of enemy forces and the terrain, including what use could be made of the landscape for both attack and defence by any force.

I observed the situation, and I did not like what I saw. I hurried to Armin and made my report to him. I said, *"Sir, the legion is currently in battle and is fighting for its life! The rebels are attacking in large numbers, and I doubt if the legion can survive if we do not break the Pannonian attack.*

The legion has river frontages on three sides of it because of the forking of the rivers! The rivers are deep and fast-flowing, presenting an obstacle to any attacking force! The plain between the forks of the rivers is flat and reasonably clear of trees and other undergrowth.

On the southern side of the forking rivers is a range of mountains. Is it possible for us to get aid from the other legions in this grouping? After all, there could be many more enemies coming yet!"

Armin now said, *"Adalhard, it is very obvious to me that we must move very quickly if we are to save the legion! We shall again launch a combined cavalry/infantry attack upon the rebels by using the cavalry and the "One Hundred" of this unit! When the enemy realises that they are under attack from elite infantry shock troops and elite cavalry forces, they will either run away or die in their positions! Again, I need you to go out on the battlefield, perform your valuable scouting activities, and then report what you find directly to me.*

As it is day-time and the sun is shining, urgent messages could be sent by smoke signals or the sun's reflection from Roman mirrors. If you can see that you are close enough to us to hear you, you may want to try sounding warning blasts on your horn!"

I want you to devise a simple code that we Can teach to all of our warriors! I want you to set up the following types of simple codes for our warriors to learn. Firstly, we could use flashes of light, which reflect the sun using small Roman mirrors or other suitable materials with very shiny surfaces. Also, devise a system of horn blasts that all have different meanings and are easy for the warriors to learn!

For example, I would like the code to consist of three reflected light flashes or three horn blasts, which should be separated by the amount of time it takes to count, one-two!

That could be used to warn us of the sudden arrival of enemy units in our areas. I shall leave the setting up of the simple codes and the teaching of them to our warriors up to you, Adalhard! By having these quick communications, it will give us another advantage over our enemies! Now go and get it all done, and then continue with your scouting missions!"

With that, the ala moved off at speed towards the battlefield. The naked warriors of the "One Hundred" were running alongside the horsemen and keeping pace with them. In time, the battlefield came into sight.

Armin issued commands. He said, *"All those of you who have horns are to use them to give loud blasts of the horn so that both the Pannonian rebels and the Romans whom we are rescuing will hear us. That should result in the Romans getting renewed confidence and also cause dismay to the enemy!"*

As noted earlier, upon hearing the horn blasts, the heavy infantry poured out of their positions and attacked the enemy forces, who now were under attack from two directions. They were under attack from the direction of the legion. The legion was attacking using its Heavy Infantry, while the ala of Armin and his men were attacking utilising the combination of specialist cavalry and elite light infantry forces.

These things combined and resulted in the Pannomians becoming confused and many of them fleeing from the battlefield. Many of them died, and a lot of them were taken prisoner. Armin discussed the events of the day with me.

He said, *"Adalhard, my friend, those eighty-four enemy prisoners were going to be sold as slaves, and that would have significantly enriched the Cherusci coffers! However, all of that has been stopped from happening because of the fool in command of the XV Legion! The Legatus Legions[9] has commanded that all eighty-four enemy prisoners are to be crucified. I told the stupid Roman fool that if he wants to kill the prisoners, then he and the Romans must do it because the members of this cavalry ala shall not!"*

Much to all Armin's unit members' disgust, eighty-four crosses bearing a crucified enemy soldier on each one of them appeared just outside of the uncompleted fortifications of the Roman camp. Armin became so disgusted by what he saw that he stormed off to see the Legatus Legionis.

He said to the Roman, *"So, you really have done what you said you were going to do! I did not think that even you could be so stupid as to waste a*

[9] Legion commander.

resource such as these men who could have made us rich by being sold as slaves!"

The Roman said, *"So there you are, Arminius! Because I am making an example of what happens to Rome's enemies, it was necessary to execute all prisoners of war in public so that the barbarians will see what happens to Rome's enemies! When they see this sort of thing often enough, the message that it is futile to defy Rome must get through their thick skulls!"*

Armin answered, *"What you are doing is to instil a hatred of all things Roman in the very people you wish to conquer! That will in due course rebound upon you, and you will end up being sorry for this cruelty and waste of lives of valuable slaves, the sale of whom would have made me much more wealthy!"*

And so it was that Armin was yet again overwhelmed by the extent of Roman cruelty! Yet, he decided to bide his time and build up his expertise and knowledge of Roman tactics. He was summoned to appear before the Legatus Legionis. When he arrived at the commander's tent lodgings, he was ushered inside it by a munifex who withdrew upon the commander's arrival.

The legion's commander spoke to Armin. He said, *"Arminius, I must thank you and congratulate you on yet another battle won and another entire Roman legion being saved by your men and yourself! This time, your efforts saved the XV Legion from certain destruction due to your fine efforts!*

The Legion was doomed until you used your remarkable tactic of using your elite light infantry as shock troops acting in conjunction with your elite cavalry! I have sent word of your deeds to the Senate in Rome, and the senators have now granted you full Roman citizenship as well as the title of Equestrian. That means you have now become a Roman Knight! May the Gods smile upon you and your fine Cherusci men!"

While the commander of the XV Legion was speaking, Armin was grim. He was thinking, *"Fucking bullshit! Your Roman gods are not the true gods of anyone on earth, and they are myths! Don't talk bullshit to me! More and more, I am becoming sickened at the cruelty you Roman arseholes commonly practice!*

Your love of either impaling people or of crucifying them just so that you poor excuses for men can watch the people you do those things to slowly die in extreme agony due to the methods of execution you pricks have devised are enough to completely sicken me! I hope not to see too much more of this sort of thing, you callous pricks!

As well, there are stories among Roman officers about the aftermath of the battle with Spartacus. Officially, Rome says that Spartacus and his men were crucified. The Romans who were there tell a different story! They say that you callous Roman pricks used thin poles to insert into the arseholes of the rebels and that you forced the poles right into them.

It is said that the rebels were then carried to their places of execution, where the free end of the pole was embedded into the ground. The man's weight would then have made him very slowly slide down the pole until such time as it almost protruded from his back. All of the time, he would have been in extreme agony until he died nearly two days later.

In due course, I will deliver my people back to complete independence from you, you callous cowards! For the time being, I shall continue to serve as a Roman officer, but know this! After I completely know all of your tactics and how best to counter them, I will act against you when the time is right!"

Marobod Establishes in Bohemia

While Tiberius was in temporary retirement from public life, Domitius Ahenobarbus was given the duty of strengthening Roman influence in submissive areas of north-western Germania. Intercourse with the local population was encouraged, fortified posts were multiplied, and a road was built from the Rhine to Aliso on the Lippe.

After Tiberius has returned from his voluntary exile on Rhodes, he took up command of the army in Germania and sent Sentuius Saturninus against the Chatti. At the same time, he tried to conquer the Caninefates on the frontier with Bravia; he was also trying to subjugate the Attuarii and the Bructeri.

He managed to obtain the loose co-operation and a luke-warm alliance with the Cherusci and persuaded them to quarter Roman soldiers among them. The Chauci were bought under Roman control by the Cherusci. These things resulted in a period of peace and prosperity. However, things were happening, which would suddenly call forth the empire's whole strength for its defence.

As ever more stories about the power of King Marobod of Bohemia and his Mark-Mannen warriors reached the ears of the Romans, they became increasingly uneasy about Marobod and his people, seeing them as a significant potential threat to Rome itself!

After Marobod made himself the ruler of Bohemia, he applied his power and influence to surrounding Germanic nations. Several surrounding tribes openly acknowledged him as their sovereign. After some time, he was able to have a standing army of force of seventy thousand infantry soldiers and four thousand cavalry troopers, all of which were drilled and disciplined on the Roman model because Marobod had been a serving Roman army officer.

Marobod was speaking to some of his army members. He said, *"Gentlemen, over the next ten to twelve years, we shall try out my army against many different enemies! We shall use our army in expeditions against distant tribes, and we will spread terror to the extremes of Germania's borders! We shall not take shit from the Romans, and if they act against us, we will wipe them out!"*

Many people had incurred the wrath of Rome during those times, resulting in those people seeking the protection of Marobod against the Romans. One of his sub-chiefs spoke. He said, *"Permission to state my mind, please, sir!"* Marobod replied, *"Permission granted. What is troubling you, Eckbert?"*

He said, *"Sir, I have noted that on many occasions, we have given sanctuary to the enemies of Rome! I cannot help the feeling in my bones that the Romans will launch military strikes against our people sooner or later and invade parts of Germania and, in particular, Bohemia!*

Many of the people we are sheltering are guilty of committing offences against Rome, which the Romans deeply resent. I get the impression that the Romans will use military strikes against us and other Germanic people because they fear us all so much! I suggest that we build up our infantry and cavalry forces and conduct constant aggressive patrolling of all of our country.

In particular, we must continuously patrol our border areas close to the Romans! They are likely to invade at any time. Suppose an opportunity arises for us to spread discord among the Romans. In that case, we should do so, before they can act against us!" Marobod replied, *"Thank you for your input, Eckbert. I agree that we must initiate aggressive patrolling programmes so that our army is always informed of Roman activity!*

Also, we have many other Germanic tribes coming to assist us if the Romans do attack. However, I totally agree that we must not let the Romans attack us or dictate any terms to us. I am considering the possibility of trying to unite all Germanic tribes against Rome, but I rather doubt if that will become possible!"

Augustus Confers with Tiberius

Meanwhile, in Rome, Augustus and Tiberius discussed the apparent dangers of various tribes in and near Germania. Augustus said, *"Tiberius, my son, I note with alarm that the German tribes opposed to Rome are presenting us with a great danger! Making things even more difficult for Romans is that Germania has vast areas of trackless forest, and there are no roads, towns, or cities that we could attack and simply take-over!"*

Tiberius said, *"Augustus, my father, things may not be as bad as you appear to think! We have established Roman domination in northern Germania, and I believe that we should take full advantage of the friendly disposition of the Hermunduri. I put it to you that we should use the Hermunduri to help us crush Marobod and his forces in Bohemia, which is only two hundred miles from Rome's frontiers! To enable Rome to do this, the Army of the Rhine's command should be given to Sentuius Saturninus. I should also be involved by leading the Illyrian legions!"*

In 6 A.D., the two leaders staged a combined assault against the forces of Marobod. Saturninus built a road across dense forest and advanced through the territory of the Chatti towards the Danube, while Tiberius marched from Carinatum along the river to make a junction with him on the frontiers of Noricum. The junction of the two Roman forces took place within sight of Marobod's advanced guard. The

Romans took up positions which were of advantage for the coming campaign.

While these things were happening, the discontent that had long been spreading among the populations in the Illyrian and Pannonian provinces became one organised rebellion under the command of two chiefs named Bato and Pinnes.

Tiberius sent for a messenger. When he arrived, the messenger was escorted in to see Tiberius. Tiberius said, *"What is your name, messenger? I have important work for you!"* The messenger replied, *"Sir, I am optio Marcus Malinois, and I shall attend to whatever task you have for me with the utmost of my abilities!"*

Tiberius said, *"Thank you, optio Marcus Malinois! I need you to travel to where King Marobod of Bohemia is and offer him peace terms which are most advantageous for him! Suppose you can get him to accept our peace terms. In that case, it will allow the Roman forces of both Saturninus and my own forces to hurry to the defence of the Italian peninsular and so alleviate the fear in Rome of yet another Germanic invasion like that of the Cimbri!"*

Rome had the good fortune of Marobod accepting the terms offered to him, resulting in the combined armies of Tiberius and Saturninus hurrying to the defence of Italy.

The rebellion had spread like a plague along the entire Pannonian and Illyrian frontiers as far as Macedonia and Thrace. Two hundred thousand infantry and twelve thousand cavalry soldiers now took up arms at the two chiefs' signal to take revenge upon the Romans.

Having called his people to arms, the Illyrian chief named Bato urged his soldiers to attack Romans, as did the Pannonian leader named Pinnes. As their forces were vast and led by men who knew Roman tactics, the situation that Rome now found itself in alarmed many Romans. The Roman Senate's emergency sessions were held, with many speeches being made by Augustus, Tiberius, and others. Such was the fear in Rome that a near panic had set in.

Augustus spoke in the senate. He said, *"Fellow Roman citizens, the Illyrian and Pannonian rebels hate us with a vengeance! They have vast forces which are being led by their own commanders who have had the experience of serving as Roman officers! They, therefore, know Roman tactics and the strengths and weaknesses of Roman forces!*

Unless they are stopped immediately, they could be at the gates of Rome within the next ten days! In order to prevent that from happening, Rome shall raise forced loans for the good of the state! Retired Roman army veterans shall be put back into service with the army! Slaves shall be given their freedom on the condition that they then serve in the army alongside the regular soldiers!

With the exception of those legions that are based a long way away from the rebellions, the Roman Empire's entire strength shall be placed into the areas of the uprisings and placed under the command of Tiberius!

The war with the rebels continued for four more years and was finally stopped by the Roman Empire, making concessions instead of relying upon conquests alone. The pacification of the Illyrian and Pannonian provinces was celebrated in Rome with great rejoicing and festivities.

Honours were heaped upon Tiberius and Germanicus, whom Augustus had placed in command in association with Tiberius. At this moment of self-congratulation and triumph, news arrived of the destruction of three entire Roman legions together with all of their supporting units. The commanders' deaths and the stopping of Roman power and dominion over central and northern Germania!

Varus as Governor of Germania

As we have already seen, Varus was removed from Syria's government and placed into new Roman acquisitions in Germania. He was mild in his manners but always habitually inactive and idle. He was obstinate, pedantic, extortionate, and grasping.

Varus Uses the Routine of his Syrian Administration to Govern Germans

Varus set up his governorship along the same lines as his previous administration in Syria. Holding court as if he was a king, he spoke! He said, *"I shall make the Germans obey Roman rules and laws! I am implementing Roman law in place of all Germanic laws and customs! The Germans shall no longer be able to use their ancient traditions, and Roman laws and customs shall be followed!*

Roman courts shall be set-up in place of the traditional Germanic judgement seats of Gau-Graff and Zent-graff. No matter if the Germans like it or not, they must obey Roman orders and adopt Roman ways of life, which includes constant bathing! If they do not do so, I shall crucify them!"

Rome's fiscal and criminal laws were enforced, with prosecutions and processes that vastly multiplied the Germanic population's contempt for all Romans! As a result of the introduction of these Roman laws and commands, a host of Roman lawyers and government officials such as tax collectors descended upon Germania like a plague of locusts. In time, Varus and the lawyers prospered.

His new settlement was complete with three of the five legions that he commanded. That left his uncle, Lucius Asprenas, in command of the other two legions, located behind him in the territory of the Ubii.

Feeling secure in his new seat of government, he set about building barracks and towns. He then assumed the state of a sovereign prince or king and summoned the Germanic chiefs to his tribunal judgements. At the Roman trial of a Cherusci warrior, Varus was the judge hearing the case.

The warrior was accused of defying Rome and being insolent towards Romans, and not respecting Roman women. In the courts of Varus, to be charged was akin to being found guilty. When Clovis appeared before him, Varus said, *"Clovis, it has come to my attention that you and many other Germanic barbarians are ignoring orders of my soldiers to move into the town that I have built around Aliso.*

Also, that you and other Germans are not respecting Roman women and even worse, you are not obeying the Roman orders. That shall not do! I consider you and your kind to be rebels, and it is the sentence of this court that you shall be crucified. You are getting that sentence because Roman citizens cannot be crucified, but Germans can.

You shall be taken to the hill just out of town in the evening, and then you shall be tied to a cross. As the night turns into day, and then afternoon, you shall experience a great thirst, and in due course, you will die from lack of water and food. Do you have any last words?"

All of the time, he directed the execution of legal sentences. As a result of this, the free-spirited Germanic warrior could see his chief, kinsman or friend treated like a slave or dying under a lictor's[10] axe,[11] if he happened to be a Roman citizen. Those who were not Roman citizens would always be impaled or crucified.

Clovis immediately answered that. He said, *"Bullshit! Get the hell out of my country, you Roman bully! Since you have come here, many people have been crucified by you and your henchmen! I know of at least three German women who were raped by you and who now have your children! Just leave my country and do not return!"*

Varus said, *"Clovis, you are condemned to die by crucifixion! As for me raping your women and impregnating some of them, you should be thankful for me doing so because at least the resulting children shall be half-human*

---

[10] An officer, official or guard in the service of the main Roman magistrates.
[11] Roman citizens were beheaded, not crucified. That punishment was for barbarians and Jews.

which is so unlike you Germanic apes! All of you German people are of a much lower class of people than Roman people, so be thankful for Romans like me raping your women because their children will all be much better than you unwashed and smelly Germanic warriors! You really must learn to bathe at least once per day!"

These things resulted in Varus and his team of Roman lawyers prospering. His scheme for quickening the new territory's pace of embracing Roman civilisation appeared to run contrary to his predecessors' timid policy. The Roman contempt for the Germanic barbarians now allowed the set-up of an extensive conspiracy within the headquarters of Varus.

Several Germanic warriors from the tribes of the Cherusci, Chatti, Ubii, Herumandi and other tribes were meeting to discuss the growing concern being felt by the Germans about Varus.

Agilman said, *"My fellow warriors of Germania, we have among us a Roman monster who is raping our women and crucifying our men! It is high time for all Germanic tribes to unite and remove the Roman pest! We can best do so by closely watching everything that Varus does and then relaying that information about Roman units' movements directly to where the Romans will go! That way, a nice hot, hostile reception committee in the form of ambushes and other impediments to their progress can be arranged!*

Conrad, I know that you work closely with the Varus headquarters! So please tell us all what your duties to the Roman called Varus are and how we can benefit from the information that you will send to us!"

Conrad now stood up before the meeting and spoke. He said, *"Thank you for the introduction, Agilman. My duties at the headquarters of Varus are those of a scribe. That is because I learned to read and write in both Greek and Latin at the early age of thirteen years!*

Because of my ability to write Latin, I get to know everything that happens at the headquarters of Varus. I am the only one who can write in Latin, in this area other than Varus himself! Varus does not want to be burdened with the writing of orders and instructions. Therefore, I have to do it for him!

So that none of you have to learn how to read and write in Latin, I have invented the first Germanic script based on the Latin alphabet! As well, I have prepared twenty small pages of parchment that you can use to revise the lessons in reading and writing of thefirst German script! All ofyou twenty warriors shall train as message writers using the German script which uses the Latin Alphabet!"

He then proceeded to go to all twenty warriors who were present and, in turn, gave him a small folder of parchment which had the basic new German script to which he was referring to within it.

He then stepped forward and drew some images on the sand at his feet. He said, *"Fellow warriors, please step forward until you can clearly see what I have drawn in the sand. I want you to think about this, and then, I want you to tell me what it means."*

Starting today, we shall concentrate on teaching you how to write words in our German language using the Romans' own Latin alphabet. This way of communicating is the most efficient way for us all to communicate now.

By us also learning to use the alphabet the Romans have, it will significantly aid our revolution!

Therefore, I shall teach all twenty of you to read and write basic words in the German language using Rome's alphabet! After you have left here, I need you to discuss all of this between yourselves and practice what you have learned during our lessons!

We shall start with very simple things. First, we look at the various sounds that the Latin characters and combinations of them make. So, this is the Latin letter "A", and it makes the sound of a: This is the letter B, and it makes the sound of "b": this is the letter c, and it makes the sound of 'ka" in German.

Now let's try using these letters to make words! By writing C plus A plus T, we have a word. Bangulf, please come forward and tell me what you think this word means!" Bangulf stepped forward as asked by Conrad.

He said, *"Conrad, you have written c, a and t in the Latin script. I think that it means cat. Is that correct?"* Conrad said, *"Yes, you are correct! By all of you learning this way of communicating and then going out to Germanic military units and teaching this to others, we will enjoy having a written communication system which will equal what the Romans have in due course! So, we shall learn the Latin alphabet, but we will write the messages in German. That will make things exceedingly difficult for Romans to understand any of our messages that they may intercept!*

The arrogant Romans know that there is no written German language at the moment, and they arrogantly think that we cannot devise our own written

209

language. So, if the Romans intercept a message that is written in the German language but using the Latin alphabet, they will not know how to read it.

So, learn what the symbols are and what they mean. Ensure that you all know it because all of our lives may depend upon us getting reliable information to and between our warrior units! Some of you may have heard of a possible deliverer of Germania from the Romans who are actively trying to conquer us! I have heard of a Cherusci commander who is highly thought of by the Romans! Could he be the deliverer?"

For the moment, the Germanic chiefs disguised their true feelings and resentment towards the Romans, pretending to show the greatest regard for Varus's decrees and pretending to admire his wisdom. The Germanic barbarians were accurate observers of individual character, and they quickly realised that the new Roman Governor was ideal to be used in their plans to rid Germania of Romans.

It was the Germanic staff of the Varus Headquarters who suggested to Varus that legions send some of their cohorts to stop pretended insurrections or to be used to clear forest tracks of non-existent robbers or to escort convoys of supplies when there was no threat coming from anyone at all.

In the meantime, the Germanic conspirators surrounded Varus, fed him incorrect information and garbled his intelligence. While they took prompt measures to instruct their followers, they prepared them for general uprisings and rebellion against Rome at a signal from themselves.

Varus was kept informed about the situation of the Roman effort in Pannonia and what the various Roman units were doing, and who commanded them. He was fully informed of the names of various commanders.

He was told of a Cherusci commander's heroic efforts who had saved the XV Legion from inevitable disaster and how he had achieved a great victory for Rome. He was speaking to a centurion about this. He said, *"Centurion, do you know what the name of this outstanding officers is?"* The centurion replied, *"Yes, sir, his Roman name is Arminius, and his Germanic name is Armin! He is a Cherusci nobleman of great ability and power!"*

Varus said, *"Centurion, go to where this Arminius is now and see his commanding officer with my written request for Arminius and his cavalry ala[12] to immediately quit Pannonia and hasten with all possible speed to here at Aliso! I want this great officer and soldier here in my service!"* The centurion replied, *"Sir, what you are asking may not be possible! The word among the army has it that Arminius is considered to be very valuable by the Praetor he is currently serving. If true, then you shall just have to do without him!"*

Varus was now shouting. He said, *"Here is my written order for Arminius and his Cherusci cavalry ala! Also contained with this is the order signed by Augustus himself that I am to have whatever and whomever I want so that the Germans can finally be conquered! Now go and make sure that you return with Arminius and his*

---

[12] Major equite cavalry unit attached to the legions at a rate of two ala per legion.

outstanding soldiers! I do not care how you do it; I just want it to be completed in the way that I have outlined to you! Bring Arminius to me!"

Along with many other secret members of the Germanic conspiracy in the headquarters of Varus, Conrad was overjoyed by what he had heard. He smiled as he spoke. He said, *"Finally, now that everything is organised, we have the news that Armin the deliverer shall soon be here with us!*

When he gets here, we will contact him and let him know that we have everything in place for a general rebellion and mobilisation of all Germanic people to rise up against the Roman invaders! Wodin and Thor must have heard our prayers, for they are being answered!"

Armin is Ordered to Assist Varus

The Praetor had Armin summoned to his tent at the Roman camp in Pannonia. After Armin was escorted in by a munifex, the Praetor said, *"Arminius, I find your assistance extremely valuable and effective! I personally would like to keep you here assisting my legions! The problem is that I have received an order to send you and all of your ala to assist Varus in Germania! The order has come from the very top, being directly from Augustus himself!*

You and your ala are to travel directly to the bases and fortifications built by Drusus on Augustus's orders at Aliso on the Lippe River. When you get there, report directly to Varus for duty assignment!

Before you go, I am promoting you to the rank of Prefectus Equitarius[13], which means that you shall be in command of all equite[14] cavalry units assigned to many legions! I need you to organise things in all of the equite cavalry units by promoting all of the most capable soldiers before you leave. You are to take the entire ala with you when you leave here and begin your journey to Aliso in Germania. Your unit will be replaced by a new one coming from Rome. I can only hope that the new unit will have just a small measure of the outstanding military success and application you and your men have had here!

Take some time for your ala and yourself to rest, then draw whatever you and your men may need from the supply officer. When that has been completed, travel to Aliso with your ala to serve Varus. Good luck to you, my friend! May Jupiter and the other Gods smile upon you!" Armin took the hand of his Roman superior and shook it. He said, *"Thank you, my Roman friend! May Wodin and his son, Thor, smile upon you!"*

Far from filling him with a fear of the unknown, Armin was overjoyed at the prospect of returning to Germania. For some time, the well-organised cells of conspirators within Varus' headquarters had been sending him written reports in Latin saying what was happening in Germania. This activity also let Armin know the names of the people he would soon be helping to rid Germania of the Romans!

---

[13] Prefectus Equitarius was in overall command of all cavalry units assigned to many legions!

[14] Equite units were non-Roman citizens in the service of the Roman army. They were often from Gaul and Germania.

As Armin and the men of his ala were riding towards Aliso, I (Adalhard) acted as the unit's forward scout. We had to be careful, and part of that is to be watchful! Then, the same as happens now, the forward scout often found out about dangerous situations before his unit got into trouble. His job was to inform the unit so that corrective action could be taken. I was peering through some bushes and located some eight-hundred paces ahead of the ala when I noticed a young Germanic looking man in the company of eight Roman cavalry troopers.

I rode out to where the young man and his Roman escort were, then I spoke in Latin. I said, *"Halt and identify yourselves!"* The young man answered in Latin, *"Thank you for asking! I am Conrad, and I work as a scribe in the Headquarter of Varus!"* He then stopped speaking Latin and spoke German to me.

He said, *"As I have said, I am Conrad. Are you with the Cherusci leader called Armin?"* I answered, *"Yes, I am; he and the rest of the ala are about eight hundred paces behind me towards the south-east! You say your name is Conrad? I think that I have seen that name many times on messages coming from Aliso to Armin!"*

Conrad replied, *"Yes, if you have been reading the messages to Armin, you will know me well! It is my pleasure to announce that there are now at least ten other Germanic scribes working at the Headquarters of Varus! Whenever we have to write out orders for Roman units of Varus, we also write a German copy that is then quickly sent to the various Germanic warrior units chosen to deal with the Romans!*

We have sent many Roman legions and their cohorts to clear forest tracks of non-existent robbers or whole Roman legions to escort supply trains through areas of non-existent rebels! We can send word very quickly to Germanic warrior units to harry the Romans, and we often do so!

At the moment, Varus, the Roman Governor, does not know if he is coming or going, because every piece of information he receives has been changed to suit our needs and not his! We have successfully set-up a comprehensive conspiracy within his own headquarters, and he does not know it and suspects nothing! Could you also please introduce me to Armin?"

I replied, *"Yes, indeed, Conrad, you shall see him very soon. I am the Cherusci Training Officer of this ala, and I shall introduce you to him! I think that he will like to meet you, the man who has been supplying Germanic forces with much information about the Roman enemies!*

I have battled much in the direct service of Armin and Rome. I know that he is the deliverer that our people are looking for. He was visibly shaken when his Roman superior officers ordered the mass crucifixion of Pannonian rebels. I heard him say, "You callous, cruel Roman arseholes! I will one day get all of you out of Germania!" Conrad replied, *"Good, I have always thought that he could be the deliverer!"* Then we went to see Armin.

Armin Reports for Duty with Varus

After I introduced Conrad to Armin and we told him about the vast conspiracy set-up within the Headquarters of Varus, we all went to Aliso with Conrad

215

and Armin accompanied by the Roman escort of Conrad, leading.

Upon arrival at the Roman fortifications on the Lippe River, Conrad, Armin, and I were ushered into the Roman Governor's presence. After the ushering munifex had guided us to where he was, we found Varus seated upon a gilded throne. The munifex withdrew, and Varus spoke.

He said, *"Arminius, I am so very glad to see you! I am at my wit's end trying to keep these Germans under Roman control! One thing that makes controlling Germania so hard is the fact that the Germans do not have towns or cities. I tried to put an end to that, and I built entire towns with houses for the Germanic people, but they refused to move into the towns and houses that I have built for them!*

They just tell me that I only built the houses and the towns so that the Germans would all be easier to control since they would be easy to find in the towns and cities! That, of course, means that the Roman army has to continue searching for the Germanic people in isolated hamlets and farm buildings!

Not only that, but these people fight us at every opportunity, and they remain unconquered! That situation must be rectified, and I think that you can be a great help in my achievement of that goal! I made a personal appeal to my Lord Augustus to have you sent here! Your reputation precedes you! Now please go and familiarise yourself with the surrounding country-side and take some time off military duties for yourself and your men!

After you have been here for fourteen days, I want you to be here with me when I sit in judgement of these Germanic barbarians! I shall need your advice on how best to deal with many situations involving the Germans. In the meantime, it may benefit you to have some interaction with the Germanic population of this area. Who knows, maybe you will find a girl to fuck! Whatever happens, be ready to assist me during my judgement of the German criminal people in fourteen days from now!

I have been in contact with your previous commander. He has written to me informing me of the fact that you are now both a Roman citizen and a Roman Knight! I know that your previous commander of the grouping of all Roman legions in Pannonia promoted you to the position of commander of all equite cavalry units in Pannonia! That being the case, I hereby promote you to your rightful place! That of the over-all commander of all equite cavalry units operating in Germania!"

That started Armin to think, *"This could not be better, you fucking arrogant Roman arsehole! By me being in your court, I can use the existing conspiracy against you and expand it greatly! I shall have access to all information going into and out of your headquarters. Together with the other Germanic tribesmen and women, I shall have the necessary means to finally throw you Roman pricks out of my country!"*

Armin quickly and accurately assessed the new governor of Germania's character, resulting in Armin attaching himself to Publius Quintilius Varus. He became an intimate associate and table companion of Varus. In Armin, Varus found a person whose conversation and manners were those of the typical barbarian frankness, which had been polished by the time Armin had spent as an officer directly fighting for the Roman army. While Varus overlooked the lessons learned and experience gained while in service with the Roman army, Armin did not!

During the next two weeks, Armin explored the country-side area around the Lippe River and spoke to many people. He was laying down the grounding of his future attacks upon the Roman invaders! He was always busy seeing new people and making a great impression upon them. Women found themselves powerfully attracted to him, for he was strikingly handsome. At first, he mentioned his scheme to liberate Germania to only a few trusted people. He instructed them to flatter the governor and to laugh at his rather bad jokes whenever Varus indulged in his humour.

He pointed out that overpowering the Roman legions was not possible at the time. The Germanic forces had to draw the Romans into areas favourable to the Germanic warriors and away from the Romans' resources. The plans of getting rid of the Romans was secretly communicated between Armin and most Germanic tribes.

Armin is Introduced to Thusnelda

In time, Armin was introduced to Thusnelda by her father, Segestes. He was very much a client of Rome and a known betrayer of his countrymen whenever he thought that he could profit from doing so. In Armin, he saw a way to further enrich himself because of Armin's reputation among his Roman superiors. So, he introduced Armin to his daughter.

He said, *"Armin, this is my daughter, Thusnelda. Thusnelda, this is Armin, the cavalry officer of whom you have heard so much!"* The effect of this meeting of the two young people was dramatic, to say the least. Both of them were enthralled with the presence of each other.

Thusnelda, forgot about the presence of her father and spoke to Armin. She said, *"Armin, I have heard of your many deeds in Pannonia and other places. I am so delighted to meet you finally!"* Segestes correctly assumed that these two young people would become lovers and voiced his opposition to it. He said, *"Thusnelda, you are betrothed to another man whom I approve of, and I want you to go ahead and marry him as it will be a perfect union for you!"* He was expecting his daughter to obey him and marry the Roman court official.

Instead of being obeyed by his daughter, he was firmly told to leave. Thusnelda was like many other Germanic women of her time. They knew that they were the equals of their male partners. Thusnelda was defiant and said, *"Pappa, you have been told this before! I shall not marry the Roman official whom you want me to marry! You do not care about me, and you are only interested in getting more money and power that my marrying a Roman can bring you!*

Let us get it quite clear that I am not interested in advancing your station in life! I shall have the husband of my choice and not your's! Now go away and leave us in peace!" As soon as Segestes had left the young couple's presence, she removed the clasp which was holding her cloak, and it dropped away, revealing her trim and firm young body to Armin.

She then removed her undergarments and placed Armin's right hand upon her left breast. Then she took his right hand and put it upon her vagina. She said, *"Armin, my love, please very gently suck the nipples of both of my tits! While you are doing that, I want you to finger-fuck me for some time until I am nice and juicy for you. When that happens, I want you to mount me and make love to me!"*

Armin did as requested, and after their lovemaking was over, both Thusnelda and Armin went to Segestes to try to initiate a good relationship of 'Father-in-law and son-in-law", with him. That resulted in Armin speaking to Segestes. He said, *"Segestes, I am in love with your daughter Thusnelda, and I wish to have her as my wife! We both would very much like to have your blessing for our coming marriage, but if we do not get it, we will marry anyway. The choice of giving us your blessing lies with you and only you!"*

Segestes wanted Thusnelda to marry a Roman court official, which would have given him a considerable amount of money and power. Now he thought that Armin and Thusnelda were stealing that prize away from him. Therefore he said, *"No, Armin, my daughter is betrothed to a Roman court official, and he, not you is the man she will marry!"*

Thusnelda now spoke. She said, *"Pappa, I do not care what you think or whom you want me to marry! Iam exercising my right as a noble-born Cherusci woman to have the man of my choice and not yours! I shall marry whoever I want to, and I want Armin, whom your Roman friends call Arminius! I shall go on seeing Armin, so you had better just get used to it all!"*

The show of defiance by his daughter both surprised and angered Segestes. As well as being grasping and cowardly in nature, Segestes was also extremely jealous of Armin's hero reputation among his Germanic counterparts and his Roman comrades. So jealous of Armin's prestige was Segestes, that he began plotting the downfall of the man who had swept away his daughter.

To Segestes, this insult was nasty because he did not see how he could profit from their relationship! He did not like what was happening between the young lovers, but true to his cowardly nature, he left the area without saying anything to anyone at all. He began to foster a growing hatred for Armin, which gave way to active plotting on his part against both of them, even though Thusnelda would also be affected badly by what he was doing!

Segestes, as we have already seen, was very pro-Roman in his outlook and was a 'Client noble of Rome'. Segestes tried to have his own friends appointed to positions within the headquarters of Varus, but he found that all of the posts were filled by people loyal to the coming Germanic uprisings.

After he had tried continuously to warn others of the future uprisings, he finally managed to speak to Varus. He was escorted into the throne room of Varus by a munifex. As Segestes and the munifex approached Varus, he spoke. He said, *"Segestes, you boring oldfool, what is it that you want now?"*

Segestes answered, *"My Lord Varus, I bring you grave news that the Germanic tribes are organised and acting behind your back! They are preparing to launch several uprisings against Rome! The traitors are being led by your deputy, called Arminius or Armin if you prefer his Germanic name! If you act quickly, you can stop the future uprisings against Rome, and that may give you enough leverage with Augustus to return to Syria where you would like to be!"*

Varus looked shocked, and then he spoke in a disparaging voice. He said, *"Segestes you old andjealous fool! Everyone for miles around Aliso knows that Armin has made love to your daughter Thusnelda and that she is about to live with him as his wife! I have personally seen the house that they have! My entire court knows of your extreme jealousy of Arminius, and we all know that you want Thusnelda to marry a Roman Court Official called Tudrus. That shall not happen! Your daughter is now like a woman married to Arminius, the commander of all equite cavalry forces in Germania. He is also both a Roman citizen and a Roman Knight!*

You have urged me to capture all Germanic chieftains and to interrogate them using torture to separate the loyal from the rebels! You have bought in other advisors who know nothing about anything and who just waste my time while they bore the living daylights out of me!

You do very little other than make false accusations against other people of whom you are jealous! And, here you are accusing a Roman citizen who is hero knight ofRome of treachery! I will have you know that Arminius is everything that you are not! Now go away, and if I ever see your ugly lying face in my court again, I will crucify you!"

The Roman Governor's conduct placed Segestes and his pro-Roman friends at the conspirators' mercy, whom Varus continued to both trust and employ as he always had.

There is no doubt that some of this was due to the Romans' habitual contempt for all barbarians' capabilities. Also, there was the overwhelming confidence that Varus had in his great army of three legions, complete with supporting units of cavalry and other specialist forces.

The Love Story Resented by Segestes

What followed now is legends' stuff, and the true love story of Thusnelda and Armin began to flower. They continued to openly live as husband and wife, much to the annoyance of her father, Segestes. When Thusnelda decided to visit her father, he wanted her to leave Armin. He said, *"Thusnelda, make up your mind and dump Armin so you can marry Tudrus, the Roman, or else stay with Armin, but leave my home immediately. Armin, who is also known as Arminius, is not welcome here!*

Thusnelda replied, *"Pappa, "What is it about the word no, that you do not understand? No matter what you say or do, I am getting married to Armin, and that is the way that things shall stay! My darling father, I love you deeply as any woman should love her own father. However, I am a Cherusci woman and the leader of the other Cherusci women. I have been the leader since the death of my mother. Why can you not just accept the fact that Armin is not only an outstanding military leader but also a Roman citizen and a Roman Knight? I thought that would please you more than someone who is only a*

Roman citizen and a stupid court official like the man you want me to marry!"

Upset, Thusnelda hurried to where she knew her love was. Having found Armin, she said, *"My Love, I do not know what to do! I want you to be my husband, but my father forbids that! While I want you as my husband, I also deeply love my father! Can you think of a way that I can have you as my husband but still be able to speak to Pappa?"*

Armin quickly thought over the matter, then he spoke. He said, *"Thusnelda, my Love, you have already seen the house that Adalhard and I have built for us. We could go there to live, and you can pretend that I have abducted you. That might reconcile your father with you. By the time we get to the house, a priest of Wodin will be there, and he shall marry us according to Cherusci law!*

The priest will be one of several people who will talk to many others, saying that we are now husband and wife, that we are legally married within sight of Wodin!" Thusnelda was happy with that compromise. She said, *"Thank you, Armin, for thinking of this marvellous solution to overcome the problem of Pappa!" He shall have no choice but to accept what we do!"*

Thusnelda thought about the situation the two lovers were in. She spoke to Armin about it. She said, *"Armin, my Love, my father, Segestes, does not like you one bit! He is actively working against us, so I am glad that you took matters into your own hands and have decided to abduct me.*

We must both be very careful of him as of now! Make sure that you and your patriots working for a

Roman free Germania never say anything at all, which my father can hear! He will take any information about you and the movement against Rome straight to Varus! He has already tried to do so several times, but so far, the Roman Governor just laughs at him, which upsets Pappa even more, all of the time!"

Armin replied, *"Thusnelda, my Love, you fret too much! We have our home already built. The building method was to lay roughhewn tree trunks down on top of each other and fill the cracks with a mixture of clay and straw. After that, we put in the rafters for the roof. After which we constructed the roof itself, using thatch to keep out the rain.*

I frequently have to be close to Varus because the fool has made me the commander of all Equite cavalry units in Germania! I am therefore privy to all discussions about all military matters involving Romans! I always know the supply and re-inforcement status of all Roman units in Germania as well as their exact locations!" There are now at least ten scribes working in the Varus headquarters who make copies of everything that is written and send the copies to a liberation unit of Germania movement official who can read Latin! As well, our warriors are being taught the new written German language which is based on the Latin alphabet."

During the course of their normal activities, Armin and his men were auxiliary cavalry soldiers under the direct control of the Governor of Germania, Publius Quntilius Varus. That made these men's lives difficult in that they had to fight against their own countrymen many times.

Armin fully realised that there was no way his warriors could successfully take on the battle-hardened professional Roman army on open ground. For that reason, he was willing to wait until the time was right before he began the rebellion.

While waiting for the right time to strike, he and his men continued to serve Rome. To the new Roman Governor, everything appeared to be normal. Armin, meanwhile, was discussing the Roman presence in Germania with many others. By doing this, he ran the constant risk of betrayal, which soon became apparent because of Armin's father-in-law's ongoing attempts of treachery.

Discussion Among the Germanic Warriors

Within Armin's inner group of people who would help plan the actual battles against the Roman enemies were his wife, Thusnelda, who greatly assisted with the planning, Armin's father, Segimer and his uncle, Inguionerus. This small group of people would often meet to discuss ways of luring and trapping the Roman army under the command of Varus. At a meeting held one night, Thusnelda addressed the gathering of plotters against Rome.

She said, *"Gentlemen, it is my considered opinion that the task of destroying the Roman army will be much easier if you lure the Romans into carefully prepared ambush sites. Which have had all of the pathways and tracks narrowed so that the enemy cannot move freely against you!*

If you placed these ambushes in areas where you will hold the advantage of having the high ground and at the same time keep the Romans confined to narrow pathways, they will not be able to bring their war machines with them! As well, we should use the members of Armin's Cherusci Equite Cavalry alae. By having them among the Romans, they will suspect nothing until Armin, and his men attack them! If we use these methods of attacking the Romans, I am sure that we shall win!

I know just the place where to do this! It is in a particularly swampy area near the Kalkriese Hill, which dominates the surrounding country-side by being elevated to over three hundred feet above it. The hill's summit has dense forest, which is the ideal hiding place for the Cherusci cavalry forces' main body. I want to be able to further assist everyone by scouting the killing ground and preparing maps of the area with the help of Armin's leading scout commander, Adalhard!"

Meanwhile, Armin's Father-in-law, Segestes, again tried to betray Armin, whom he hated with intensity, directly to the Roman Governor Varus. Segestes said to Varus, "Sir, I have news and even proof that your Auxiliary Cavalry Prefectus Equitarius is speaking against Roman rule in general and against your governorship in particular. He is directly speaking out against you at all opportunities, and I know that he is trying to set up a rebellion against you and Rome!"

Varus answered, "Segestes, you fucking stupid old fool! It seems to me that we have had this discussion before! Do you not think that I know of your hatred for Arminius? Do you not realise that I know the reasons you hate the hero so much? Do you actually believe that I can take the word of a man who is well known to be a coward, *a liar and a thief? Do you not realise that I know of your ambitions and that Arminius stands in your way?*

Do you not realise that you have contributed nothing to Rome's greater glory, while Arminius is a Roman citizen, Hero and a Roman Knight? Now go away, you boring old fool and do not ever again bother me with your petty jealousies, you disgusting old fart!"

Varus sent word of this meeting with Segestes to Armin. Who now began thinking, *"So, as expected, my father-in-law is a traitor in our midst! It is a situation that I shall have to monitor closely to make sure that the old bastard can't damage the rebellion before it even starts! However, not only will it begin, it will be very successful, and I will liberate all of Germania in due course!*

For the time being, I must continue playing up to Varus' vanity and make him think that my men and I are indispensable parts of the Roman army if he is to hope to remain as the Governor of Germania. I have a small following now, but it will become bigger. I will work towards obtaining a much larger following and establishing alliances between the Cherusci, Bructeri, Marsi, Sicambri, Chauci and Chatti."

The next morning, Armin was summoned to join a conference with Varus. He was escorted to the Vaus throne room by a munifex. Upon seeing him, Varus spoke. He said, *"Thank Jupiter that you are here, Arminius! Some minor tribes have started a rebellion in the north-west of Germania! I need you and your cavalry forces to go there and stop this rebellion before it even has a chance to start!"* Armin replied, *"Yes, sir, it shall be as you desire!"*

He was thinking, *"Very well then, I shall put a stop to the rebellion by making the rebels my allies, and in doing so, it will be the beginning of my rebel forces! You will only hear that the rebellion has been stopped, but you will not know that I have recruited the rebels to my cause of throwing the Roman bully out of my country!*

I know that I have much to lose in that I am a Roman citizen and Roman Knight and also that my wealth shall be lost as well, but that is a risk that I must take to liberate my country, you fucking callous Roman prick!" So it was that Armin and his ala set off to bring the rebellion in the north-west of Germania under control. He sought and was granted an audience with the leaders of the rebellion in the north-west. Armin stood before a gathering of the leaders and spoke.

He said, *"Leaders and warriors of the resistance to the Roman invasion of Germania! Firstly, let me introduce myself to you! I am Armin, and the Romans call me Arminius. I am of the Cherusci tribal nation. I am presently working within the headquarters of Varus, the Roman Governor! Working with me in his headquarters are ten German scribes who write out correspondence for Varus. Because of my status as the commander of all Equite Cavalry forces in Germania, I always know which Roman Legions are deployed and where they are! We garble all intelligence received by the Romans, and we send their legions out on wild goose chases!*

Please keep up your outrage against the Roman bully, but do not try to do anything about it yet! Our time will come, but first, we must all train and prepare things such as sites where we can successfully ambush and wipe out entire Roman Legions! Once we have united the forces of the Bructeri, Chatti, Cherusci, Chauci, Marsi, Sicambri and others, we must train in earnest. Among the things that our warriors must learn is discipline!

I have no doubt that many of you will say, "The Romans always have their war machines of ballistae[15], catapults and scorpios travelling with their legions." *While all of that is true, it is also true that the war machines travel on either their own wheels or are mounted on wagons. In the case of ballistae, they are transported on wagons in pieces, ready for assembly at their destination.*

In all cases, the war machines require good roads for their successful transport, and they are therefore vulnerable to our attacks. The strength of the Roman Legions is in engaging enemies out in the open. First, the Roman Heavy infantry will hurl their javelins at their enemies and immediately follow that up with a sword and shield attack!

So, we shall lure these arrogant southern fools into areas of our choosing where their war machines cannot go and where our forces can get very close to the Romans! That way, we shall deprive them of the use of their javelins and so disrupt their favourite tactic!

The Roman Pila[16] have soft iron blades that will bend upon striking the Romans' enemies' flesh! That makes the Roman Pila a weapon which is very difficult for the affected person to withdraw and renders him/her an easy target for the Roman infantry who will assault and

---

[15] The ballista was an ancient form of artillery in that it was a machine which could hurl a missile like a spear over extremely long distances.
[16] Latin name for Javelin.

finish off the affected person. That is another reason why we have to be in close quarters with the Romans when we finally attack them! Also, we should not let them see until we attack them, other than to make them chase us into our chosen areas!

You now have among you, some men who have been trained in the use of the Latin alphabet to write simple words in German. These men are to teach many others this form of messaging and give our liberation movement a communication system that will become the equal to what the Romans use. In time, by the addition of refinements, this shall form the basis of the written German language!

My cavalry units and I will stay among the Romans. I shall send messages of importance about Roman military matters directly to you by means of running messengers or carrier pigeons.

I will now appoint men to positions of instructors and trainers who will travel to wherever they are required for our warriors' training and get them to combat-ready status! From time to time, I shall visit various units and personally train specialist warriors such as the "One Hundred", who will assist every cavalry ala.

Let's all work together from today onwards and rid our country of the invading Roman oppressors!" With that, the assembled warriors returned to their homes and, in the following times, began to train as Armin wanted. They focussed on matters of discipline, the arts of swordplay and the use of both short and long spears and shields.

The more capable young men were put into prestigious units such as the "One Hundred", which were attached to Germanic cavalry units. Other than that, the general population of Germania were at home or attending their fields. That gave the outward appearance of everything being peaceful. There was nothing to alert the Romans to the coming storm of vengeance!

Armin and his Men Return to Aliso

Armin and his men returned to the fortifications on the Lippe, and he reported to Varus that the rebellion in north-west Germania was over. Varus said to Armin, *"Thank you, Arminius, my friend. I think of you as the most valuable resource that Rome has in this part of the world."* Armin said, *"Sir, may I now go home to my wife, Thusnelda? I have not seen her since you sent my men and me out to put down the rebellion in the north-west!"*

Armin now went to his home just outside of the fortifications on the Lippe and spoke to Thusnelda. He said, *"Thatfool Varus, sent my cavalry units to the north-west of Germania to put down a rebellion there, and we have reported that it was completely crushed! While it is true that the uprising has ended, for the time being, the tribesmen and tribeswomen of the north-west are now training in Roman tactics of conducting warfare!*

I am making sure that our men are fully trained in all Roman tactics as well as my favourite tactic of using light infantry such as the "One Hundred" mixed in with the cavalry units! When the Romans encounter this sort of force, they will not know what to do because nothing like it has been used against Romans before! My ala and I used this with great effect against the Pannonians when

I rescued the XV Legion from inevitable defeat. However, the Romans have forgotten all about the way I was able to rescue that legion, and that mistake shall cost those cruel and arrogant pricks very dearly!

I will personally select and train all men for entry into the elite 'One Hundred', and I fully intend to have as many of these highly trained and extremely fit elite light infantry as possible. I shall put at least two of these "One Hundred" light infantry shock troops into every ala, thereby doubling their strength! The Romans do not know it, but they have played straight into my hands by giving me the overall command of all Roman army auxiliary cavalry alae in Germania!"

Thusnelda said, *"Come to me, my love and make love to me, my hero. I will help you plan what we must both do to rid our land of the Roman bully forever a bit later. For now, make love to me and be with me. Later on, we will plan the end of the Roman presence in Germania for good!"* so it was that they again made love. Unknown to both of them, Thusnelda's father, Segestes, was hiding within their home, and he overheard their conversation.

As usual, he was true to his grasping and cowardly nature. He began thinking, *"So Armin, you have told lies to Varus, and instead of putting down the rebellions in the north-west, you have in fact set up major future uprisings against Rome. Not only that, but you are continuing to set-up rebellions everywhere you can. I am sure that this information will get me a lot of Roman money if I can only get the Roman Governor, Varus, to listen to me! Not only are you a rebel yourself, but you have corrupted the mind of my daughter to the point where she is openly anti-Roman and supports you!"*

Segestes sought an audience with Varus but was told, *"Segestes, his excellency, the Roman Governor has decreed that you are never to be admitted to the presence of himself at any time, now or in the future! Publius Quintilius Varus is too busy to bother with wastes of time such as yourself. You are not welcome here, so go away, you stupid old fool!"*

Segestes replied, *"Munifex, you are the lowest rank in the Roman army! Yet here you are speaking down to me, a nobleman of the Cherusci nation! Get me an audience with Varus, for I have information that is of critical importance to Rome!"*

The munifex replied, *"A nobleman of the Cherusci nation? Come off the grass, Segestes, no-one likes you or wants to talk to you. Everyone knows that you are full of shit! Your hate for the hero of the Roman army, Arminius, is well known. I will not escort you in to see Varus! However, if you are willing to take the chance that he will not execute you, you will find him at the end of the great hall where he is sitting in judgement of two Germanic princes!"*

Segestes went to the great hall where Varus was. As Segestes entered, he could see and hear Varus. Varus was sentencing. He said, *"Prince Ansel of the Chatti and Prince Alajos of the Bructeri, this court finds both of you guilty of treason against Rome! Do you have anything to say before the sentence is passed?* Prince Ansel yelled, *"Up your's, you Roman arsehole! I am a prince, and I do not bow before the likes of you, Roman pig!"* That encouraged Prince Alajos of the Bructeri to call out, *"To hades[17] with you, Roman pig! May you suffer long and die a prolonged and shameful death, Roman! Long live the Germanic revolution!"*

As usual, Varus was very calm when sitting in the judgment of others. He said, *"You will now both wish that you were Roman citizens. The worst that can happen to Romans is to be beheaded. However, in both of your cases, you are Germanic barbarians, and therefore, both of you shall either be impaled or, if you are lucky, you will be crucified instead! Guards take both of these rebels away and impale them both right away on top of the hill just past the river!"*

Then as he was finishing, he noticed Segestes. Varus rolled back his eyes, and while sighing, he said, *"What is it now, you stupid old fool?"* Segestes said, *"Sir, it is with great alarm that I must let you know the true motives of Armin and what he is really up to behind your back! When you sent him and his men to crush the revolt in the north-west, not only did they not crush the revolution, they ably assisted it, and they continue to do so!*

In fact, they united the north-western and recruited the rebels to the cause of ridding Germania of all things Roman and Arminius continuing to get more allies and recruit more rebels to his cause. Unless you quickly take action against him and his men, you will rue the day that you heard of the name Arminius!"

Varus was almost stunned by this news, but he decided not to take notice of what Segestes said. Varus

---

[17] Meaning hell.

said, *"Segestes, you old shit-headed fool! I find your presence here to be both tedious and disturbing! I told you before to stop your baseless accusations of the hero who saved the XV Legion! Now go away before I have you beheaded! I do not want ever to see you again!"*

Armin Gathers Strength for his Rebellion

Suddenly awakening in the very early hours of the morning, Thusnelda said to Armin, *"My love, you know the areas around Kalkriese Hill? I have been thinking of what you told me of how the only way for us to successfully take on the Roman armies is to use the countryside and terrain against them!*

By so doing and seeing to it that they cannot have their war machines with them, we can hide our warriors so close to the Romans that they shall be overwhelmed before they can apply their tactic of hurling their javelins followed by an infantry attack. This way, we can also prevent the Romans from using 'defence in depth'.

I have been in the area of Kalkriese Hill, and I get the impression that this area is ideally suited to our purposes! You have told me that our revolt is still undermanned, and I know that it would be a good idea for us to form an alliance with Marobod! By doing so, you will obtain the use of his Mark-Mannen, who have excellent abilities of fighting in swamps and marshy areas!

So, my love, please go and see Marobod in Bohemia and successfully form the alliance with him, which will help determine the successful outcome of the war of independence of Germania!"

Armin replied, *"Thank you for your input Thusnelda, my love. I am sure you are correct! The Roman Governor of Germania wants me and my cavalry alas to go to Bohemia anyway to stop the activities of Marobod! That is ideal because we can use the excuse that we are going to Bohemia to reign in Marobod to further set up more alliances and active resistance cells or units all over Germania!*

I want you to go to the areas around Kalkriese Hill and carefully take note of all of the terrain there. It would help if you were looking for things like the track's width through the forested and swampy areas. Where we could best hide large bodies of fighting men very close to the Romans in such a way that they will not see them until it is too late!

We shall then kill those arrogant and cruel Romans for what they have done and for what they continue to do to our people! No-one will suspect that you are putting in the ground-work for the rebellion. However, there is a lot of closely growing vegetation in the areas near the Kalkriese Hill, and therefore, I think it would be a good idea to have my main scout, called Adalhard, and ten of his warriors go with you.

I would like it if both Adalhard and you could write detailed reports about what you find in the Kalkrieser Hill area. Although we now have some writing in the German language, it is still in its infancy, and therefore I think that the report must be written in Latin to ensure that there are no misunderstandings.

In particular, I want maps showing where the paths through the forests and swamps are, also where there are large areas where we can dig away the swampy side of the tracks, thereby making them very narrow.

The sods from the swampy side shall then be used to build a sod wall behind which our archers and spear throwers can hide. That will enable them to remain out of sight until the approaching Romans are within the range of their arrows and spears, which will then rain down upon the Romans! Thus, Thusnelda began preparations for the Kalkriese Hill journey and obtained the scouting services that I was honoured to give her while Armin went to see Varus latter on the same day.

Upon being ushered in to see Varus, Armin said, *"Sir, you told me to do something about that nuisance called Marobod and his Mark-Mannen (Men of the Swamps). With your blessing, I will leave for Bohemia today, after I have obtained more men and equipment!"*

While he was saying this to Varus, Armin was thinking, *"I will equip my revolution with Roman arms and armour which you are supplying. Over the next few months, I will continuously be absent from this area because I shall be selecting and training warriors in the Roman military ways and the use of Roman weapons and German weapons, which we will then use against you! In the end, you will pay the ultimate price for invading my country, you Roman pig!*

This time, you will not be able to use catapults, ballistae or scorpios, so there will be no supporting barrage of large rocks, burning materials, large arrows, and spears, which will take away important Roman advantages!

You will no longer enjoy the benefit of Roman soldiers having armour while facing Germanic warriors who do not have armour and often fight naked because I am supplying as much Roman chain mail and plate armour as possible directly to Germanic warrior units! Also, there shall be Mark-Mannen hiding under the water of swamps and rivers while breathing through hollow reeds near the edges of the track through the killing areas! My forces shall rehearse the ambush of Varus and his legions until such time as I am completely confident that my warriors will beat all Romans!"

Armin left and was soon on his way to meeting with Marobod in Bohemia. While that was taking place, Thusnelda and I went to the region around Kalkriese Hill, and we scouted the whole area, which took us over a week because we drew detailed maps noting that Kalkriese Hill was a three hundred and fifty feet high hill.

That made it ideal for the siting of observers who would signal Armin and the other rebels using flashes of reflected light from Roman mirrors, smoke signals and loud sound blasts from horns/trumpets if Germanic units were within earshot! The Kalkriese Hill is located just out from the northward range of hills, and any Roman military units had to detour by some two miles in order to go around it.

Anyone who takes this route will find themselves in an hourglass-shaped area that is about half a mile wide at its middle. There are numerous wide and muddy streams that meander across it, flowing north from the hills into a great swamp.

The Kalkriese hill itself is, in many places, very steep and has both pools and many swampy areas that will slow any progress. In many places, the forest is so dense that marching formations have to split in order to allow their soldiers to move around trees and cautiously avoid exposed roots. We went further into this area and noted that only a strip of sand mixed with other soil provided a solid footing. We also noted that it was only about one hundred feet at its widest.

Thusnelda, and I discussed what lay before us. She said, *"Adalhard, it seems to me that if we could lure the Roman Legions and their supporting units into this area, our warriors would be able to get very close to them and attack them before they could use their javelins, which would then place the Romans into a disadvantageous position!*

As the Romans move forward through this area, they shall be forced to march along the narrow passage, with forested slopes of the left-hand side, while the right-hand side is bordered by the great swamp containing stands of willows and alders. Near the edges of the track between the hill's slope and the swamp are many reeds and tall grasses." I immediately agreed with her and said, *"Yes, Thusnelda, this is the place for Germania to wipe out three Roman legions and their supporting units in one battle! Here, where the track narrows even further, is ideal for the ambush!*

Here, we must deepen the swamp areas' water cover so that the Mark-Mannen can hide under the water standing up while breathing through hollow reeds. We must now make good maps of all of this, and we need to write reports about it for later presentation to Armin!"

We set about drawing the maps and writing the report as Armin had instructed us. Both Thusnelda and I knew that we had to keep these documents and maps away from Roman eyes!

Armin Makes an Ally of Marobod

Meanwhile, Armin was being ushered into the hall where Marobod was seated on a golden throne. He slowly walked over to the throne and knelt before Marobod, saying, *"Mighty Marobod, my name is Armin, and it has come to my attention that you would like to be rid of the Roman bullies in your lands! As some people know, I am a Roman Knight and cavalry commander, which gives me a good insight into what the enemies of the people of Germania are constantly faced with.*

I have the ears of the Roman Governor called Varus. I am planning the destruction of all Roman forces in Germania, and for this to become successful, I need your help!" Marobod was interested and said, *"Armin, I am interested in what you are proposing, but I need to know more about this if I am to become involved in it. Please tell me how you are planning to accomplish this great feat and how we can help each other to beat the invaders!"*

Armin answered, *"Marobod, I am planning to wipe out as big a Roman force as possible by luring the Roman Legions active in Germania to an area where they will not be able to use their war machines or even march in their usual formations of three men abreast of each other!*

A major Roman tactic is to march men three abreast[18] , and if attacked, the column will simply pivot and face the enemy, with the first rank hurling then hurling their pila[19]. That is normally followed by the second rank hurling their pila and so on until all ranks have hurled their pila, and then the whole column will engage the enemy in combat using their gladii[20]. If we are to beat them, we must get close enough to burst upon the Romans before they can organise themselves to use their javelins (pila)."

Marobod replied, *"Armin, where are you planning on doing this and why?"* Armin answered, *"Marobod, do you know of a large hill called Kalkriese Hill?"* Marobod said, *"Yes, I do know it, and I think you are correct in your assumptions. There are many streams, swamps, and bogs in that area, and I know from personal experience that the pathways through the swamps and marshes are narrow, and this would be the perfect place to stage an ambush of up to four; legions and be successful!*

I think that it would be a very good move for us to dig away the ground from the edges of the marshes and swamps to make sure that the Romans only have very narrow paths and that they can never march in formations greater than a single file! As long as you, today right here and before me, swear to bring me the head of the cruel Roman Governor called Varus, I am happy to provide immediately up to five hundred and eighty of my Mark-Mannen. I will send them to your area next morning!"

---

[18] Known as the triple line.
[19] Latin for javelin.
[20] Short Roman swords. Singular is gladius.

Marobod continued, *"I suggest that you immediately put them to work in digging away the ground from the edges of the tracks through the marshes and swampy areas. I agree with what you are proposing and would like to see the sod constructed earth wall on the forested side of the marsh where our men can hide behind to throw their spears and fire their arrows when the time comes! I am sorry, but for now, five hundred and eighty men is all I can spare! Is that all right with you, and will you swear to bring me the head of Varus when the battle is over?"*

Armin replied, *"Marobod, I accept what you are proposing. I hereby swear upon my honour and that of my father, Segimer, and before Wodin and Thor, that not only shall I defeat the Roman army, but I will personally cut the head off Varus, the Roman Governor of Germania and either bring it to you in person or have it sent to you by my subordinates!"*

That was followed by feasting on venison and the drinking of beer. The next morning, Armin was on his way back to Aliso and the headquarters of Varus. He was now approaching full confidence that his campaign for Germania's total liberation would be completely successful in about four months afterwards.

Armin now went to Varus's quarters and was ushered into where Varus was seated upon his throne by a munifex who departed upon Armin and Varus beginning their conversations. During his discussion with Varus, Armin was interrupted by the arrival of a messenger from

243

his Alae[21]. The messenger spoke, he said, *"Sirs, I am Bogart, and I have urgent news for the ears of Arminius alone!"* Armin said, *"Governor Varus, please excuse me momentarily while I attend to whatever this messenger has to say! After that, we should continue our discussions."*

Armin and the messenger went to a secure and private area when the messenger spoke. He said, *"Sir, I have some urgent news which you have asked us to keep you informed of. Firstly, the force of five hundred and eighty Mark-Mannen from Marobod is now at the location near Kalkriese Hill. Secondly, our scouting party made up of your wife, Thusnelda, Adalhard and the Cherusci escort often warriors are also in that area. They are now organising the Mark-Mannen to deepen the swamp close to the track.*

On the hillside of the swamp, they are constructing a sod wall from the earth taken out of the swamp's edges to deepen it. At the moment, the sod wall on the side of the swamp opposite the hill is at the height of a man's chest! Thusnelda has instructed me to give you the completed maps of the area. Thusnelda and Adalhard jointly drew these up!"

The messenger then gave Armin the maps, and he closely examined them. After a while, Armin spoke. He said, *"Messenger, you have done well! Now get some rest and refreshment and then return to Thusnelda and Adalhard. Tell them to keep on with what they are doing. I have noted their suggested 'Killing Area', and I agree*

---

[21] Several Equite cavalry units attached to Roman Legions. Ala means single while alae is plural.

that these are the most suitable places to wipe out up to four full Roman Legions and their supporting units!

Also, tell both of them that I want the track through the area to be narrowed such that only one man at a time can proceed through the area! Also, inform them both that they are to see to it that many impediments to the progress of the Roman legions are placed in their way. For example, I want many trees to be weakened to fall across the track through the swamp, thereby making things difficult for Romans! Make sure that everyone there knows the Romans shall be there in twenty-one days from now!"

Armin returned to where he had left Varus. Seeing him, Armin said, *"Sir, it has come to my attention that a major rebellion is breaking out in the north-west and central parts of Germania! The rebels have a very large force of fierce warriors, which include Mark-Mannen from Marobod! If you are to stop this rebellion, you will need all legions and auxiliary forces available! The area where the rebels' are active and causing so much strife has narrow tracks, streams, and many marshes and bogs!*

Because most of the tracks in the region are through the marshes, the tracks will not bear the weight of heavy wagons! That being the case, you shall have to leave the war machines behind. But then again, you have three legions and the support of several unattached Roman army cohorts and auxiliary equite units helping you break the rebellion! You will have your normal support from my cavalry units, and I don't think you will need anything else!

As the putting down of this new rebellion is of great importance to Rome, I suggest that you lead as many legions as you can get and take them all with you to the Kalkriese Hill area of north-western Germania. That is within an area called the Teutoburg Forest! Just imagine Varus, that we wipe out the German rebels! Augustus will be so pleased that he may send you back to Syria as you want him to!"

Having finished saying that to Varus, Armin was thinking, *"Yes, you rotten Roman pig who is not welcome in my country, please accompany your legions to their doom. So that I can keep my promise to Marobod by cutting off your head and then bringing it to him! The time for the vengeance of the Germanic people is approaching you, rotten Roman pig!"*

Varus now said to Armin, *"Arminius, please go and check out possible alternative routes in the Kalkriese hill area and get back to me with that information! I agree with you that I should be with the legions for the destruction of the troublesome Germanic warriors! By doing this in person, I will get the glory and money that will come from the Germans' total subjugation, which is sure to follow my success in wiping out the tribesmen in the Teutoburg Forest!*

As you know, I have three fully manned and well-armed legions at Aliso, which also have supporting units of Roman and equite cavalry, archers and other specialist soldiers! My three legions at Aliso are the best of the Roman army. I also have another two legions under the command of my uncle further to the south of Germania.

I have sent messengers to him, asking him to send his two legions to assist me if that is possible. After all, we now have a chance to wipe out the German warriors! If my uncle's answer is that he cannot spare any legions, I will go after the Germans with my three legions and all supporting units! Either way, the Germans shall obey Rome!" Hearing Varus say that made Armin rejoice. He was thinking, *"Better and better, you Roman pig!"* He then set about organising the trap.

Armin sent a message to his father, Segimer and his uncle Inguionerus to meet him at Kalkriese Hill's summit in fourteen days from then. His message to them was, *"Father and Uncle, the works on the killing ground at the ambush site near Kalkriese Hill are nearing completion. We must meet and work out the fine details. I will tell you what I have in mind when we meet in fourteen days from now. – Armin."* That resulted in Segimer and Inguionerus leaving for Kalkriese hill with many more conspirators.

Armin, who was satisfied that things were going according to his plan, now left the company of Varus and travelled to meet Thusnelda. She was delighted to see him, and they immediately made love. Both of the lovers discussed the new revolution.

Armin said, *"My love, things are going according to plan, and I am confident that soon, we can rid Germania of the Roman yoke forever! That is what I want so that my people can be free! I also think that it would be a good idea to permanently unit the people so that Germania can finally have its own army and naval forces! We must see to it that things like the Roman invasion cannot happen in Germania again! However, I think that things will have to wait until after we have victory over the Romans!"*

Early on the following morning, Armin and the seven hundred and forty members of his ala left Aliso on horseback, other than those who were the light infantry. As they were leaving the area, the Cherusci nation's women were lining both sides of the track on which the force was travelling. Some of the women had dis-shrivelled hair and were imploring their husbands and boyfriends to win the fight so as not to let the women become the playthings of the enemy! Leading this large grouping of women was Thusnelda and her friend, Erminlinde.

After a period of nine days, Armin rode to the Kalkriese Hill, deep within the Teutoburg Forest. Arriving there, he camped upon the summit of the hill and awaited the arrival of Segimer and Inguionerus and their escort. He did not have to wait for long because he could see the approaching figures of his father, uncle and their escort while the men were still about two miles away from his position.

As the men got closer to his position, he lost sight of them completely because they were now in areas where they had swamps and marshes on one side of them and forested sloping hillsides of the other side of them. Armin made notes of this because he knew that it was one of the critical things about this site, giving his men the advantage and victory in the final battle when it came.

He began thinking, *"I know from the experience that I have gained from my knowledge of using this terrain, that my father and uncle plus their escort will now be near the bend in the track at the foot of Kalkriese Hill, just where a large stream flows into the marshy bog. I shall ride towards them. There is no way they can mistake who I am because I am wearing my Roman army armour, including my Roman helmet with red tufts on the top of it."*

As he got closer to his relatives, he saw that Segimer was wearing chain mail armour, and animal skins to keep warm. He was also wearing his Germanic battle helmet, which had horns protruding from it. His uncle, Inguionerus, was formidable looking in that he was also wearing chain mail armour and animal skins.

His helmet was a Germanic helmet which had wings attached to the sides of it. Inguionerus believed that he needed to wear a winged helmet, so that if he died in battle, the wings on the helmet could take his soul up to the heavens, close to the Valkyries, who would then take him to Valhalla.

Valkyries were blond maidens who wore chain mail and a battle helmet. They were supposed to ride down from the sky in which Valhalla is located and offer slain warriors a place on their horses, behind them. A fallen warrior was never to look a Valkyrie in the face, as this would spell certain doom for eternity.

As Segimer and his brother Inguionerus and their entourage came into sight on the track, Armin greeted them, saying, *"Hail Father and Uncle Inguionerus! As you have seen, things are prepared, and when the attack upon the Roman army has begun, there will be no chance of any Romans surviving, other than the ones whom we choose to let live! They shall be selected from the prisoners we take unless they are needed as sacrifices.*

I want some Romans to live so that they will go back to Roman camps and command centres and take the word of the defeat of three entire Roman legions plus all of their supporting units back to Rome! That shall mean that three-fifths of the entire Roman army in Germania has been destroyed! I now want you both to come with me because we are going to plan the assaults onto the Romans by our men, and it is very important that you both play your parts in this glorious quest!"

He said to both men, *"Father and Uncle, please dismount, for I now have to draw some mud maps and give both of you orders which must be carried out, no matter what the circumstances happen to be!"* Armin drew the map on the sand of the track. He said, *"As you rode along the track through the marshes and swamps, you should have noticed that that the track has been narrowed down so that only one man or horse can proceed along it.*

That has been done to stop the Romans from using their 'Triple Line' formation in which three men are marching abreast. When the 'Triple Line' is attacked, the whole line pivots. That is followed by the first line throwing their pila (javelin) and then crouching. The second line then throws their pila, and then crouch, followed by the third line doing the same after that, the entire three lines or triple line charges forward and attacks their enemies using the gladius.

The use of the 'Triple Line' in this way had been the key to Roman successes because if one rank fails in obtaining its objectives, it is replaced by the second and, if necessary, the third line and the fight goes on until the objective has been achieved.

We have excavated away the soil sods from the swampy side of the track for a distance of three Roman miles[22] , and with the sods of earth removed from the swampy side of the track, we have constructed an earth wall which is at the height of a man's chest. This low wall is ideal for our spear throwers and archers to hide behind until they hear our trumpets' and horns sound, which shall sound the attack. By taking on the enemies in this way, we can grab them by their belts and wipe them out!

Segimer, I want you and your cavalry to ride down the right side of this hill and wipe out all Romans that you encounter, take no prisoners, just kill the Romans!" He went on to speak to his uncle. He said, *"Inguionerus, I want you and you men to sweep down the left side of the hill and kill Romans! I also need you to take some one-hundred men, prisoner. The prisoners are for sacrificing to the Gods of Wodin and Thor, but mainly we shall release many of them so that they can take the news of the defeat of the most respected legions of the Roman army directly to Rome!"*

Inguionerus was a little overwhelmed by this and said, *"My nephew, I am astounded by the earthworks and other preparations that you have made. How on earth did you manage to get all of this done and still train out warriors? Did you somehow get more men that I don't know about?"* Armin's answer was, *"Uncle, I have been able to obtain the services of an extra five hundred and*

---

[22] A Roman mile was 1,000 paces.

eighty men called Mark-Mannen from Marobod. These 'Men of the Marshes' are just what we need for operating in boggy country."

That prompted Inguionerus to exclaim, *"What? Are you fucking mad? Have you really gone into a deal with the arsehole called Marobod? Don't you realise that he cannot be trusted and that he is likely to turn on you as quickly as he does to the Romans? Hell and damnation young man, what has that poor excuse for a man asked for in return for the use of his men?"*

Armin answered with, *"Uncle, you fret too much! Marobod has given his word that he will fully support us, and we cannot back out of things now, even if we want to! The only things he has asked for is that I pay his men while they are in our service and that I bring him the head of Varus! As far as I am concerned, bringing the head of Varus is a small price to pay because I am happy to do that for nothing! In fact, if I could only get the Roman Emperor here, I would be glad to add the head of Augustus to the list!"*

He now said, *"Now let's get back to planning the attack. We must get this correct and final. The decisions we make now shall be set, and there will be no deviation from them. Both you and my father have your orders; make sure that you both obey them and do so on time!*

The signal for you both to begin your respective sweeps down the hillside will be three blasts from the horn of Adalhard. That will be preceded by a series of mirror flashes from Kalkriese Hill's summit as the Roman column moves forward.

My cavalry alae will be at the front and rear of the column, attacking it there, when you and your men arrive, much of the Roman column will have been killed due to attacks from spears and arrows of my men behind the earth wall and the Mark-Mannen at the edges of the swamp.

The Romans will not see these men before they are attacked, due to the fact that the Mark-Mannen will be below the surface of the water, breathing through hollow reeds and very close to the Romans. When you hear the three blasts from the horn of Adalhard, there will be a co-ordinated attack on all parts of the column.

The sides of the column will be attacked by having spears and arrows rain upon them from the men behind the earth wall, while simultaneously, the Mark-Mannen will come out of the water and attack the Romans. While that is happening, my cavalry alae will attack the front and rear of the column!"

Signal Communication Using Mirrors

Armin continued, *"To get instructions to our units quickly, we shall use light reflections from Roman mirrors! Just make sure that you both know what will be happening. Make sure that you and all of the men in your respective commands know our simple codes!*

Firstly, if you see a single flash of light and no follow-on flashes, it means that units are still moving into position. Secondly, Two reflections of sunlight from Roman mirrors located on the summit of Kalkriese Hill simply mean that the units intended to be in positions on various parts of the hill are in place and are ready for battle. Two long flashes of light followed by a short one will mean that the units are in position, and they can see the other units with whom they are to co-ordinate the attack.

Three long flashes indicate that you must immediately attack! If it is cloudy and there is no sunlight to reflect from mirrors, we will use a smoke signal system from Kalkriese Hill's top. The signals will be the same as those we use if there is sunlight available. See to it that you and all of the men in your commands are up to speed in these forms of communication. As soon as you return to your own areas, begin intensive training of all warriors in communications as outlined here! The battle and all of our lives may depend upon it!"

Rehearsing the Attack

My leader, Armin, was a great tactician. He knew that although it is not natural for men to attempt to kill each other when they have never seen each other before and that while fear may be present, it will be significantly nullified if the men know exactly what to do.

He knew that training, practice and constant rehearsal were the keys to lowering fear in the men and making them much more effective soldiers. The Roman enemy was dangerous because it was both highly trained and highly disciplined, making the Roman army a very effective fighting force.

Armin was discussing the need to change the military habits of the Germanic warriors. He said,

We must change the way Germanic warriors traditionally do battle! Our warriors have always rushed toward the enemy, and then they attempt to overwhelm him using

strength and numbers of men. That sort of thing plays straight into the hands of the well-trained and highly discipline Roman legions! As of now, all Germanic warriors shall at all times instantly obey orders without question! Our warriors will continue training for long days until they become disciplined and effective!"

Armin came over to me and told me what he wanted in the training of the men. He said, *"Adalhard, see to it that all men of all ranks continuously train by doing foot and weapons drills as wells as infantry and cavalry minor tactics. See to it that everyone knows and can use signalling by mirrors, smoke signals and horn blasts.*

I shall personally inspect the men performing the drills. I also want constant practice of tactics and contact with enemy units drills! Once our men have had enough practice, everything will become second nature to them, and they will be feared warriors by even the Romans! I am returning to Aliso, where I have to report to Varus and make sure that he continues to suspect nothing!"

To ensure that all warriors knew what they were supposed to do, Armin left instructions for all units to train under their tribal superiors' direct control. All men were trained in areas that were the speciality of their people and districts. For example, the Mark-Mannen were mainly trained in ambush techniques and lying-in wait by submerging just below the surface of the dark and murky water in the swamps and bogs while breathing through hollow reeds from the marshes.

So, it was that there was a constant rehearsal of placing the ambush. The Mark-Mannen would practice hiding in the water very close to the edge of the swamp, while the spearmen and archers of the Cherusci and other tribes would practice crouching down behind the earth wall and throwing their missiles upon hearing three horn blasts.

Armin had returned from Aliso. He said, *"Adalhard, I am going to watch our men training from the summit of the hill!"* He then went to the summit and sounded three horn blasts to see if his plan looked effective. Upon the horn blasts, spearmen and archers hiding behind the earth wall let fly with their weapons. Simultaneously, the Mark-Mannen armed with swords and lances arose from under the water of the swamp and rushed towards the centre of the track.

That was followed by cavalry riding down the slopes and encircling the track, while the archers and spearmen from behind the earth wall also ran towards the centre of the track. Armin said, *"Fine, gentlemen, the plan appears to work well. I need you all to continually practise the drills until everyone knows instinctively what they must do and when!"*

It looked like Armin was happy with what he had seen. He said, *"Adalhard, keep the men training like that, but also get some of them to act the part of the Roman enemy! I want all future rehearsals to be practised using wooden weapons and sticks; after all, we do not want more casualties from training!*

Make sure that the men who are acting the part of Romans are continually rotated with other men. Rehearse the attack upon the Roman column daily for the next twelve days, and make sure that you have the men close to their positions! I have to return to Aliso! I shall be back in the company of Varus and his three legions plus supporting units. We tried to get all five of the Roman legions in Germania to come here, but the other two are required in southern Germania!

I want the spearmen behind the earth wall to have at least twenty-five spears each. That should give the attack enough deadly force when combined with the arrows of the archers! After the men behind the wall, the Mark-Mannen and the cavalry coming down the hill's slopes have done their work, the combined effects should well and truly wipe out the Romans. To make sure of it, I and my cavalry alae shall be attacking the front and the rear of the Roman column!

Over the next ten days, expect to see small units of Romans coming to and from the Kalkriese Hill. When you see them, let them pass unhindered because it will help our cause if the Roman scouting units report to Varus that everything is even worse than what he thinks.

If possible, let the Roman scouting units see our warriors being drilled and disciplined on Roman military ways! Let the Roman scouts see that we have vast numbers of men being trained in weapons and foot drills. All of that should result in Varus being informed that the Germanic warriors' capabilities are far greater than he could imagine!"

The Trap is Sprung

Having arrived safely back at the Roman army headquarters at Aliso, Armin reported to the governor. He said, *"Sir, the threat from the rebels is a lot greater than we believed. Their warriors are not only vast in number; they are now also well-disciplined and very capable! I have seen them openly performing contact drills[23] and also foot and weapons drills, just like we do in the Roman army! That is most disturbing because the Germanic forces appear to be at least as good as all members of the Roman Legions!"*

By giving the information to the Roman Governor, Armin made sure that Varus would take the bait and march his legions straight into the trap he was setting for the Romans! Armin had organised the maximum number of black-smiths who were now producing as many steel and iron weapons as could be produced as long as three months before. He had also organised much Roman plate and chain-mail armour to be directly delivered to his Germanic units.

As well, Armin had organised that the heavy Roman shields were produced in great quantities and issued to his units. Some Germanic units chose to use their very light shields, which were only a raw-hide stretched over a wooden frame. To Varus, what Armin had told him was appalling news which he did not believe was possible, due to his own arrogance making him think that it was impossible for the rebels to become as efficient as Roman soldiers, still, the news bothered him enough to speak.

He said, *"Thank you for this information Arminius, my friend; I was originally just going to send a legion, which has been strengthened by the addition of some detached cohorts from other legions to deal with the rebels near Kalkriese Hill. It looks to me like raiding the*

---

[23] A contact drill is a rehearsal of what must happen when contact is made with enemy soldiers.

isolated small groupings of three to five houses on the hills surrounding Aliso and then placing all of the people in the homes onto crosses like I did in Judea might fix this revolution!

The rebels will think twice before attempting any more uprisings when I nail their men, women, and children upon Roman crosses! I am implementing a programme of continuous patrolling by Roman Heavy Infantry units to gather more information about the enemy near the Kalkriese Hill.

Soon, I will personally lead three full Roman legions and all of their supporting units and as many unattached cohorts as I can find to that area of the Teutoburg Forest, and I shall wipe out the rebel scum! Please tell me how many men do you think we will need to completely destroy the rebels?"

Armin replied, *"Sir, I am sure that you will need all of your Roman army units in Germania for this task, as well as all of your auxiliary units! Because the track through that area is so narrow and very boggy, in most places, we will not be able to bring the catapults, ballistae[24] or scorpios with us because the ground in that area will not support the weight of the wagons carrying these war machines. It will be difficult enough just to have supply wagons moving with us and keeping pace with our forces! The fact is that for both ease and speed of movement, it will be far better to leave the war machines behind, here at Aliso!"*

---

[24] Plural of ballista.

While he was saying this to Varus, he began to think. He thought, *"Your arrogance, Roman bully, is overbearing, but you will soon pay for your crimes against the Germanic people, and just as you have shown them no mercy, you shall also not receive any! We will wipe out every man in your army; this means that Rome will lose more than twenty thousand men.*

Something that you do not know or will be able to discover is that already, up in the hills, some fifty Roman miles away from Kalkriese Hill, some of my units have built dams across the streams feeding into the swamp area near Kalkriese Hill. They will open the sluices, thereby drowning many Romans when I give the order."

Varus suddenly asked Armin, *"Arminius, when do you think we should commence operations against the rebels?"* Armin wanted the Roman governor to move his entire three legions and their supporting units against the Germanic warriors by fifteen days from then, as he had organised both the ambush for then and the training of his forces would be complete at that time.

Therefore, Armin said, *"Sir, from here, we have about three days marching in order to arrive at the Kalkriese Hill area. My information is that the rebels will be at their strongest and most concentrated at the Kalkriese Hill by fifteen days from now! So, if we were to get the provisions ready for travel within the next few days and begin marching within twelve days from then, we should arrive just in time to catch most of the rebels, of whom you could then make an example of what happens to the enemies of Rome to the German people!"*

Varus was beside himself with joy at the prospect of making the greater part of the Germanic rebels captives and then crucifying or impaling all of them. He said, *"Arminius, go and organise everything needed for marching the three legions that we have here to the Kalkriese Hill area, and for us to arrive there within the fifteen days from now you have specified. Thank you for your suggestion of leaving the war machines behind, because the German people do not have towns or cities, we shall not need them, as they will only slow us down. Thank you for this valuable contribution to my plan of bringing the rebel scum to Roman justice! You have made things a lot easier! In fact, I shall personally lead my three legions and so get more glory for destroying the rebel scum!"*

Hearing that made Armin smile. He thought, *"Thank you, Wodin and Thor, for making this Roman bully think along these lines! It is exactly what is needed to destroy him and all of his legions when they march into the trap!"* He then found his messenger. He said, *"Messenger, travel to the hills located abut fifty Roman miles from the Kalkriese Hill swamp. When you find my men there, tell them to open the sluice gates in all of the dams during the middle of the night in fifteen days from now!"*

As planned, after twelve days, Varus and his three full-strength legions plus supporting were marching towards Kalkriese Hill during the third day of September in 9 A.D... The Roman column was made up of the three legions reputed to the professional heavy infantry's crack legions. These were the XVII, XVIII and XVIV Legions which were further strengthened by the addition of six more cohorts[25] of heavy infantry. The Roman units were also supported by equite[26] units specialising in spear throwing, light infantry, cavalry, and many other applications.

Under the command of Armin were two cavalry alae per legion or six alae in total. Each of Armin's cavalry alae also had two units of the elite "One Hundred" light infantry soldiers. Each legion proudly carried its traditions on a staff that bore the Legion's name and an image of the Imperial Roman Eagle, which the soldiers were willing to fight and die for. Varus and his Roman army were marching forward, feeling extreme contempt for the Germanic tribesmen they were hoping to wipe out.

During an 'Information and Orders Group' called to discuss how the German warriors could best weaken the army of Varus, a Suebi sub-chief called Eberhard spoke. He said, *"We have information that the three legions and their supporting units of the army of Varus have received many more soldiers by the addition of six more cohorts. That means our revolution shall now face at least three thousand more Roman Heavy Infantry soldiers! We must disperse these additional Romans before they can harm our revolution!"*

He was answered by another sub-chief from the Usipete tribe called Haribert. Haribert said, *"Eberhard, we are all warriors here, and we are making sure that*

---

[25] There were ten cohorts per legion. The number of men in the corhorts ranged between five hundred and seven hundred and fifty men, depending on its prestige.

[26] Equite units were units raised from the population of provinces and they could be from Britain, Spain or anywhere the Romans thought they had conquered.

nothing can adversely affect the plans of Armin! There are several Roman tax-collecting centres between here and Aliso, which are very lightly guarded! I propose that we attack all of these posts and kill as many of the Romans within them as possible!

As well, we should send constant messages to Varus saying that all Roman posts between the mouth of the Rhine and Aliso are under constant attack and that Aliso may fall to the rebels unless Varus sends Roman cohorts to help against the German rebels!"

These things resulted in Roman posts being attacked all over Germania and pleas for immediate military assistance from Varus to counter the German threat to all Roman posts. Varus was still confident that the Roman justice system's terrors would continue to protect him and other Romans from the barbarians! He issued charges against the offenders against Roman Law and continued his march despite the traps now closing around him and his army. The Germanic chiefs continued to follow Varus and his army while pretending to be his friends. Still, they sent out detachments of their warriors to erect impediments along the Roman march route.

As well, trees were cut through so that only a bare minimum of wood was still holding them upright. That resulted in many trees falling across the track at the next wind. Some of them fell upon the passing Roman soldiers of Varus's army. To add to the Romans' woes, the Roman supplies from the rear had been entirely cut-off. The weather became rainy with the onset of the cold autumn rains. Problems and disputes kept on arising between the Roman soldiers and what Varus thought were his Germanic allies.

These problems combined caused Varus to call yet another 'Orders and Information Group'. Varus was addressing his officers. He said, *"Gentlemen, the problems of disputes and friction between our Roman soldiers and our Germanic allies are just mere camp quarrels. However, if they keep on happening, we must stop them because they could disrupt our alliance with the Germanic equite forces, which would cost Rome very dearly!*

My Roman scouting units have informed me that we shall soon be quitting the open country, in which Roman army units are unbeatable and going into areas where there are steep forested slopes on one side of us and swampland and marshes on the other side. The scouting units have also reported that the numbers of barbarians have grown to alarming proportions and that their fighting ability is now the equal of Roman soldiers!"

He was interrupted by the arrival of a messenger. Varus said, *"Yes, messenger, what is it?"* The messenger replied, *"Roman outposts are now under attack between Aliso and the Rhine as well as towards the east! It appears that that tribes called Usipetes and Suebi are in revolt and are being led by Eberhard, Eburwin, Gaufrid and Gebhard. The Roman garrison at Aliso is undermanned and may soon become the subject of attack!"*

Varus answered, *"By Jupiter, when things go wrong, it does not just rain; it pours!"* He had barely finished saying that when suddenly, a sentry reported to Varus. He said, *"Sir, a large number of Roman refugees have arrived here seeking shelter from further barbarian attacks! It appears that there have been co-ordinated attacks upon several Roman posts and outposts!"*

Varus replied, *"It is just as well that besides my three legions, I also have six cohorts which add up to another two-thirds of a legion which can be used for emergencies such as this! Therefore, the first of the XVI Legion's six cohorts shall provide security for Roman outposts and these refugees that you speak of! The rest of the cohort from my Uncle's command in southern Germania with patrol and provide security for Aliso ad the Roman post between there and the Rhine! All my other forces shall continue to the Kalkriese Hill area, where we shall wipe out the rebels!"*

At the centre of the column, the leadership was located, consisting of Varus, his Roman army officers and the equite auxiliary unit officers. The personal bodyguards of Varus surrounded him at all times. At the front and rear of the long column were Armin's cavalry units which were complete with their special light infantry support. From his horse, Varus could only see a small part of the very long column as it made its way along the track.

Varus was instantly recognisable because of the purple plumes on the top of his helmet. Other Roman officers were also distinguishable by their helmets, having coloured tuffs on top of their helmets. Usually, these were a red colour. Armin also had red tuffs on the top of his helmet, and because he was a serving Roman Auxiliary Equite Officer, he also had Roman armour, as did all of his troopers. His amour included chain-mail armour and an inscribed breast- plate as was befitting to his status of the 'Commander of all Roman Auxiliary Units in Germania'.

Varus now held an 'Information and Orders Group' which was called to discuss the situation the

Romans now found themselves in. Addressing his officers, Varus spoke. He said, *"I have a bad feeling that our presence here is going to result in even more attacks upon Romans by the Germans! We shall now close up the distance between various units, which will make it seem like we have changed direction.*

We shall continue our present course, and our objective of wiping out the German forces remains the objective! Our Roman soldiers are tired from this constant marching, and we are marking out and building a fortified camp where we can all rest for a while. That shall help restore the confidence and discipline of the Roman Heavy Infantry, which is becoming increasingly important because of the German forces' almost hourly attacks upon Roman soldiers! I have noticed that as the spirits of Roman soldiers decline, the courage and audacity of the German warriors is increasing!"

Varus next sought Armin. Having found him, Varus spoke. He said, *"Arminius, my friend, please go ahead and try to rally some of your tribesmen to join us in the putting down of this rebellion; if we can get their aid, it will make our task a lot easier! Once you have done so, return and lend assistance to whatever we may encounter!"*

Armin answered, *"Yes, sir, your wish is my command, and I shall do as you have ordered!"* But he was thinking, *"This could not be better! Thank you, Wodin and Thor, for this opportunity for me to make contact with my men who will soon be killing you, Roman bully!"* So, Armin and his cavalry units departed from the Roman column, and they were all soon reunited with their countrymen.

Armin sought out his father, Segimer and spoke to him. Armin said, *"Father, my men and I will now depart back to the Roman column, where we shall pretend to obey Roman orders! I have given orders to Adalhard to sound two horn blasts when I am seen in the centre of the Roman column! I have organised a team of horn blowers to transmit Adalhard's horn blasts along the entire three miles of track.*

When I hear the two horn blasts, it will result in my leaving the centre of the column and travelling to the front of it where I shall meet with one-half of my cavalrymen. The other half will be at the rear of the column and will wait there until Adalhard makes his three horn blasts in quick succession. When Adalhard makes his three horn blasts in quick succession, it shall be the signal that the front and rear of the entire Roman column is under simultaneous attack by all of my cavalry units.

That will surprise and confuse the Romans because we are all equite auxiliary Roman soldiers, and therefore, we all wear Roman armour and have Roman weapons! You and Uncle Inguionerus are to begin your sweeps down your respective sides of the hill and attack the middle of the column as soon as you hear the three horn blasts of Adalhard or those who relay his horn blasts! You shouldfind that much of the work will already have been done because of the spearmen and archers behind the earth wall and the Mark-Mannen under the swamp's water.

As soon as they hear the three horn blasts, the Mark-Mannen will rise out of the water and attack the Romans with swords and spears! They should wipe out many Romans before you and uncle Inguionerus arrive

267

because they shall be so close to the Romans! I shall now return to Varus at the centre of the column, and I shall tell him that I could not find anyone willing to support the Roman cause!" With that said, Armin and his cavalry left to return to Varus.

As Armin and his men re-joined the Roman legions, they could see the reflections of the sun gleaming off the armour of all members of the Roman column. As the column moved along the narrow track, Armin's cavalry alae split into two halves, with the first half going to the front of the column and the second half of the alae going to the rear of the column.

Varus called for an 'Orders and Information Group' to be held. He said, *"Gentlemen, our Roman scouts have informed me that it would be best if our baggage wagons are left behind in this fortified position under the guard of one cohort! The rest of the three legions and supporting units shall continue the march to wipe out the Germans!"*

The three legions and their supporting units moved slowly but relentlessly forward. They made much noise due to the pounding of the soldier's hobnailed sandals upon the narrow track where the Romans found that they could only march in a column of a single man, or sometimes, two men abreast of each other. As the column moved further forward, it was found that large trees were often in the middle of the track, causing more delays as the soldiers had to move around them. Making things even worse for the Romans was Armin's advanced units now opening the dams' sluices in the mountains. That released a great gush of water which even flooded the tracks through the swamp area.

Varus became uneasy because he had also observed the light flashes coming off Roman mirrors being used by Germanic warriors informing each other that the column was entering the ambush site. Varus said, *"Arminius, there are many little flashes of light coming from the summit of the Kalkriese Hill. Is this a brewing problem for us? What do you make of it?"*

Armin replied, *"Sir, I think that I should go to the front to better control my cavalry forces because I get the impression that the rebels are about to attack. Once I am located with my men at the front of the column, it will be easy for me to deal with any situation. I am useless here in the centre! I have to be with my men in order to command them!"* That prompted Varus to say, *"Very well, Arminius, go to the front of the column and do what is necessary!"*

Armin set off for the front of the column, all the time noticing that mirror flashes were signalling about his progress as he rode on. The Romans also noticed the increase in mirror flashes, and they were becoming more nervous all of the time. Varus was in the centre of the column, and he was feeling very secure due to having Roman soldiers all around him.

To Varus, everything seemed fine, and he was confident that he would crush the German rebels before the end of the day. It never once occurred to him that his trusted auxiliary cavalry commander could be in the process of implementing the destruction of Roman forces in Germania. As far as he was concerned, he and his army were marching to complete Germania's conquest. He forgot all of the warnings about Armin that were given to him by Segestes.

Although the Roman soldiers were uneasy, they would have been far from happy if they could see through the higher ground's earthen wall. For behind it were the spearmen who had twenty-five spears per man and among them were archers who had steel-tipped arrows.

The chest-high earth wall extended for three miles of track which had the great swamp on the lower side of it, and the spearmen and archers had been placed all the way along it. The archers and spearmen behind the wall were waiting for the three blasts from my horn to attack the Romans on their lower side.

The five hundred and eighty Mark-Mannen were in position under the swamp's water and breathing through hollow reeds. Because the track and ambush site's length was three Roman miles, a series of signalers and horn blowers was organised to relay the three horns blasts signalling the attack when it came.

I could see that Armin had left the centre of the column and was on his way to the front of it. I could also see the mirror transmitted signals that told me that Armin was now very close to the front of the column. I waited a short time, then I could see Armin at the front of the column, so I sounded the three blasts from my horn. The spearmen then threw their spears towards the track. They were joined by the archers who shot their arrows into the Romans on the track below them. While that was happening, the Mark-Mannen got out of the water and attacked the Romans with their swords and short spears.

Meanwhile, the Cherusci cavalry under the commands of Segimer and Inguionerus swept down their various sides of Kalkriese Hill and closed with the remaining Romans on the track below. Armin and his alae surrounded the front and rear of the Roman column and attacked all Romans they could see. The German spearmen behind the earth wall quickly threw their twenty-five spears each into the Romans below them, and then they charged into the middle of the Romans from the high ground and killed many of them using swords and battle axes!

Some Romans could now hear the Cherusci cavalry's galloping approach commanded by Ingionerus and Segimer bearing down upon them from opposing directions. Meanwhile, the front and rear of the Roman column found that they were under direct attack by Germanic warriors and the Roman auxiliary equite cavalry alae!

The German warriors darted in from behind trees, striking out at the Romans with short spears, long swords or swinging their battle-axes at them. The narrow track the Romans were on deprived them of the use of the 'Triple Line', and indeed, the Romans could not pivot and hurl their pila from even just one line of Romans! Thus the Romans were deprived of being able to apply 'Defence in Depth'.

Hundreds of Roman soldiers were impaled by the thrown spears and fired arrows of the warriors behind the earth wall. Many died instantly, while others screamed in agony as they desperately tried to pull spears or arrows from their bodies. As more German warriors realised that their Roman enemies could not mount a defence against them, they moved in closer, killing Romans with their battle-axes, swords and spears.

The Roman army of three full legions who were reputed to be the best of the Roman army had most of its members lying on the ground and dying of wounds unless they were already dead. As a result of this, the ground was blood-soaked, and much of the water in the great swamp and the marshes now also were the red colour of blood.

While some German warriors had chain-mail armour and helmets, the majority did not. That and their light-weight armaments gave the Germans high mobility and speed. They depended on the effectiveness of their axes, spears and long sword. If this action had been fought out in the open plain, the Romans would have won! The surprise attack which the Germans sprang upon the Romans was carried out in confined and boggy environments, which favoured the Germanic warriors while putting the Roman legions into a severe disadvantage.

It was only now that Varus and his commanders realised that they had walked straight into a trap from which there was no escape. In his desperation and fear of what was happening, Varus was beginning to feel the fury of Armin and his German warriors. However, he did not think that he and the Romans were the aggressors; instead, he blamed everything upon the Germanic people!

A Legion Commander and his tribune spoke to Varus. The legate said, *"General Varus, your three legions have been wiped out! This column's front and rear have come under direct attack from Arminius and his Roman Equite Cavalry Alae! Elsewhere, the three Roman Heavy Infantry Legions have been reduced to some cohorts fighting for their very lives! They cannot hold out much longer!*

Along the entire three miles of track, Romans are dead or dying. Away from the front and rear of our column, our legionnaires are further harassed by the Cherusci cavalry units commanded by Segimer and Inguionerus, who are sweeping down the slopes of the Kalkriese Hill and killing all Romans who have not yet fallen to the warriors behind the earth wall and the Mark-Mannen who have attacked our men after they emerged from the great swamp!"

Varus was visibly shaken. He said, *"Legate and tribune, is it only bad news that you have for me? Is there no good news at all?"* the Legate answered, *"No General Varus, there is no good news, the best that we can hope for is to die honourably!"* Varus replied, *"Oh, fuck it!"*

As the full realisation that his entire Roman force of twenty thousand men killed by the Germanic warriors, he had vowed to destroy, hit home, Varus dug a hole into the ground near where he was standing. Next, he placed the hilt of his gladius into the hole and then placed loose soil between it and the edges of the hole.

That was followed by Varus compacting the soil surrounding the hilt of his sword. Now that the sword was fastened to the ground by its hilt, Varus committed suicide by exposing his stomach area and then falling upon his sword's sharp blade.

The army commanded by Varus numbered over fifty thousand soldiers. Still, less than half of those legionaries were with him when he walked into the Teutoberg Forest trap (Kalkriese Hill area). The slaughter of Romans was not confined to the area where Varus and his army died.

273

Detachments of his soldiers were cut off and killed in other areas near Kalkriese Hill. As well, large numbers of Roman civil officers, advocates and procurators now fell victim to the oppressed Germanic population, which directly exacted revenge because of the insults and hard life under the Roman Governorship of Varus, who use torture and beheading of Germanic princes as a punishment for not obeying Roman Laws as well as the crucifixion of the Germanic people of the lower ranks and classes.

Tribune Caeditius was in command of a detachment of two cohorts from the XVIII Legion. Varus had ordered him to provide security for the army of Varus by attempting to secure the southern flanks of the army. Where he and his cohorts were stationed, they could hear but not see the battle. Accordingly, Titus Caeditius spoke to his officers and men.

He said, *"We must know what is happening to the main units of our army under the command of Varus. Things do not sound like the gods are on our side! Optio Sevenoius, take a half-century, find out what is happening, and report your findings immediately! Do not attempt to engage the enemy; your job is to find out what is happening and to get the information to me as quickly as possible."*

The optio answered, *"Yes, tribune, it shall be done as you command!"* and he left to carry out his orders. After some hours later, he returned to the tribune. The Optio said, *"Sir, the situation is that the entire army of Varus the Roman General and Governor has been or soon will be wiped out to a man! You can save the men under your command by withdrawing from here and silently walking to a distant field.*

That is possible because the Germanic warriors are too intent on gaining booty from the slain Romans. If you were to get out of here safely, you could then order your trumpets to sound. That may make the barbarians think that the uncle of Varus, called Asprenas and his legions are close at hand." Tribune Caeditius took the advice of the optio, resulting in himself and his units escaping from the slaughter in the Teutoburg Forest.

Asprenas immediately advanced cautiously to aid the embattled Romans when he was informed of the disaster, which resulted in the wiping out of the Roman Army of Varus. The situation was simply that all three legions of Roman Heavy Infantry and all of their supporting units were trapped and facing inevitable defeat.

After making several observations of the barbarian forces' activity and progress, he called for an 'Orders and Information' group to be held. He said, *"Gentlemen, we are too small a force to successfully try to stop the progress of the triumphant Germanic warriors! We only have one legion and four cohorts, which is too small a force to take on the victorious Germans! Therefore, we shall withdraw to the Rhine, partly to ensure our Roman soldiers' well-being and partly to keep down the Cis-Rhenane[27] Germans, who may have the disposition to follow the examples of their former countrymen."*

---

[27] Cis-Rhenane Germans were Germanic tribes who has settled in Gaul and taken up the ways of their new Gallic neighbours.

The Roman prisoners were dealt with in accordance with the whims of their German captors. A few Romans were offered sacrifices to Wodin and Thor, while the rest were divided out among the Germanic warriors as slaves and were taken to centres where they could be sold.

The captured Roman lawyers were put to death after they had endured the insults, torture and degradation from the Germanic tribesmen and women. The booty in the form of armour, weapons and treasure was equally divided among the Germanic people. The eagles of the defeated legions were given to the Chatti, the Marsi and the Bructeri.

The body of Varus was found, and it appeared that the Roman soldiers had made an attempt to pay the last honours to the body of their fallen leader, even though they were in the midst of desolation and death themselves! While many of Varus's officers continued to fight to the end, others among them also suicided after they witnessed what Varus had done.

Segimer and Inguionerus met Armin at a place near the middle of the killing ground with some of their men and shook hands. Armin said, *"Welcome, my dear Father and Uncle. Today is a great day! The sun is shining, the Roman bully called Varus is dead! That is the callous arsehole over there! Marobod asked me to bring the head of Varus to him, so I am now going to cut off his head!"*

With that said, Armin walked to the body of Varus and using his long broadsword, he removed the head of

Varus from his body. Having completed that, he wrapped up Varus's head in cloth and placed it into his saddlebag.

The Germanic warriors began moving among the dead and dying Romans. Often they killed those Romans who were not already dead, while in some cases, the Romans would become prisoners. The fortunate ones among the Roman prisoners were simply let go and told, *"Roman pig, today is your lucky day! We are letting you go unmolested so that you will take the news of the defeated of the Roman army of three legions plus supporting units back to Rome! To help you in this, and to make sure that you do not get lost or attacked on your way back to Roman held areas, we are taking you as far as five Roman miles from the Roman frontiers of Italy and Gaul! There we shall release you! Make sure that you tell as many Romans as possible of the defeat of Varus and his large Roman army!"*

Armin returned to Thusnelda at their home near Aliso, and they embraced. He said, *"My love, we have been triumphant, and Varus, along with his army of three legions, no longer exists! I have his head wrapped up in cloth inside a container attached to the saddle of my horse. I shall have to leave here in about a half day from now in order to keep my word to Marobod and bring him the head of Varus!"* Thusnelda said, *"My darling, come, take me into your arms and make love to me. Let's go to bed and make it all happen!"*

Armin Sends Varus's Head to Marobod

So, it was that Armin and Thusnelda went to their bed and made love. After a half-day had passed, Armin was again mounted on his horse along with his and along with his entourage, was on the way to Bohemia to visit Marobod. A messenger approached Armin and told him that he was urgently required back at his own cavalry units to sort out some problems between the warriors, which, if left unattended, could have had severe effects upon the discipline of the units concerned.

Armin ordered that Egilhard report to him for duty immediately. Egilhard reported to the German leader. Armin said, *"Egilhard, I have an urgent task for you to perform! Over there, on the table, is the head of Varus wrapped up in white cloth! You and the rest of the men in this entourage are to continue travelling to Bohemia, where you shall take the head of Varus to Marobod! Make sure that you deliver the head to Marobod and then return to Aliso!"*

Egilhard did as he was ordered and arrived at the large longhouse that was being used as a residence by Marobod. Egilhard was ushered into the presence of Marobod by one of his servants. Upon seeing Egilhard, Marobod said, *"Where is Armin? How did the fight go, or has it not happened yet?"* Egilhard said, *"My name is Egilhard, and Armin has sent me to deliver the head of Varus to you! He cannot be here himself because his presence is urgently required with his cavalry units. In answer to your question about the fight with the Romans, it went very well, and the Romans have lost an estimated twenty thousand soldiers due to it!*

Not only did we close with and kill the Roman invaders, but we have wiped out three of the most feared legions of the Roman army! These were the XVII, XVIII, XVIV and an additional six cohorts of heavy infantry from the two legions based in southern Germania.

Regarding prisoners, some have already been sacrificed to the Gods while many others have been set free so that they will take the word of the Roman defeat back to Rome! Armin is grateful to you for supplying your Mark-Mannen. Opening his saddlebag, Egilhard said, *"Here, Marobod, is the head of Varus like you have specified!"* He then took Varus's head out of the saddlebag and placed it upon a small table near Marobod. He said, *"There you go, Marobod, the head of Varus as you have requested!*

During the fight with the Romans, your Mark-Mannen suffered forty-five deaths. The remaining five hundred and thirty-five warriors should be returning here within two to three days, once the feasting and drinking celebrations of our victory have been completed. Now then, if that is all, I would like to return to my wife!"

Marobod said, *"Egilhard, thank you for the head of Varus. I am now happy to send you back to your wife, whom I am told has the name of Adalheidis"*[28]

As soon as Egilhard had departed, Marobod spoke to his servants. He said, *"Rewrap the head of Varus in clean white linen and take it to the Roman Emperor, Augustus, in Rome itself! I want you to observe the reactions of the Romans near and around Augustus, and I want to know about the reaction of Augustus himself!*

Marobod just did not want to be in possession of a trophy as dangerous as the head of Varus, and besides, he wanted to be in a position where he could have more

---

[28] Adalheidis is the ancient form of Adelaide.

influence on Augustus and use that to his advantage. That was the main reason that he sent the head on to Rome!

The Reaction in Rome to the Loss of Three Crack Legions

Tiberius was successful in stopping the rebellions in Pannonia and Dalmatia, something that took him almost three years to complete, at the cost of many Roman lives. The Senate had approved the holding of a triumph for Tiberius. The preparations for the celebrations were well underway when the first reports of the Roman army's disaster became known. Soon after that, the head of Varus was delivered to Augustus by the warriors of Marobod.

The Roman commanders on the Rhine had been sending positive reports, which led Augustus to believe that the Germanic people east of the Rhine were at last completely under Roman control. After all, had he not appointed Varus to oversee Germania's final pacification and make it a typical Roman province? As soon as he heard of the disaster, he began fearing his Rhineland bases and all Roman possessions in Gaul.

Only four years before, the Illyrian Wars had caused mass panic among the Roman population, who were increasingly nervous about the possibility of Germanic forces attacking Rome itself! Augustus was receiving reports coloured by propaganda and false information. Even so, he could not have believed that a military force such as that of Armin and his Germanic warriors, which had wiped out the flower of the Roman army's elite legions in one single battle, could be stopped by a river.

He could not have believed the weak remnants of the Roman Army of the Rhine, which had been weakened by the demands made upon it to reinforce Roman units taking part in the Illyrian War, could withstand sustained attacks by Germanic forces, in particular if the Rhenane Germans joined with the forces of Armin.

A Senator was speaking in the Senate. He said, *"My fellow Romans, I have news of a disaster which has befallen the Roman army! The Roman Governor of Germania and all of his three legions of Heavy Infantry, complete with all supporting units, as well as another six cohorts from the two legions in southern Germania, have been wiped out! Given that there are ten cohorts to a legion, it means that of a total of twenty-eight legions to maintain Roman supremacy in the world, we have lost more than three and a half of the best legions in our army!*

That also means that almost one-eighth of the total forces of Rome have been wiped out! Friends and Romans, let that sink in for a while, and you may also begin to fear what could happen from now on!

The facts are that Arminius is still alive and out there in Germania, Gaul, or the Norican passes, and he is a real threat to our existence! I call upon Augustus and Tiberius to do something about these appalling states of affairs before we all end up being dead men because the Germans may want revenge !"

Augustus and Tiberius were discussing the situation. Augustus said, *"Tiberius, my son[29], The Germanic people have wiped out all major Roman*

---

[29] Augustus adopted both Tiberius and his brother Drusus.

military units operating in Germania! Germanic warriors are currently threatening the Italian peninsular with a war which is like that of the Cimbri and Teutones threats of many years ago! We must somehow reduce the possibility that the Germans will take over Rome!"

Tiberius was silent for a time, then he spoke. He said, *"Augustus, my father, I have thought over what you have just told me, and I am sure that we must immediately post guards all over Rome; to discourage sympathetic uprisings among the foreign residents of Rome as the news of the disaster that has befallen our army spreads among the population! I also recommend that you sack the German mercenaries acting as your Praetorian Guard and in all of Rome's cavalry alae! If these men are still here when the Germans attack, it will greatly aid them if and when the Germans in the service of Rome attack Romans! I further would like you to state in public that we shall be sponsoring games and that we shall honour Jupiter when calm is restored!"*

Augustus was so bothered by the loss of his elite legions that he let his beard and hair grow for months after the disaster. He could often be heard wailing, *"Quintilius Varus, give me back my legions!"*

The Response of Augustus

In order to stabilise the situation on the Rhine frontier, Augustus sent Tiberius to take command of the legions there. Tiberius set about the redistribution of Roman forces in the Rhineland and decided to improve the military base's defences that he controlled.

Tiberius called for an 'Information and Orders' group to take place. When it started, he spoke. He said,

"Gentlemen, we shall campaign across the Rhine and operate against the Bructeri and the Marsi. Finding them shall prove difficult as always due to these Germans not having towns or cities.

So, we must look for isolated small groups of up to five longhouses! Operating against the Germans like this has little to no effect upon them, but what we are doing is showing the Germans that Romans still control the West Bank of the Rhine and that we can freely move onto the eastern bank at any time we choose to do so.

I am sending Roman patrols into the Rhine's eastern side, intending to find and burn the German people's crops and homes! Any Germans that we manage to take prisoner shall either crucified or impaled!'

Tiberius did as he discussed with his officers at the 'Information and Orders' group. Germanic homes were found by Romans and burned along with the crops which may have been in the area. These new actions by the Romans rekindled the hatred and contempt that my people felt for the Romans. That resulted in armed clashes between my people and the Romans commanded by Tiberius, no matter if Roman historians say otherwise.

All of the time, Rome's cost was increasing in both the number of Roman soldiers killed whilst on active service and the amount of money necessary to maintain the offensive against the German people. Some Roman history writers claim that Augustus left a statement ordering that the Roman empire must not be expanded beyond its present boundaries.

I know for sure that such a document never existed. Remember that I am a ghost, and I visited

Tiberius's headquarters when he was in conference with his officers. Tiberius said, *"Gentlemen, you have all done very well, and Rome is the only power in the world! We have a major problem. The Germans remain unconquered, and they are always willing to fight and kill Romans at all times. The campaigns in Germania are too expensive, and if Rome does happen to win something, it is of little value and usually has been bought at a great cost of Roman money and lives. I can see no point in continuing to waste Roman lives and money on trying to do the impossible.*

I propose that we withdraw to the Rhine's western side and keep our outposts fully manned and active. We shall be able to very quickly move between the posts due to the Roman roads between them that are already built. From time to time, Roman legions shall still be able to move into Germania whenever Rome wishes that to happen." I saw and heard all of that happen because I can move freely in time and space as a spirit. No-one can see me unless I chose to let a person do so.

Campaigns of Germanicus in Germania

In 13 A.D., the year before he died, Augustus sent Germanicus, the son of Drusus, to take command of the Rhine legions. Tiberius stayed in Rome because he was aiding Augustus by being the co-Emperor and helped in controlling the empire. The duty of avenging the death of Varus and his legions fell upon General Germanicus.

While Tiberius was in command of the Rhine Armies, he redeployed the Roman army's forces, which resulted in eight legions being stationed on the Rhine frontier. Four of these were in lower Germania – the V and XXI at Xanten and the XX and XVI near Cologne. There were four legions stationed in upper Germania- the II, XII, XIII and the XXVI. These added together were one-third of the entire Roman military forces.

Detachments were sent across the Rhine to garrison the castles and outposts built by Drusus to observe the Germanic tribes in Hessia and Westphalia. Caius Silius commanded the Upper Rhine's Roman army, and Aulus Caecina commanded the Lower Rhine's Roman army. Germanicus was given command of both of these armies by Tiberius.

First Expedition of Germanicus

The Roman armies of the Rhine had been recruited, and it was necessary to lead them into action immediately. Germanicus, therefore, assembled twelve thousand legionnaires and eight squadrons of cavalry as well as twenty-six cohorts[30] of auxiliary soldiers at Casta Vetera and going through Caesia Sylva set out for the country of the Marsi under the command of Caecina.

A messenger rode to Caenina and was escorted to see him. The messenger said, *"Sir, I and the rest of the scouting units of my legion have important news for you to consider!"* Caecina said, *"Very well, messenger, please slow down, relax and tell me what you have to say!"* The messenger replied, *"Sir, you have now left the dangerous forest behind you, and your forces are in a more open country. I am Optio Cassandra of the II Legion, where my duties are those of leading the reconnaissance units. We*

---

[30] A cohort had between 500 and 750 men, depending on its prestige. There were ten (10) cohorts per legion. In this case, the 26 cohorts added up to 2.6 legions.

have intelligence that Germanic warriors have been eating and drinking all night last night and that they are likely to do the same tonight!" Caecina replied, *"Optio, you have done well, now refresh yourself have some food and then take this critical information straight to General Germanicus! My forces shall move ahead and surprise the Germans. We will make them pay for killing Romans!"*

The Romans moved quickly and silently through the forest, and they had the blessing of a bright moon and starlit night. The small hamlets of the Marsi were surrounded by Roman soldiers who were thirsty for the Germanic people's blood to exact revenge upon them for the loss of three Roman legions and the death of Varus.

The Romans spared no-one. The aged, the women and children were all slaughtered without mercy. The country for miles around that area was ruined for generations to come because the Romans worked salt into the soil of the area. The Roman soldiers did not even suffer a wound because they had completely surprised the sleeping German villagers. The Romans recovered the three eagles belonging to Varus' legions after being found in the sacred grove of Tanfana, where the Marsi and Bructeri had deposited them as trophies of the victory over Roman legions.

While returning to the Rhine, the Romans had to repass the Caesian Forest where the Bructeri, Tubantes and Usipetes were waiting for them to exact revenge for the wanton murders of their unarmed and sleeping families. The Germanic warriors remained motionless until the entire Roman army had marched into the forest. Lothar, who was a sub-chief of the Usipetes, spoke. He said, *"My warriors, ahead of us is the Roman XX Legion and its auxiliary units. They are acting as the rear-guard of the Roman army! We and other Germanic warrior units shall attack the Romans in as great a force as possible! That should confuse the Romans, at least! So, move out and close with and kill all Romans near to us!"* The Germanic warriors did that, and it resulted in the Romans becoming confused to the point where it was only the leadership of Germanicus that saved the Romans.

Germanicus put himself at the head of the XX Legion and charged the Germans with such vigour that he drove the enemy into open ground where he killed many of them. In the meantime, the main part of his army emerged from the forest and erected a fortified camp, allowing the Romans to sleep safely that night. The Romans continued their retreat to the Rhine in the morning without more attacks from the Germanic warriors.

The Second Expedition of Germanicus

Germanicus was in conference with his officers. He said, *"The recovery of the lost eagles of the three destroyed Roman Legions of Varus accompanied by the slaughter of Germanic women and children is the Roman reward for the sacrifice and work of our first expedition! We shall continue to hunt down the rebels when and where we can do so!"*

It was now the year 15 A.D. and the year appeared to offer some advantages to the Romans. The old feuds between Armin and his Father-in-Law, Segestes, arose again, resulting in fresh outbreaks of feuds between them. The allies and friends of Segestes had already been pushed to their limit by Armin, and now the Chatti were clearly showing their desire to join with Armin and his confederates.

Germanicus, therefore, ordered Caecina, who had command of four legions of Roman Heavy Infantry and five thousand irregulars, to attack the Cherusci and Marsi while he and the other four legions attacked the Chatti. He encircled and burned Mattiacum, which was their main village and restored the fortifications of Drusus on mount Taunus and put into place a merciless campaign of pillage of the open country, slaughtering my people who were just non-warrior farmers and other assorted civilians. He then returned to Moguntiacum laden with plunder.

Meanwhile, Caecina attacked and defeated the Marsi while preventing the Cherusci from giving assistance to the distressed Chatti. However, all of this did not stop the resistance of the Germanic tribes, who had no relaxation of hostility towards the Roman invaders. A munifex walked to where Germanicus was and said, *"Sir, there are messengers from Segestes who are imploring to see you! Segestes is wanting immediate assistance against his enemies and in particular against his son-in-law, called Arminius!"*

That was like music to the ears of Germanicus, for he saw the problem of the Germanic resistance to Rome as the obstacle it was. In particular, he knew that Armin was inspiring his country-men and their war-like attitudes by keeping alive the hatred for Romans. They had been the oppressors of his country as well as the recent butchers of defenceless German wives and children.

Germanicus decided to get input from others about how best to exploit the feuding between Segestes and his Son-in-Law. So, at a conference with some advisors, Germanicus spoke. He said, *"Gentlemen, I have been asked to provide immediate assistance to Segestes, who is the Father-in-Law of Arminius! I need you to consider a number of things about this that you may not know yet and advise me as your opinions of how best to deal with this gave matter!*

Firstly, let us consider that Segestes is trying to excuse the part he played in the action against Varus. No matter what he says, he can neither disguise it nor deny it! Also, many other Romans and I are not at all happy about his excuses. He is known as being greedy, grasping and cowardly. I also know that his daughter, Thusnelda, who is the wife of Arminius, also deeply loves her father, and she is currently living with him in his house, but I have no idea of where that may be.

I am proposing to have a renewal of connection between Segestes and Rome, which will in due course give us Arminius or at least his wife, Thusnelda! Gentlemen, I hereby am turning this problem over to you. If you recommend a renewal of contact with Segestes, that will please me.

If not, I will go along with your decision! Whatever you decide, do so quickly, for time is wasting!" His advisors discussed what Germanicus had said, and then they voted to agree with him. As a result, Germanicus held an audience with Segestes and re-established contact with him.

Germanicus Meets Armin's Forces Twice

Between 14 A.D. and 16 A.D., Germanicus launched several major campaigns across the Rhine into Germania, where the Roman legions again faced Armin and his forces. Germanicus wanted revenge for the destruction of three Roman legions, and he was not trying to expand the Roman Empire contrary to Tiberius's orders. Although there were many more battles and countless skirmishes, they did not alter the new boundaries set by the defeat of the Roman forces in the Teutoberg Forest in 9 A.D...

In 15 A.D., the Roman army under the command of Germanicus, during his third campaign, clashed with the warriors of Armin during two major confrontations. During an 'Information and Orders Group', Germanicus expressed his concerns.

He said, *"Gentlemen, we are going east into the interior of Germania to exact revenge for what the Germans have done to Varus and his legions! As we are going to take on the Germans deep within their own country, we will be at a disadvantage of not knowing the countryside and having no knowledge or maps of the areas that we shall be in!*

There are also other major problems associated with our invasion of Germania. One of the main problems is the length of our communications lines, which will affect our supplies adversely. Because of our supply lines' length, I have decided to use soldiers who shall march east into Germania from our Rhineland bases. They shall be reinforced by other soldiers who shall sail up the Ems

River from the North Sea in ships that have been built for that purpose.

So it was that while some of his soldiers were marching eastwards in Germania, other soldiers were taking it easy and sailing up the River Ems. The plan was for both of these groups of soldiers to meet and then attack both the Cherusci and Bructeri. During that summer campaign, Germanicus and his army visited the battle site at Kalkriese Hill, located deep within the Teutoberg Forest.

When the Romans arrived there, they were horrified at what they saw when they got to the battlefield. Countless bones had been placed into specific orders by the German warriors in order to appease their gods. Many weapons were scattered upon the ground, with most of them being of Roman origin because the Germanic warriors had only lost a few men in comparison to the losses suffered by Rome.

At a location that the Romans called 'Pontes Longi'[31] , Armin and his men attacked the Romans with the fighting lasting for two days. The Roman general named Caecina had disturbing dreams, which resulted in him wanting to get out of the area where Varus and his legions had died. The general had dreamt that he watched Quinctilius Varus rise from the marshy and waterlogged area, splattered with blood and calling upon him to leave that part of Germania immediately. Neither side could win a decisive victory in this battle because both were evenly matched.

---

[31] Latin for Long Causeways.

With Germanicus commanding eight legions and supporting auxiliary units, he marched them into Germania's interior from his bases on the Rhine. They were soon joined by the men who had sailed up the Ems River as and men who had sailed up the Weser. The Roman army was approaching the Weser from the west, while Armin and his warriors approached the Weser areas from the east. With the Roman army was Flavus, the brother of Armin.

Segestes Betrays Thusnelda

Both Thusnelda and Armin were watchful of Segestes, who had constantly proven himself to be a major source of irritation in so much that he was always trying to betray his daughter and son-in-law to the Romans. Armin, my friend, and leader, had captured his father-in-law and was holding Sesteges prisoner in a substantial building near the forest surrounding Aliso.

Segestes was a nobleman of the Cherusci nation, and he had some friends who thought that they could advance their lives by swearing allegiance to him, and so, in may of year 15 A.D., they managed to send a messenger through to Germanicus who was happy to receive the messenger.

Germanicus asked the messenger, *"Well, messenger, what is it that you have to tell me?"* The messenger replied, *"Sir, I come to you bearing grave news! Segestes, the father-in-law of Armin, whom you know as Arminius, has been captured by him, and he is imprisoned at a location near Aliso. Segestes wants you to hurry and release him from his confinement! In return, he will lead you straight to the house where Arminius is!*

Sir, just think of the glory that will be yours in Rome if you capture Arminius!"

Germanicus answered, *"Thank you, messenger, I have long wanted to capture or kill Arminius! Return to where Segestes is and tell him that his release from his imprisonment is imminent! It shall be particularly satisfying to capture Arminius, especially because he is the Germanic people's guiding light! It is his dauntless spirit that keeps the Germanic warriors fighting us, even when we vastly outnumber the Germans!*

Messenger, you have done well; go to my field kitchen, have some food and refreshments and then return to Segestes with the message I have given you!" the messenger departed and was quickly on his way back to Segestes.

It was late evening when Germanicus went to the aid of Segestes and freed him from the building which had been his prison. He said to Segestes, *"Where the fuck is Arminius? He is the one I want!"* Segestes answered, *"He and my daughter Thusnelda are in my house, here in Aliso! It is now night-time and very dark outside. There are some holes used for storage along the way to my home, and I can safely guide you and your men past these straight to my house. I suggest that we have no more than twenty men in our party because of the noise of our approach alarming both of them and allowing them to escape!"*

That resulted in Germanicus, Segestes and eighteen Roman soldiers walking towards the house of Segestes, where Armin and Thusnelda were. While the group of twenty men were walking towards the house, they caused many of the household dogs in Aliso to start barking.

I had for a long time the feeling of Segestes being totally untrustworthy, and now I was alarmed with a sense of imminent danger approaching. Let's face it, the reputation of Segestes being a coward and traitor to even his own family was richly deserved. Because of my disquiet and a sense of approaching danger, I was still in my chain-mail armour suit and had all of my weapons at the ready.

Armin and Thusnelda were both asleep and naked in the next room. Then I heard the dogs barking, and I went to both of them and said, *"Hurry up and get dressed, both of you! Armin, here are your weapons and armour. Put them on quickly and meet me outside, where I have two tethered horses waiting for us at the rear of this house. Hurry, judging by the barking of the dogs; enemies are on their way here and close by!"*

Armin quickly got dressed, and then he assisted Thusenelda to dress herself because she was heavily pregnant. Having finished dressing, Thusnelda took up her shield and battle-axe and then she stood just behind the front door while Armin and I walked through the rear door and went to the horses. Armin and I had just got into our horses' saddles when we noticed the first of the Romans trying to cncircle the house.

That made me say, *"Look over there, Armin, your father-in-law has betrayed you and Thusnelda again! I just saw the worthless arsehole leading this detachment of Romans!* I had barely finished saying that when a

Roman soldier lunged at me. I drew my sword and cut off his head; then we galloped our horses away into the night.

During this time, Armin presented a fantastic sight! He had replaced all of his Roman army items with Germanic ones. His Germanic helmet had metal wings attached to the sides of it. He had a long red full beard, and his weapons consisted of his favoured long broadsword and a battle-axe, and he was wearing a full-length chain-mail armour. He also had a Roman shield that he used to smash into Roman soldiers to stun them just before killing them. He looked every inch the Germanic warrior whom the Romans so feared.

Meanwhile, Segestes had seen that Armin and I were killing the Romans with ease, so he ran off to find Germanicus and finally found him. To Germanicus, he said, *"Sir, come quickly, Armin and Adalhard are killing your soldiers, and it looks like they will get away unless you move your arses and get them now!"*

Germanicus said, *"Segestes, you prick, it is to my great advantage to use you, but I do not like you, you cowardly prick. I really cannot stand traitors such as you; the only reason you are still alive is that your information about the enemy is useful. Now lead the way to Arminius but remember that I consider you to be a gutless arsehole!"* With that said, Germanicus followed Segestes to the house in which Thusnelda was living and assumed Armin was also there, again enjoying her company.

Together with eight Roman soldiers, Germanicus burst through the house's front door to find that Thusnelda, who was heavily pregnant and very defiant, confronting them at the door and banishing a battle axe. She said to them, *"You are too late, my husband has gone, and he will exact revenge against all Romans for the shit work you gutless arseholes have done this night!"*

Germanicus now spoke, saying, *"Thusnelda, wife of the traitor Arminius, you are now under arrest in the name of Tiberius, the Emperor of Rome, unless the emperor grants you amnesty, you will become a slave and so will your unborn child. You shall have much to regret for being the wife of the man who has destroyed a large part of the entire Roman army and killed Varus, the Roman Governor of Germania!"*

Thusnelda remained both proud and defiant and said to Germanicus, *"I am a princess of the Cherusci Nation and I will never willing be with any cowardly Roman bully. I may be made a slave, and I may have to submit to sexual advances from who-ever owns me, but I will never give my owner satisfying sex or love, for all of that is the right of my husband and hero, Armin!"* Germanicus now said, *"Why do you call him Armin? His name is Arminius!"* Thusnelda said, *"That is as false as is everything Roman! His name is Armin; you Roman bullies added ius to his name and called him Arminius; that is not his name!"*

Germanicus said, *"My men have seen what you and the Germanic warriors have done to the bones of the three legions that you Germans butchered! All of my soldiers are extremely angry that you Germans have killed so may Romans and then arranged their* bones in fashions that will appease your Gods of Wodin and Thor!

Many of my soldiers want me to turn you over to them to teach you not to attack Romans! However, I will not allow that because they will rape you until you die! Instead, I am giving you to the detachment of eighteen soldiers who helped me to capture you. They will have you for the next night. You should prepare yourself to be raped repeatedly! That will be your just deserts!

Germanicus now said to Thusnelda, *"I am taking you to Rome, and when we get there, you will be paraded throughout the city as a prisoner of war. In particular, three Roman Triumph Parades will feature the display of "The Wife of Arminius, the terrible Germanic warrior who destroyed three Roman legions and killed the Governor of Germania. Publius Quinctilius Varus."* The loss of his wife and the great love of his life caused Armin to grieve over the loss of his beloved Thusnelda, and he never remarried, choosing instead to remain loyal and faithful to 'The Love of His Life.'

First Triumph of Germanicus on 17/May/17 A.D.

The Roman historian Strabo wrote about the Triumph of Germanicus on 26/May/17 A.D... He wrote, *"In dealing with these people, distrust has been a great advantage, whereas those who have been trusted have done great harm, as for instance the Cherusci and their subjects, in whose country three Roman legions, with their general Quintilius Varus, were destroyed by ambush in violation of the treaty. But they all paid the penalty and afforded the younger Germanicus a most brilliant triumph in which their most famous men and women were led captive, I mean Segimuntus, the son of Segestes and Thusnelda, the wife of Arminius, the destroyer of the three Roman legions commanded by Varus the Roman Governor of Germania!"* This was, in fact, Roman propaganda which sort to glorify everything Roman and too make everything about the enemies of Rome appear to be despicable.

With the Roman Senators and the general Roman Population wanting good news, the Roman Propaganda machine worked overtime. It published posters proclaiming the coming triumphant parade of Germanicus as a significant victory over the Cherusci, Chatti and Angrivarii and all nations between the Rhine and the Elbe.

Pictures were painted of the mountains and rivers that were crossed, and exaggerated accounts of battles fought against the Germanic people were written, with all of these being outright lies. Still, it was what the Romans wanted to read and hear, so all that was exhibited to the Roman population. Many Romans were very interested in seeing the woman who was the wife of the warrior who had destroyed so much of the Roman army in Germania, and they were even willing to pay for the privilege of being afforded room along the parade route to see her.

Thusnelda was a woman who was more like her husband's heart, instead of her father, Segestes. She stood before the Roman Crowds without tears, fearless and proud. She only tried to conceal her pregnancy's appearance as it may have added more zest and lust to the triumphs, which were essential to the triumphant Roman crowds' eyes. That was for the first of the triumph processions.

Segestes abandoned his daughter without reluctance to the Roman Triumphs' disgrace and mockery and was present during all triumphs, witnessing his own daughter's degradation. He left it to the Romans to determine if she should be treated as the daughter of a friend or an enemy's wife.

There were three triumphs for Germanicus involving Thusnelda. When the third Triumph Parade for Germanicus took place, which also featured her infant son, named Thumelicus, and in which Siegismund and Sithiacus, the sons of Segestes and Siegemir, also exhibited, as well as Libys, who was a priest, and Theuderich, who was a chief of the Sicambri. As well, there were also other captives of the long-standing following in the procession.

The Birth of Thumelicus

In her cell, Thusnelda was running a slight fever, and then her contractions began. As she was a prize exhibit to be used for future triumphant parades involving Germanicus, a midwife was organised for her. The midwife attended to Thusnelda and bathed her forehead continuously with cool water to lower her fever. She said, *"Thusnelda, I am Julia Sentuius, and I am a Roman lady. I am going to help you to have your baby. Make sure that you just relax and try to do as I tell you, and all should be well!"*

Thusnelda answered, *"Thank you, Julia. I am having some pain associated with this birth. Do you have any wine on hand that could help me dull the pain?"* Julia said, *"Yes, there is some wine on hand, but try to do without it for now. Let us concentrate on getting the child out of you! I can see that your contractions are becoming more frequent and closer together. Using a scale of one to ten, with one being nothing and ten being unbearable pain, what would you say your current pain level is?"*

Thusnelda said, *"The pain level is about six on the scale you have mentioned."* Julia said, *"Very well, Thusnelda, I am pouring a goblet of wine for you".* She then proceeded to do so and offered the full goblet of wine to Thusnelda. Julia said, *"Thusnelda, do you think your child is a boy or a girl?"* Thusnelda replied, *"I am sure that this child is a boy! When he is born, I shall name him as Thumelic. He shall become known as the 'Son of Arminius', the destroyer of Three Roman Legions of heavy infantry!'"* Soon afterwards, at mid-morning of 26/May/17 A.D., Thumelic was born.

Julia said, *"Congratulations, Thusnelda, you have a fine son just like you predicted! I already know that you are naming him as Thumelic. Germanicus has asked to be kept informed of this birth, and I have sent a runner to tell him of the birth of Thumelic. Have you hade any dreams about him?"* Thusnelda said, *"Yes, I have dreamt that he shall become as big a pain in the arse to Rome as is his father, Arminius! The problem is that the dream becomes confusing because I was thinking that I saw Thumelic looking like a gladiator, and in the dream, I heard Romans call him Thumelicus, even though I have named him as Thumelic!"*

At that moment, a runner from Germanicus came into the cell where Thusnelda was now nursing her baby son. He said, *"Thusnelda, your son has been renamed by Germanicus as 'Thumelicus' because he thinks that your chosen name of Thumelic sounds too Germanic. By changing it to Thumelicus, the name can pass as being Latin. When your son is a toddler and about three years old, both of you shall be in a final Triumphant celebration for Germanicus. After that, you and your son shall be sold as slaves to the highest bidder at the Central Slave Market in Rome!"*

The most splendid ornaments of the triumphs of Germanicus were the degrading exhibitions of Thusnelda and her infant son Thumelicus. He was aged three years by the time of the final Triumph of Germanicus. Segestes was allowed to continue at large and was rewarded with a grant of land near Castra Vetera, where he continued to live under Roman supervision.

It was known that he obtained women for his own use at this property and that he was drunk many times and given to excesses. That happened after he betrayed his daughter for the land grant and money rewards.

The Auction is Held

The slave trader could see that he would make a lot of money from Thusnelda and her son's sale. In a loud voice, he said, *"The bidding shall commence at five thousand sestertii*[32] *or five hundred denarii*[33] *or five aurei!"*

Romulus Fancetii yelled, *"I bid twenty aurei!"* The Salve trader smiled, knowing his fortune was being made. He yelled, *"I am bid twenty aurei, remember that this is for Thusnelda, the wife of the murderous German who wiped out three Roman legions and her son! Do I hear thirty aurei?!"* There were excited and lively discussions among the Romans.

The bidding resumed with Silverio Caeponius yelling, *"I bid thirty-five aureus, but I only want the woman! Someone else can pay for the boy!"* The slave trader said, *"I am bid thirty-five gold aureus for the woman alone! Will someone offer fifty gold aurei for her? Remember, she has a son, and I can include him in the price!* That prompted Julius Montegarios to speak. He yelled, *"Fifty-five gold aureus for the woman and her son!"*

At this point, the slave trader nodded towards his private guard. His guard called Markus Titus Outassius, who then began also to bid. He called out, *"I bid seventy-five gold aureus for the woman and her son!"* the slave trader said, *"I am bid seventy-five gold aureus for the woman and her child?"* Outassius said, *"I bid ninety gold aurei for the woman and her son!"* that resulted in the salve trader calling, *"I am bid ninety gold aureus, any further bids?"*

---

[32] There were 100 sestertii per gold aureus or 25 silver denarii.
[33] The silver denarii were valued at 4 sestertii.

From the rear of the crowd came a loud voice. It said, *"I am Titus Flavius Comptomius, and I bid One-hundred gold aureus for the woman and her son!"* The slave trader called, *"I am bid one-hundred gold aureus for Thusnelda and her son! Are there any further bids?"* Having said that, he again nodded to his guard. Outassius yelled, *"One-hundred and ten gold aurei for Thusnelda and her son!"*

No-one spoke or moved. After some silence, Comptomius again bid. He shouted, *"I bid one hundred and twenty-five gold, aureii!"* The slave trader said, *"Sold to Titus Flavius Comptomius for one-hundred and twenty-five gold aureii! So, Titus Flavius Comptomius, collect your slaves and take them home!"* Comptomius said, *"Make sure that you immediately dress Thusnelda, she is now my property, and I do not want other people ogling at my merchandise! I am, in fact, quite disgusted and upset at the way that many Romans leer at many women. I would very much like it if the lower classes of Romans were to learn to behave a lot better!"*

The slave trader spoke to his guard. He said, *"Well done, Markus, because of your 'dummy' bidding, the price for Thusnelda and her son has been forced to reach one hundred and twenty-five gold aureii! Thank you!"*

Armin Reacts to the Capture of his Wife.

Armin was both furious and incredulous at the betrayal of his wife, Thusnelda, by her own father, Segestes and her resulting capture by Germanicus and the enslavement of both his wife and their then-unborn child. Accordingly, he was heard to yell out in a booming and disgusted voice, *"Oh dishonourable father-in-law, Oh, Great Roman Emperor and associated arseholes, and you disgustingly gutless Roman army, you pack of cowardly curs!*

All of you have achieved nothing, except the abduction and capture of one poor woman who was so heavily pregnant that she could hardly move! Whereas I took apart three entire Roman Legions numbering twenty thousand men by force of arms using man to man combat in open battle! The trophies of my deeds can be seen to this day in groves of Germania in honour of our gods! Your vileness and cowardice disgust me to the core!

Let my Father-in-law, Segestes cultivate the land grant at Castra Vetera which he received for betraying his own daughter and let him get back the priesthood for his son! My people, never forget that through Segestes and others like him, you have been compelled to witness the rod and the axe and the toga of Roman lictor³⁴ between the Elbe and the Rhine.

As to other nations at a distance from us, who may be ignorant of the Roman Government and its ways, remember that once you have felt them, you will be most sorry. You will have to shake them off, no matter if the Roman Emperor you have to deal with is Augustus or Tiberius, for they are equally as bad!" (Greenwood, 1836)

---

³⁴ Lictor was a Roman court official – executioner who beheaded Roman citizens.

Disastrous Retreat of Caecina

Germanicus saw the clouds of the gathering storm and knew that he had to do something to disperse the tribes he knew could join together, forming a powerful force if they became united. To prevent this from happening, he dispatched Caecina with forty cohorts of infantry to march directly to the Ems. At an 'Orders and Information Group', called to discuss the growing Germanic menace. He said, *General Caecina, take four legions (forty cohorts) of heavy infantry and march directly to the Ems River."*

At the same time, Pedro with Roman Cavalry took a route through the territory of the Frisii towards the same point. Meanwhile, Germanicus himself, with four legions, boarded ships on the Rhine and sailed through the canal of Drusus and the Zuyder-Zee, reaching the mouth of the Ems by sea. The hereditary enemies of the Cherusci, the Chauci, now accommodated the Romans. Stertinius, with several light troops, suddenly attacked the Bructeri and finally managed to recover the beaten XXXI Legion's eagle. (Greenwood, 1836)

After his force had ravaged the entire area between the Ems and the Lippe, Germanicus spoke to Caecina. He said, *"Go towards the Teutoburg Forest and the Kalkriese Hill area and survey the land. I want you and your legions to build roads over the swamps!"*

Varus and his legions had perished at the exact point due to their violation of the Germanic people's high spirits and honour, and heaps of white bones marked the spot. There were some half-ruined mounds showing places where the slaughter of the Roman forces had been the greatest. The Roman army now performed the rites of burial while there were loud lamentations of the whole army because no one knew if he was burying a relative or stranger's remains. With eyes, which were flowing with tears, and with revenge in their hearts, the men of the army of Germanicus set off in pursuit of the Germanic tribesmen.

Armin knew that his country's strength lay in the woods and marshes, and for those reasons, he retreated to a position that was open in the front of it but was covered by swamps. His flanks and rear were protected by dense forests, hiding the majority of his infantry forces. At the open ground at the front of his position, he only showed small numbers of warriors hoping that the Romans would attack. Germanicus did precisely that, directing his cavalry and light infantry to charge the front of the Germanic position. The result of this was that the Romans found themselves attacked by the Germanic warriors on both flanks. They had suddenly and in large numbers attacked the Romans from the woods, putting the Roman cavalry to flight.

Meanwhile, the Cherusci cavalry squadrons were attacking the Roman Auxiliary Cohorts. A chief of the 'One Hundred' called out to his men. He yelled, *"Look at how the Roman cowards are running from the fight! Our cavalry has gone past many of them, chasing after the Roman leaders! Men of the 'One hundred', forward and smash everyone you see who is not of Germanic blood!"*

That resulted in the mass of Roman soldiers and horses being pushed back until they were on broken and uneven ground, which aided their Germanic enemies. Suddenly, a cheer went through the Roman ranks as Germanicus broke through a section of the line with his cavalry. Germanicus and his horsemen did not wait around, but they retreated to the Ems River.

Having successfully retreated to the Ems, Germanicus and his men embarked onto ships while Caecina proceeded overland to his quarters at Castra Vetera. Trying to lighten the load over the flats at the mouth of the Ems, two legions under the command of Caecina left the ships with orders to march by the coast road to a point where the Roman fleet could take them back on board.

Due to the Romans' ignorance and their Germanic enemies' activity, both of these legions' retreat was a great disaster. Armin adhered to the type of warfare that had already proved to be so effective against the Romans and was so well applied by his countrymen.

The march of Caecina was in part along an ancient and decayed causeway, initially constructed by Domitius Ahenobarbus. That was made of wooden beams laid over a marshy tract and was about ten miles in length. The soil on either side of this was slippery bog or slime, and that was skirted at long way away from there by gently rising hills which were covered by dense forests.

Armin and his lightly armed men, having left everything which could impede their progress behind them, moved quickly through their well-known forest paths and so were in advance of the Romans, who were marching slowly towards the same point weighed down by baggage and without light infantry who were capable of coping with the Germanic Warriors. Caecina now found the causeway was so rotten that it was necessary to reconstruct it.

A scout from his heavy infantry legions reported to Caecina. He saluted his Roman general and spoke to him. He said, *"Sir, we are in a lot of trouble! Although you have located this camp on the firmest ground available, it is still not firm ground, and it may give us much trouble!*

Many of our men are complaining of being attacked by leeches, and there are viper snakes that have bitten some of our men. Worst of all, we are surrounded by German warriors who appear to be at a strength that is more than five times the number of soldiers we have!"

Caecina replied, *"Decanus, return to your unit and make sure that all of our soldiers understand that we must work to restore the rotten causeway. One legion shall provide protection, while three other legions shall perform the work!*

There shall be armed combat units with all working parties! Other combat units shall patrol the perimeter of the causeway and provide continuous roving protections for the work parties. As well, there shall be stations at intervals to provide protection where there shall be reserves on hand. So, do not worry yourself too much, for our safety is at hand!"

The Cheruscian Warriors were accustomed to using their long spears with great effect on even the most slippery ground and, at extraordinary distances, avoided close combat. The Roman soldiers had to have firm footings to be able to hurl their javelins with any advantage. Also, the Romans were wearing heavy armour found that they had to struggle to make progress because of the swampy ground on either side of them.

However, Caecina was not Varus, and throughout the first day, his soldiers continued to fight their Germanic enemies. Darkness falling upon them did not give them any respite because the Germanic enemy was active and alert all night. They had managed to dam up the waters on the high grounds, and then they opened up the sluices, thereby flooding the stations and drowning the works of the Romans who now had their labours made doubly exhausting.

Due to dejection, which was quickly spreading through his army's ranks, Caecina realised that inaction was fatal and therefore made a strong effort to clear the forests on his flanks. He formed part of one legion on the right and a second on the causeway's left sides and placed a strong advanced guard on the partly finished road. He organised a second legion to protect the rear. A narrow bit of firm ground between the forests and the marsh areas enabled him to do this. The baggage was sent forward along the outskirts of the woods.

After a day of non-stop fighting, much bloodshed and great fatigue, he succeeded in reaching the marsh's outer edges and camped for the night on this stronger ground. On this night, like the first one, it was spent in constant watchfulness and many alarms.

From the forested areas came the sounds of festivities being had by Rome's Germanic enemies and their triumphant yells. Simultaneously, the Romans' fires burned dimly, and the legionnaires were talking in whispers while they were lying dejectedly if they could or just wandering around from tent to tent expressing their anxiety.

Elated Germanic Warriors Attack Caecina

The dawn showed no better prospects for the coming day. Germanic warriors had repeatedly broken through the Roman line of march, and the Roman soldiers became confused and disoriented. The Roman army's baggage had now sunk so far into the unstable soil that it was immovable, and then Armin was seen cheering on his warriors to battle. He was heard to exclaim, *"Look at that; it is Varus and his legions again, let these new invaders of our country have the same fate!"* (Greenwood, 1836)

At an 'Information and Orders Group', held to discuss the Germanic attacks, Caecina issued orders. He said, *"All Roman soldiers must go back into their trenches and resist the expected attack of the Germans!"* That resulted in the worn-out and dispirited Romans silently returning to their stations in the trenches. Meanwhile, the German warriors were pressing their commanders to lead assaults on the Roman camp. Armin argued against that.

He said, *"I realise that many of you want to get stuck into the Romans yet again because you feel that they are in a weakened state due to their losses of men! However, I am cautioning you all to abandon your ideas of assaulting the Roman camp! It will be far better for us to let once again the Roman pigs march! By doing so, we shall have minimal casualties while we inflict maximum casualties among the enemy!"*

His uncle Inguionerus answered him. He said, *"Armin, let us not mess about with your old tactics of surrounding and harassing the enemy! There is only total victory to be had if we attack the Roman camp, which will give us much booty and many Roman prisoners! Armin, you are too cautious, and I do not like that! My men and I will attack the Roman camp now, no matter what you say!"* That suited many of the members of Inguionerus' unit because they were greedy for plunder. So, he organised the attack, and at the break of day, the Roman lines were fiercely assaulted.

The Roman soldiers were dying quickly under the Germanic warriors' spears. The Roman cavalry was sliding about upon the soil, which was slippery due to the blood soaking the ground because of the slaughter. Caecina suddenly had his horse killed under him, and he narrowly avoided falling into the hands of his enemies.

The lust for plunder among the Germanic warriors was once again the Roman army's salvation, and a large part of the baggage was abandoned to them. While the barbarians were intent on their plunder, the Romans obtained enough time to erect defences strong enough to give them a degree of protection for the night. The loss of many of their entrenching tools rendered the work tiresome and inefficient, as well; the tents and dressings needed by the wounded soldiers were now in the hands of the enemy.

That night a horse broke free from its tether and ran through the Roman camp, accompanied by the shouts of those trying to catch it, now spread panic throughout the camp, resulting in the whole army rushing towards an opposite gate to the one where the disturbance with the horse had taken place.

Caecina was the first to realise that this was a false alarm, so he ran towards the gate shouting orders and assurances, but to no avail, and he threw himself across the gate's opening in such a way that his soldiers would have to pass over his body if they continued their cowardly running away from the battle. His leadership, by example, was successful, and both order and discipline were restored, but his soldiers were still without hope and feeling dejected.

Caecina ordered, *"We shall now retreat as far as the Rhine! While we are retreating, we shall have constant patrolling of our line of march to ensure that we are not surprised by unexpected enemy attacks upon us!"* That resulted in the Roman army reaching the Rhine without further attacks upon them. There were reports that Caecina had been cut off and that he was about to lose his legions as well. While at Roman posts along the Rhine, the garrison soldiers broke down the bridges and abandoned their posts.

Then, an alert sentry went to his decanus. He said, *"Decanus, I think that we are saved! Approaching is Agrippina, the wife of Germanicus and her escort!"* The decanus replied, *"Very good! Munifex, go and introduce yourself to Agrippina and then take her to see our centurion!"* the munifex did as ordered, and soon Agrippina was among the soldiers, giving out food and dressing their wounds. In general, her presence lifted the spirits of the dejected Roman soldiers. She also gave out dressings for those men whom she did not treat herself.

The Retreat of Vitellius

The retreat of Germanicus by sea also had dangers. Due to their ignorance of the tides and the onset of the autumn gales, Vitellius and his two legions lost all of their baggage and camp equipment and many soldiers drowned before they reached the place where they had to disembark from the ships.

After the army entered its winter living quarters, it was found to be so greatly reduced in the numbers of men and equipment that the entire resources of Gaul, Spain and Italy were required to resupply the losses in arms, men, horses, equipment and treasure. The expedition was disastrous to the Romans, even though it had been skilfully planned. Tiberius was speaking to Germanicus. He said, *"Germanicus, my nephew, I like your standing as a soldier, but the fact is that you now have had three expeditions, all of which have been failures!*

Your third expedition has been so great a failure that it requires Gaul, Spain, and Italy's combined resources to resupply the losses of soldiers, their arms, horses and equipment, and even the treasure of two legions!

So, whatever praise is due to you for your being a good soldier, it is lessened by your failure in three successive campaigns, which have also shaken your standing as a statesman. On top of that, as the Emperor, I am anxious about the losses sustained by the army. Which is leading me to look at sounder views!" The

Germanic tribesmen, on the other hand, had decisive successes. My great leader, Armin alone, stands out as the wisest and most able of the Germanic generals.

Germanicus said, *"Tiberius, you are the Emperor, and you have my complete allegiance. I am aware that you must now consider removing me from my command. However, I still wish to recover the conquests of my father in Germania. If you let me do so, I want to recruit a Rhenish corps from among the Rhenane Germans who settled in Gaul. By using them against their former countrymen, it could even things up for Rome! I am willing even to use my fortune to help to pay for a fourth expedition!"*

Tiberius said, *"Very well, Germanicus, go ahead and recruit your Rhenish Corps. I shall stand by you, and Iam permitting to use the entire resources of Italy, Spain and Gaul upon this fourth expedition! Just make sure that you are successful this time, or even I cannot help you!"*

The Fourth Expedition of Germanicus

By now, it was found that the neighbouring Gallic provinces were incapable of supplying the necessary stores, horses ad baggage wagons for the distant and expensive land campaigns. Addressing his soldiers, Germanicus spoke. He said, *"We are going into Germania. I know of the dangers of a long march or retreat through that place because it is a place without roads, and it has deep rivers, swamps intersect it, and it has dense forests! Therefore, I have had a fleet of ships built which are large enough to transport my entire army and its provisions for the season!*

I am moving six entire legions to Aliso, which is under siege from the Cherusci and their confederates!" A Roman scout from Germanicus forces was with his contubernium[35] when he quietly called for his decanus. When the decanus arrived, the scout said, *"Decanus, look through this bush; towards the creek in front of the forest over there! You will see two women in the company of an older Chatti warrior! What do you want us to do?"*

Decanus Sentitius looked and saw the women and their lone male escort. He said, *"Munifex, there are eight of us Romans here, and we can easily overcome those three people. The two women among them should give us all a goodfuck when we rape the bitches!"* That resulted n the eight Romans firstly surrounding the group of two women and one older male warrior, after which they killed the warrior and raped the two women. With the two women now held captive, the members of the contubernium returned to their legion and reported to their Optio.

Decanus Setitius said, *"Optio, we captured two Germanic women. What do you want to have done with them?"* The optio said, *"Take them both to our centurion! I just hope you have not done anything to your two female prisoners because we are currently in a war situation with several Germanic tribes! What we do not need is more tribes joining the actions of the rebels against Rome! If these women turn out to be Chatti, it may go against you*

---

[35] Contuberium was an eight man tent unit and the smallest sub-unit of the Roman army. Similar to the American squad or the ten man infantry section of the Australian army.

or result in your promotion depending upon what is decided by the centurion."

Centurion Bascilius was in his tent when Decanus Setitius reported to him. The decanus saluted his officer and spoke. He said, *"Sir, we have captured two Germanic women! They are both outside!"* Bascilius said, *"It is good that I can speak a little of the barbarous German language. Bring the two women in, and I shall try to find out who they both are and what they have been doing!"*

The two women were bought into his tent, and the centurion said, *"I am Centurion Bascilius, my commander is General Silius, and he is under Germanicus command. I want to know who both of you are and what you have been doing so close to Roman army units!"* The women spoke. The older one said, *"My name is Gude, and I am the wife of Theobaldric, the chieftain of the Chatti! When my husband finds out that both myself and my daughter have been raped by your soldiers and taken prisoner, you shall find the Chatti joining the Cherusci and other Germanic tribes to hunt you Romans down and to kill you!"*

That prompted the younger woman to speak. She said, *"I am Liepmayt, and I am the daughter of the chieftain of the Chatti! When Pappa hears of how you Romans have raped and abducted my mother and me, you shall be most sorry!"* The centurion spoke to the other Romans near him. He said, *"Take these two German wenches to General Silius! He can have the responsibility of correctly dealing with these probable threats to the existence of Roman units!"*

Silius was impeded by stormy weather and therefore only collected a small amount of booty. Other than that and the two women's capture, he and his legions pressed on towards Aliso. The Cherusci were watching the Romans and simply abandoned their siege of Aliso and withdrew from in front of them. The Romans now found that the Germanic people had demolished the funeral mound erected to Varus's legions' memory.

Germanicus was in conversation with Silius. He said, *"Silius, all Romans under my command, including your legions, shall now restore the altar to Varus and his lost legions! After that, our combined forces shall re-establish communications between the fortress at Aliso and the new series of fortified posts linked by Roman roads! After that, I and my four legions shall move into the territory of the Batavi, and then we shall embark onto my fleet of one thousand ships which we shall sail into the North sea and finally land at the mouth of the Ems River!"*

The Angriarii were in revolt, and it was successfully put down by Germanicus. They now marched directly towards the Weser River, where Armin had taken up positions with the intent of forcing the Romans into battle. With the Romans was the brother of Armin called Flavus.

The Meeting of Armin and Flavus

When the Romans came into sight of the Germanic warriors, Armin sent a request to interview his brother to Caesar (Tiberius), who approved it. Flavus having Caesar's permission to do so, met his brother on opposite sides of the river which was flowing between the hostile armies.

Flavus had lost an eye while in the service of Rome, and it caused Armin to enquire, *"Where did you cop this injury to your head, losing your eye?"* Flavus replied, *"Well, my brother, that happened while I was in the service of Tiberius chasing down and killing the rebels of Pannonia in much the same way as you had done before me. I was a little too slow to stop a sword blow that was swung across my front, and it was only my Roman helmet that saved me from losing much of my head and dying. As it was, the other fellow died instead of me!"*

Armin asked, *"And what has been your reward? Did you get an increase in pay, a crown and other military distinctions?"* Flavus said, *"No, none of those things, just the normal pay of a junior officer of the Roman army as you have done. Rome is ready and willing to give clemency to repentant rebels. I can assure you that if you were to return to the embrace of Rome and again swear allegiance to Rome, then neither your wife nor child would be considered to be enemies of Rome, and they would receive mercy!"*

Flavus could see that he had touched a raw nerve in his brother's heart. He said, *"Yes, Armin, that is correct, your wife has given birth to your son. They are both well, and they are slaves and the property of Titus Flavious Comptomius. They are living in his villa at Ravenna. Thusnelda named your son Thumelic, but Germanicus had him renamed to Thumelicus because he thinks that Thumelic sounds too Germanic and could become a danger in the future!"*

Armin did not bother replying to such selfish considerations. He said, *"Flavus, your country of Germania claims you. The ancient liberties and our gods of Wodin and Thor call upon you to end this practice of being a traitor of your people. Our mother joins her voice with theirs and implores you to take your natural place as a chief of the Cherusci and not remain an alien and traitor to our people, kindred and friends!"*

These attempts at persuasion by both brothers failed, and they now began angry name-calling and verbally menaced each other. It was only the wide river flowing between them that stopped Armin from closing with and killing his own brother on that day.

Flavus was so worked up and angry that he called for a horse, his armour and weapons, and having obtained them, he began to cross over to where Armin was waiting for him. Both men had blood and murder in their hearts, and it was only stopped from going further when the commanding officer of Flavus, the Roman General Stertinius, intervened. He said, *"Flavus, have you taken leave of your senses? Arminius is by far the most capable fighter for miles around here. He still moves like a cat, and he still has the agility of a leopard! On the other hand, you have been wounded and have lost an eye while your brother is unharmed!*

He moves very well, and if you meet him in your current condition, he will surely kill you! You have lost an eye, and that is something else that will give Arminius the edge over you! I am hereby ordering you to return to your tent and to clean your weapons! Do not fret over what your brother is calling you.

Words are just that, and they cannot hurt you, but Arminius certainly can and will do so! When you have finished cleaning your weapons, I want you to clean my weapons as well. That should keep you occupied and out of harm's way. You will thank me for this one day!" Without further ado, Flavus returned to his tent and cleaned his weapons as he had been ordered. He was still seething from the verbal attack of his brother, but he now saw the good sense of what his commanding officer had told him.

The Romans Attempt to Cross the River

The next morning, the Germanic warriors appeared on the opposite river bank and drew much Roman attention to themselves. A decanus reported to Germanicus. He said, *"Sir, there are large numbers of the Germanic enemy drawing our attention to themselves! They appear to want to fight us for possession of the river! What you want us to do, sir?"*

Germanicus said, *"Think you for the information decanus. Now it is time for you to return to your sub-unit. On the way back, you are to deliver a message from me to General Stertinius. You must tell him to hurry here and confer with me about the situation with the German warriors!"* The decanus said, *"Yes, sir, consider it to be done!"* He then left for the lodgings of General Stertinius and found him. Upon finding the general, the decanus saluted and spoke. He said, *"Sir, Germanicus has ordered your presence at a conference immediately!"* He then saluted the general again and departed, returning to his sub-unit.

General Stertinius entered the tent of Germanicus and saluted him as he was walking into the large tent. He said, *"Germanicus, my liege, what is the problem?"* Germanicus said, *"It is good that you are here, Stertinius. We are having some major problems with the Germanic warriors from across the river. I need you to go across the river at the ford located about a thousand paces from here, and then I want you and your cavalry forces to sweep both sides of the river between here and the ford. Make sure that you clear all enemy warriors out of that area. That is so that we can build a bridge which our army can use for a line of retreat if things go against us!"*

The Roman cavalry did as ordered and proceeded to sweep both sides of the river. Meanwhile, the barbarians retreated into the forest and let the Romans complete their bridge without further attack. A decanus and his contubernium reported the findings of their recent scouting activities to Germanicus. The decanus saluted his general, and then he spoke.

He said, *"Sir, my contubernium and I have been scouting the whole area, and we have found that your army is almost in the lap of the German army commanded by Arminius! It is now night time, and if you were to go outside of your command tent, you would be able to see the campfires of the enemy through the foliage of the trees here. That is how close we are to the enemy! Arminius and his forces are close by, and he will likely attack us in the morning or even possibly during the night!* Germanicus said, *"Oh, I see! Thank you, decanus, for bringing this to my attention!"* He then put on a disguise and walked through his army camp that night, listening to his soldiers' conversations.

What he heard convinced him that his army resected him and hated the Germanic enemy. With the half-expected night-time attack not taking place, Germanicus retired to his tent and thought about making the customary pep talk delivered to Roman soldiers on the eve of a battle and how best to stimulate the courage of the Roman soldiers. He assembled his soldiers and spoke to them. He said, *"Officers and soldiers of Rome! We are here to do the glorious work of hunting down and killing the Germanic warriors who have wiped out a large part of the Roman army and killed the Roman Governor of Germania! The Germans are both lightly and indifferently armed, and also, they are nothing but cowards! So, when you face them in the morning, you should easily be able to beat them!"*

Over on the other side of the river, Armin was likewise addressing his warriors. He said, *"These Romans are nothing but the shit from the army that produced men like Varus. These men have mutinied against their own officers. They now have scars on their backs from the disciplinary action of flogging, which was taken against them as punishment! These cowardly skulking Roman pigs have come by sea to avoid facing us on land because they know that you will beat them again and again!*

They also have their ships anchored on the river to give an alternative escape route when we beat them again! Remember their cruelty and greed. Remember what these poor excuses for men have done to your women, children, relative and infirm people of many areas! Bear in mind that you now have no option except to maintain the liberty of Germania or die!"

The Battle of Idistavista

Armin's army was in strong positions on the plain, which the Romans called Idistavista, and it lies between the Weser River and some hills which form an irregular line. Most of his army was at rest in open forest, with the greater part of it concealed by the forest. The wings were made up of Cherusci cavalry, which took up positions on the high ground in front of Armin's position and was ready to flank the Roman attack.

While Germanicus was preparing for battle and before his army was committed to the assault, Inguionerus, Armin's uncle, threw caution to the wind and attacked Germanicus' army. He abandoned the defensive system that worked so well for the Germanic tribesmen and charged the Romans. At once, the Roman cavalry charged them in the flanks and the rear, resulting in a great slaughter of Cherusci cavalry. After that, the main body withdrew into the forest while some units were pushed into the river. Armin was wounded, and Inguionerus only escaped by cutting his way through Roman enemies.

The Romans now erected a mound as a memorial of their victory against the Germanic people, complete with the names of the beaten tribes inscribed upon it. That insulted and infuriated the Germanic warriors. They ignored their wounds and the shame of suffering a defeat at Roman hands, resulting in them making a sudden and well-planned assault upon the Romans. They succeeded in throwing the Romans into disorder. The following day, Armin's army was again in position between the river and the forest. The front of his position was only accessible through thickly forested areas, and Armin's cavalry forces were out of sight but ready to attack the legions.

Germanicus surveyed the line of his enemies and called an 'Information and Orders Group', during which he addressed his officers. He said, *"General Tubero, take you cavalry forces and penetrate the front of the Germanic forces before us! While you are doing that, I shall be leading other legions to attack the opposite wing!"*

The fighting was heavy, and the Roman losses were such that Germanicus called another 'Information and Orders Group'. He spoke to his soldiers. He said, *"We are withdrawing all Roman units from engaging the enemy! All Romans shall be removed from combat until we can get our war machines into position on the open ground in front of the Germanic positions."* When that was done, the Germanic warriors had no resistance to these ancient artillery types and were swept from the battlefield. That allowed the Romans to enter the forest in that direction while the infantry opposite and the cavalry in front established themselves on the open front of the Germanic position.

The Romans were located between the river and a line of hills occupied by Armin's army. The contest between the two armies was obstinate and bloody. Armin was disabled by his wounds and did not take part in the battle. His uncle, Ingeruionerus, rushed from one part of the battle to another, encouraging all by his presence.

On the opposite side, Germanicus was exposing himself in front of the battle without his helmet. He was calling out encouragement to Roman soldiers. He said, *"Roman soldiers! Keep on slaying the Germanic warriors, and do not give them any mercy! Just kill them all! We must kill the Germans because nothing but the complete extermination of the Germanic warriors and their families can end this war!"* During the evening of the day, Germanicus ordered a legion to withdraw from the fighting and prepare a fortified camp so that the Romans could sleep safely for the night.

The Roman historian called Tacitus wrote, *"The cavalry fought with doubtful success, and no booty was taken other than a small number of weapons."* He then wrote what has since been described as pure propaganda, possibly from being ordered to do so by Germanicus or Tiberius. He wrote, *"The army of Tiberius Caesar, after vanquishing all Germanic nations between the Rhine and the Elbe, erected a monument to Mars, Jupiter and Augustus!"* This written passage has been proven to be a pack of lies!

What really happened was that Germanicus and his army never reached the Elbe River, and they had not been in contact with the Germanic nations along the way. Germanicus decided to retreat out of Germania, even though the military operations season was only about half over. He withdrew his army to the Ems River, and there, he embarked half of his forces onto the fleet of ships anchoured there. At an 'Orders and Information Group' that was called to discuss the tactical situation between officers, Germanicus spoke. He said, *"Gentlemen, half of this army is boarding the ships before us for easy transport to the Rhineland bases, while the remaining half shall march overland to the quarters on the Rhine."*

Soon after departing for the Rhineland on the Rhine's west bank, the fleet found itself in the path of a great storm. Many of the Roman ships filled with water and sank. Other ships were wrecked upon the coasts of the Chauci and Angriarii. Meanwhile, many other ships were driven into the ocean and sought refuge in barbarian Briton ports. All of this resulted in the heavy loss of men, horses, cattle, and stores. Germanicus collected a small squadron of the surviving ships and searched for his shipwrecked army's scattered remains.

The news of the destruction of the Roman fleet quickly reached the ears of the Germanic warriors. Germanicus was in conference with his officers. He said, *"Gentlemen, we must impress politically, the Roman Senate! In order to do so, it appears to me that a sudden attack upon the Chatti is necessary for us to prevail in Rome! In particular, it is essential to impress Tiberius!*

It does not matter how much we may try to disguise it; the fact remains that the entire Fourth Expedition has been a very costly total disaster! The only thing that we achieved has been the recovery of the last of the missing eagle of the legions of Varus!

There were some brilliant successes, but they were not decisive! No ground was gained, and the defeat of Varus has not been avenged! Arminius remains at large, and he still has a large, capable army which is an increasing security problem for Rome! What is even worse is that Germania remains unconquered and free! I now command all Roman army units to leave Germania, and they are never to return!"

War Between Armin and Marobod

There was an outbreak of war between the Mark-Mannen commanded by Marobod and Armin's forces, soon after Germanicus and the Romans left Germania.

Armin's uncle Inguionerus had for a long time been highly jealous of Armin and his abilities. He became aggrieved at taking orders from his nephew, and he thought it was derogatory for him to be serving under the command of someone who was younger than himself. He wanted to be leading the Germanic army himself and thought of himself as being more worthy of the leadership role than was his nephew, Armin. He, therefore, simply deserted Armin's army and went over to serve Marobod.

A great battle was fought, which had severe consequences for Marobod. The right wings of both armies were devastated with great slaughter, and by the end of the day, things were finely balanced, making both armies look forward to the following day to improve their positions. Marobod did not want to risk everything on one battle and withdrew to stronger ground. That was a mistake because it resulted in his men seeing it as a confession of defeat, and so, they deserted him.

Having been beaten, he wrote to Tiberius, asking for assistance. Tiberius was happy that Marobod was having difficulty. So, the Roman Emperor replied, *"I know of no claim you can make for assistance from Rome to help you in your fight against Arminius and his Cherusci, seeing that you were actively allied with Arminius's forces when he was at war with Rome. When Rome was fighting Arminius, you supplied him with five hundred and twenty to five hundred and eighty of your Mark-Manner warriors, and they did much to assist the wiping out of the three best legions of heavy infantry and all supporting units! I lost more than twenty thousand men in the battle of the Teutoburg Forest!"*

As everyone around him had now forsaken him, Marobod decided to throw himself upon the protection of Tiberius. Therefore, he went past the Danube and into Noricum. There, he wrote to Tiberius, *"Tiberius, I remind you that I have always preferred an alliance with Rome rather than the Germanic upstart called Arminius! I was only in association with him because Rome would not give me an alliance!"* Tiberius replied, *"You may rely upon a safe and honourable retreat in Italy if you choose to reside here. If your affairs happen to take you elsewhere, you may come and go as freely as your circumstances require."*

That same day, Tiberius spoke in the Roman Senate. He said, *"Fellow Romans, I have duped the leader of Bohemia, known as Marobod, to come and live in Italy! If he does come here, he will be imprisoned immediately because he is dangerous and close to Rome's frontiers! He is as dangerous to us as was Philip of Macedonia had been to Athens and as dangerous to Rome as is the other big danger to us of Arminius!*

He went on to enlarge upon the talents of Marobod, the fierce and warlike character of the nations he once ruled over and their closeness to Rome. Tiberius then praised up his management of the affairs that were likely to bring down this formidable power. Marobod, relying on the solemn pledge of safety and freedom he received from Tiberius, went to Italy. Upon arrival in Italy, Marobod was taken prisoner and detained at Ravenna for the purpose of using him as a bargaining tool in case the Suevi people should again become restive and attack Romans.

The Death of Arminius

Armin was now aiming at sovereign power and becoming king of the United Germanic Tribespeople. He was aiming at uniting the Germanic tribes into a single and powerful nation. Rome greatly feared that possibility. His desire to become the king of a united Germania put him at odds with his countrymen's independent nature;

they did not want a king of anywhere telling them what to do or how to do it!

Armin called a 'Council of War' and addressed us all. He said, *"Welcome, dear comrades, we have achieved much, and the threats from the Roman bullies no longer trouble us, for they have been crushed! Our most recent threat has comefrom one of our own countrymen, namely, Marobod! He has also been crushed! He sought assistance from the Roman Emporer Tiberius, and he deserves what Tiberius has done to him! He is now locked up in a Roman prison cell, and I hope that he rots there!*

Many others from other Germanic tribes have joined the Cherusci people, and as a result, we have become very strong! Now then, many of you are clamouring to return to the old ways whereby all tribes were completely independent of each other and not part of any nation or empire! Those times are past now, and we must unite and become a single country complete with its army and navy to make sure that never again can bullies like Romans invade us! Hear me and consider carefully what I am saying. I have been the best leader you have ever had, and under my leadership, Germania has become free of the Roman pest and all other intruders! As a single nation with me as the king, Germania will become stronger, and our people will, at last, have the security and the luxuries that they want!"

Armin had barely finished speaking when an interjector shouted, *"No, and bullshit to everything you say! I do not want any king from anywhere telling my people what to do, not ever! Not only that, but I am putting you on notice, Armin, that I am going to do everything in my power to bring you down, and that includes killing you if that should become possible! As far as I am concerned, all tribes in Germania must remain free and totally independent of each other! As you know, I have already fought against you, on the side of Marobod. I am going to make sure that your bid to become the king of all Germania will fail!"*

I looked around the assembly, and I noticed that this was being said by Armin's uncle Inguionerus and I began thinking, *"Now then, what the hell is the matter with this traitorous arsehole? He has already been fighting against Armin by going over to Marobod!"*

There were now some mutterings among the assembly of warriors, and it soon broke up into small groups discussing the pros and cons of what Armin had said. Such was Armin's charisma that only he could have gathered enough support to become king of the Germanic people at that time. That was well-known to his father-in-law, Segestes and his uncle Inguionerus. Both of these men now formed a group of plotters who were determined to kill the hero of Germania at the first opportunity.

I went to Armin and said, *"Armin, you know that you can always count on me and that I will do whatever is necessary to make sure that you remain as the leader of the Germanic tribes! We must from now on be very careful because a group of conspirators led by your uncle Inguioerus and your father-in-law, Segestes, have been openly heard to say that they both want you dead!"* I had barely finished saying that when a group of eight Germanic warriors burst into the building where Armin and I were having our conversation.

We were both in our chainmail armour, and we had our weapons with us. So, we both drew our swords while I yelled, *"Armin, take the traitorous arsehole on your left while I dispatch those two on your right-hand side!"* That having been said, we charged the intruders and killed all eight of them. I said to Armin, *"Armin, it is high time to get the fuck out of here! There are more of the arseholes outside, so we have a fight on our hands!"* We went outside the house to where our horses were, mounted a horse each and escaped.

We had only gone a short distance when Armin said, *"Thank you, Adalhard, for delivering me from those arseholes! I noticed that both my father-in-law, Segestes and my uncle, Inguionerus, were outside the house, directing their men! Great, just great, when a man's own family turns against him! I am absolutely disgusted!"*

Four days after our escape from the plotters, I became sick. I was violently ill and completely bedridden. Armin and I were both resting in the home of a friend called Alafuns. Two men approached him, and one of them spoke. He said, *"Armin's uncle Inguionerus has ordered us to attempt to get Armin to go to the home of Inguionerus at the next village about five miles from here. If you know where Armin may be, tell him that both his father, Segimer and his uncle Inguionerus want him to go to the home of Inguionerus to try to patch up the differences between them and to end up with a stronger Germania!"*

Adalfuns went back into the house, and I clearly heard him tell Armin what the messengers from Inguionerus had said. That resulted in Armin now saying, *"Adalfuns, my right-hand man, Adalhard, is currently too sick to move anywhere, and I have to leave him here to recover. I am both surprised and disappointed that my uncle Inguionerus would work against me. It is reassuring that my own Father, Segimer, shall be there; otherwise, I would suspect that the proposed meeting is a trap! I feel that I must attend this meeting, and I am taking you with me as my bodyguard!"*

Adalfuns and Armin arrived at the home of Inguionerus, and immediately, Armin was uneasy. He said, *"Adalfuns, I can see twelve horses near the home of my uncle, and I suspect a trap! If not for the presence of my father's horse among the other ones, I would immediately leave here! The presence of my father reassures me. So, before we enter the house, we shall both have our sords in our hands!* Both men drew their swords and proceeded to enter the house with their weapons in their hands.

Armin saw his father Segimer, who rose from his seat and embraced him and held Armin's arms down to his side as they were entering. While he had his arms pinned down by his father, Armin noticed that both his uncle Inguionerus and his father-in-law Segestes stood up and moved towards Armin. Suddenly, Adalfuns hit Armin on his side with a sword because he was one of the conspirators. Although the blow stunned Armin, it did not kill him. He broke free from his father's embrace and loudly spoke. He said, *"My father, why are you here among the conspirators who are trying to kill me? This is really a trap, which is what I expect from my father-in-law and my uncle, but to see you, my own father, among the traitorous scum trying to kill me is heart-breaking! You are all traitorous murdering conspirators, so fuck all of you!"* Having said that, Armin attacked his enemies, and he killed three of them. Armin fought on, but he was surrounded by enemies who were pressing in from all sides. One of the conspirators managed to plunge a short spear into the back of Armin. It was the cowardly Segestes who did that, and he called to the other conspirators. He said, *"I have put a spear into the back of Armin! Now is your chance to kill him using your swords because he will be a lot weaker now!"*

That is how the liberator and hero of Germania died, murdered by the jealous members of his own family who were very envious of him! Armin shook the entire Roman Empire, not when it was weak and building up its strength, but when it was at the height of its power. He was killed by the conspirators, which included his father, his uncle and his father-in-law. He was aged thirty-eight years at the time of his death. His memory lives on in the stories and songs of the Germanic people to this day.

Thusnelda and Thumelicus as Slaves

Both Thusnelda and her three-year-old son, called Thumelicus, were delivered to the villa of Titus Flavius Comptomius near Ravenna and began their service as slaves of that Roman. Titus's wife, named Octavia, immediately disliked Thusnelda, seeing her as a potential rival for her husband's affections. After Thusnelda had been the slave of Titus for three weeks, she was visited by Flavus, Armin's brother.

Flavus said, *"Thusnelda, you husband, my brother Armin, has been successful in driving all Roman army units out of Germania! However, that has not done him any good because his own family members have murdered him! You no longer have to undergo the degrading triumphs for Romans like Germanicus, and as long as you do not actively work against Roman rule, all will go well for you!*

That made Thusnelda say, *"Oh Armin, my love, you have liberated our people from the Roman yoke just as you always said you would! Your brother Flavus tells me that the members of your family murdered you! I shall always be utterly faithful to you, my love, and I shall never remarry, even if I can stop being a slave. If my owners demand that I have sex with them, they can force me to do so, but they shall never have the love and satisfying sex that I have given you, my love. I am yours forever!"* Thusnelda then became sadder and sadder over time. Eventually, she steadied herself down and began to live to nurture and educate her toddler son, Thumelicus.

Thusnelda, went on with educating Thumelicus with the aid of some Roman teachers. He learned Roman history and how to both read and write in Latin. The main duties of Thusnelda were those of being a personal slave attendant to both of both Titus and Octavia. That is how Thusnelda was occupied for the next seven years. A Messenger from Tiberius arrived. His message said, *"By order of Tiberius, Emperor of Rome, Thumelicus shall enter the gladiator Academy at Ravenna immediately because he is now aged ten years!"*

Some weeks later, her owner Titus, called her into his villa. She could immediately see that Titus's wife was not present, and she began to feel uneasy. Titus made sexual advances to her, and Thusnelda responded by asking, *"Titus, I fully realise that you want to fuck me, but I do not want to have sex with you. Your wife, Octavia, has made it very clear to me that she does not like my presence anywhere near you, and she may cause us both a lot of trouble if you persist in trying to fuck me!"*

Titus replied, *"I have discussed this situation with Octavia. She has told me that if I fuck you, she will do the same thing to you simultaneously, using her dildo! What she wants to do is to fuck you using her dildo while you are bent over, with your arms around my waist, and while you have my prick in your mouth giving me oral sex! She is actually in the next room, and she has bathed herself and made herself both attractive and pleasant smelling!"*

Just then, Octavia walked into the room where both Titus and Thusnelda were. She said, *"Thusnelda, take off all of your clothes right now!"* She was reluctant to obey, so Octavia said, *"Thusnelda, you are a slave, and you have to do whatever Titus or I want! Get your clothes off and then kneel in front of my husband and undress the lower parts of his body. When you have done that, you shall place his penis into your mouth. You shall then wrap your arms around his waist, and you will then raise your body until such time as you are standing but bent over with your arms around his waist and his prick still in your mouth! With you being bent over, it will allow me to insert my dildo into your vagina, and I then fuck you from behind you while Titus is fucking your mouth! You will suck his prick until he comes into your mouth!"*

This rather upset Thusnelda, who was feeling very despodent due to her losses of her husband and her son. She did not want to have sex with either one of the Romans, let alone two at once! All the same, she pretended to do as she had been ordered. Thusnelda, knelt in front of Titus and lifted his short tunic, exposing his penis. She then gently stroked his penis and licked it several times before she placed it into her mouth. She then began to suck it while she stood up but was still bent over with his penis in her mouth. Octavia had meanwhile inserted the dildo into herself, and she now inserted the other end of it into Thusnelda's vagina.

Octavia said, *"Titus, my husband, fuck her mouth until you deposit your semen into it and really cheapen this Germanic bitch! Hold her head in your hands while you fuck her mouth! Jam using my dildo to fuck her from behind her at the same time!* Meanwhile, Thusnelda felt both very cheapened and aggrieved by what these two Romans were doing to her. She was very dismayed that she was being abused by the two of them at the same time! Thusnelda became so disgusted that she bit Titus on the head of his penis as hard as she could!

That resulted in Titus screaming in pain, and he felt onto the floor. Thusnelda now kicked him into the testes as hard as she could. She removed the dildo from herself and then grabbed a gladius hanging on the wall and used it to stab Octavia repeatedly. Thusnelda knew that when she was caught, the Romans would crucify her. She got dressed and went into the kitchen area of the villa. There she found a lot much hemlock and proceeded to take it. Hours later, other slaves arrived to do their chores for Titus and Octavia.

They discovered the bodies of Octavia and Thusnelda. Titus was still alive, although he was in pain. Titus said to a slave, *"The fucking German bitch assaulted me and killed Octavia! She then took her own life so that we cannot crucify her! Take the son of Thusnelda and take him to the gladiator school in*

Ravenna! I should have listened when I was informed that Tiberius wanted that to happen from the beginning!" Runner, take a message to Tiberius that Thumelicus, the son of Arminius, is now in the Gladiator school at Ravenna!"

Gladiators

Gladiators did not always fight to the death. If the losing gladiator had put his effort into the contest and therefore provided a good show, it was usual for the crowd watching to demand that his life be spared, and the gladiator concerned lived to fight again another day. A gladiator could signal that he was yielding to his opponent by holding out his hand with a finger extended. This submission was often allowed because combat-ready gladiators were valuable property.

The gladiators took their name from the Latin word describing the Roman short sword, the Gladius. There were a number of different types of gladiator. The gladiator was a professional performing sportsman in ancient Rome. The gladiators originally performed at funerals at Etruscan towns and cities, when two or more of them would fight to the death, probably for the purpose of providing the dead person with armed attendants in the afterlife. During gladiator performances in Rome, these shows became very popular.

There were several different types of gladiator, and we will start by looking at the Dimachaeri. These types of gladiator were often barbarians who fought against other gladiators using two swords at the same time. There was the Eques, who was a gladiator who specialized in fighting on horseback with swords.

The gladiator known as Essedari fought against other gladiators from a war chariot, which was at times armed with blades protruding from each axle for a distance of up to a yard or more in some cases. This would have made things rather difficult for the opposing gladiator, as he had to contend with the weapons used against him from the chariot, but he also had to stay out of the reach of the blades attached to the axle of the chariot.

The hoplomachi was a gladiator who had a complete suit of armour.

There were gladiators known as Laquerarii if talking about several gladiators fighting as a group, and they would fight their opponents using lassos. The gladiators known as Paegniarius would take on other gladiators using a combination of whips, clubs and shields. One of the gladiators that was considered as one of the most dangerous of them was the retiarius (singular) or retiarii (plural).

This gladiator was armed with a trident and a net. He also usually had chain mail armour over one arm and always fought without a helmet, which gave him better visibility than some of his opponents. Upon the contest beginning, the retiarius would try to entangle his opponent with the net he held in one hand and finish him off with the trident he held in his other hand. The mirmillones were armed with a sword and helmet in the Gallic style and took their name from the fish in the helmet's crest.

The Samnite fought with a large oblong shield, a visor and a plumed helmet and a gladius. The Thraces gladiator had a small round shield and a long-curved dagger. The Secutor (also known as pursuer) was the normal opponent of the retiarius, and he wore a loincloth, and wide belt, a greave on his left shin, to safeguard it. His right arm being protected by a thick wrapping of linen held by leather strapping or possible chain mail armour over the right shoulder and arm. He also had the protection of the heavy Roman shield and often used this to smash into his opponents. His weapon was the gladius.

Velites were gladiators armed with spears, which would fight other gladiators as opposing groups and to death. The manager or organizer of the gladiators was called the Lanista, and he was the overall manager of the gladiators and would supervise their training, their food and whom they were matched with. He would recruit new gladiators and see to the welfare of his existing ones.

The gladiator, particularly the trained and combat-ready ones, were considered valuable assets. They could usually come and go at will as long as they returned and put on a good show for the Lanista. As well as all of the above, gladiators sometimes went into battle with other gladiators while blindfolded.

The Threat to Rome's Security Deepens

Germanicus had sent news of the birth and renaming of Thumelicus directly to Tiberius. He became alarmed. He said, *"By Jupiter, how can this be? Are you really telling me that the destroyer of the Roman*

Governor and his legions now has a son? I find that most disturbing and dangerous for Rome because when he grows up, he can easily unite the Germanic clans behind him and do to Rome what his father has done! That must not be allowed to happen! What is his name, and how old is he?

Tiberius was told, *"Sir, he is now almost four years old. He is living in Ravenna, in the villa of Titus Flavius Comptomius, who owns him and his mother called Thusnelda!"* Tiberius relaxed a little and spoke. He said, *"I do not like taking things from the Roman citizens! Send an armed escort of soldiers to the villa of Titus Flavius Comptomius and take the son of Arminius. He was renamed Thumelicus by Germanicus to the Gladiator school at Ravenna when he reaches the age of ten years!*

I want him to be a gladiator, and when he is aged between fourteen and eighteen years, he shall face a champion gladiator who will kill him. That will end the problem of Arminius and his son once and for all time! Suppose we kill him in this sort of fashion. In that case, it should be accepted by the Germanic tribesmen because they place courage, martial ability and honour of the warrior above everything else!"

Thumelicus Trains as a Gladiator

While he was still living with his mother, Thusnelda, Thumelicus was to witness the humiliation and the rape of Thusnelda by her owners several times. That resulted in the instilling of hatred of the Roman ruling classes into the boy who was now nearing his tenth birthday.

Shortly after the initial interview between the Lanista[36] named Priscus, the Lanista spoke to him. Priscus said, *"My boy, I am taking a personal interest in your training! I want you to become the best of the best gladiators and to win your freedom! The only way you can do that is to win many fights and stay alive by doing so!"*

Thumelicus already liked the older man, and he spoke to him. He said, *"Mighty Priscus, I have heard of your deeds in the arena, and I am honoured that you are taking time to teach me how to survive and become successful at this occupation of being a gladiator! You can count on me to always strive to perform at my best and return wealth and prestige to you and your Gladiator Academy here in Ravenna. In fact, I shall become so good a gladiator that I will be asked to perform at the Colosseum in front of the Emperor!"*

Priscus now said, *"Thumelicus, come with me; we are going to the training yard where the first thing we must do is to strengthen your arms and back! To do that, you shall start by doing a minimum of twenty push-ups per morning, followed by another twenty at night. You shall increase the push-ups by two per day until you are capable of one hundred and twenty of them without a break and at any time! That shall be followed by you learning sword drills and practising the use of the gladius. You will be taught how to move and feint your blows in such a way as to completely hide your intentions from the man or men you are facing! You will also be taught to behave in the ways of respected gladiators and how to die in the way that is respected by Romans! When*

---

[36] Operator or main instructor of the Gladiator School or academy.

you are about to die, it must be with honour, and I shall teach you how to do that! Your training will teach you how to die bravely and to show no fear!"

And so, the older ex-gladiator and the boy he was training moved out into the training yard. In the yard were two poles. One of them had a swinging arm attached to the top of it. At the end of the arm was a length of chain that had a timber piece attached to it. Sometimes, the piece of timber would be replaced by a dummy to represent another gladiator. The structure was used by the training gladiators who hit the timber piece, which would swing out of the way and revolve to another point that was sometimes behind the training gladiator.

Thumelicus hit the timber piece with his gladius, and the training equipment moved to a point behind him. It was now that the cat-like agility of Thumelicus became apparent because he side-stepped and jumped in a circular motion, resulting in his again facing the piece of timber from in front of him. That resulted in Priscus yelling out, *"Very well done, my boy! I had no idea that you can already move so well! Keep it up!"* Next came the requirement for Thumelicus to perform his twenty push-ups. He completed the task with some difficulty.

Priscus said, *"My boy, tonight and tomorrow and the next day and even for the next few years, you shall experience muscle pains and aches which may make you think that you are going to die. However, it will only be your body adjusting to what you shall be asking of it from now on. Just ignore the pain and get on with your life, for pain is part of it. Remember, as long as you feel pain; you are alive.*

The second pole, called a palus, was a timber pole at which the training gladiators called novicius would practice moves like thrusting at it and hitting it with their shields and wooden training swords known as a rudus. To further strengthen his arms, Thumelicus was using the rudus, which was a lot heavier than the steel gladius the gladius used by both the gladiators and the Roman soldiers in battle.

Priscus said, *"Thumelicus, my boy, I am happy with the way that your arms are strengthening and the fact that now after nine months, you can do up to two hundred and ten push-ups without stopping for a rest! That is outstanding at any age, and you are not yet eleven years old.*

Now then, I shall give you personal instruction and practice in using the Roman short sword called the gladius! Please make sure that you always remember that the gladius is a stabbing weapon, whereas the long swords used by the Gallic and Germanic tribesmen are slashing weapons. When you are facing someone, who is armed with a longsword, get in as close as possible and stab your opponent to death before he can swing his long sword. Always remember that the favoured mode of attack by someone using a longsword is to make a sweeping arc either at the neck of his opponent or by using a swinging arc downwards from over his head towards the opponent's feet!

You will now be matched against others of your age and level of expertise in swordplay and the use of other weapons. Both you and your opponents shall be using the rudus for training purposes because we want you to build up your arms' strength further and because gladiators are valuable particularly the trained and combat-ready ones!" Thumelicus now found himself checked out very closely by the Medici[37] of the academy, who examined Thumelicus for any medical problems and to see if he could withstand training and combat rigours.

Priscus said, *"Thumelicus, I like the way you move, and I think that we should concentrate on getting you ready for two possible gladiator roles. Namely those of Samnite and Secutor roles. That shall, in due course, make you prepared to go against the dangerous retiarius (Net Man). Assuming that you are successful in these and other fights, it will make me a lot of money! With your catlike reflexes, you should beat all opponents, including the dangerous retiarius. Your training will intensify later this afternoon, now get some rest!"*

So, that afternoon after he had rested for an hour, he went on for the remainder of the day with his training. Thumelicus always surprised his opponents at the academy with his speed and agility. After training like this for almost a year, Thumelicus was approaching his eleventh birthday.

Priscus said, *"Thumelicus, my boy, you respond very well to training. You have natural cat-like movements, and you are very strong! I have been asked to provide entertainment for a group of Roman Senators here in Ravenna but not here at the academy; it shall take place in the amphitheatre in Ravenna tomorrow, and if you do well enough, you can be performing at the Colosseum in Rome in about twelve months from now. Tonight, is the eve of your first performance as a gladiator.*

---

[37] Medici was the medical officer for a group of gladiators or soldiers.

Therefore, you will be provided with a woman to fuck, even though you are only aged eleven at the moment! Please take advantage of all of this and do your very best tomorrow; the reputation of my Gladiator Academy is at stake!"

Sure enough, just as the final rays of sunlight appeared and twilight was approaching, a guard came to his cell and opened the door to let in a young woman who was to spend the entire night with him. As she entered, she introduced herself as Frida. She explained that the Romans had captured her during one of their Germanic longhouses' raids, which housed several families.

They instantly liked each other, and Frida removed the clasp holding her over-garments, which dropped away, revealing her naked body to the eleven-year-old Thumelicus. Thumelicus said, *"By Wodin, Frida, you have a marvellous looking body. I want to love you, but I do not know what to do. I need you to teach me what you girls want us, males, to do!"* Frida replied, *"Thumelicus, take off all of your clothing.'* He did so, and she came to him and spoke. She said, *"Tonight is the eve of your first fight, which could result in your death if you do not please the crowd!"* She now took his hand and placed it upon her breast.

She said, *"Gently manipulate my nipples and my general tits. Then I want you to put one of my nipples into your mouth; when you have done so, gently suck my nipple until I move your mouth to my other nipple. Then do the same to that one. At the same time, insert your index finger into my vagina and perform an up and down motion. That is what some people call finger fucking. I like having that done to me and having both of my tits sucked at the same time as I am being finger fucked because that is the way to make a woman want sex. When you get me ready for it, I will show you what else has to be done.*

Thumelicus did as she requested and inserted his index finger into her vagina while he was gently sucking her nipples. Sometime later, Frida was fast becoming aroused sexually.

She said, *"Thumelicus, stop what you are doing for a moment and then step backwards and look at me closely. Look at my tits, and you will be able to see that both of my nipples are now enlarged and sticking out erectly. Can you see what I am talking about?"* Thumelicus answered, *"Yes, I can see that your nipples have undergone a change, and they are now both elongated and erect.* Frida said, *"It is good that you can see that. It means that I am aroused now, and that now is the time for you to fuck me. Come to me, Thumelicus, and again finger-fuck me for a while as you gently suck my tits again."* She now reached down to his penis and gently stroked it. Thumelicus quickly became aroused, and his penis stiffened. Frida bent over and spoke. She said, come over here, my love and insert your prick into my vagina. I will help you achieve that. And so, the young couple made love and enjoyed each other's company.

After they had made love a second time, Frida said, *"Thumelicus, as you know, I am a slave, but what you may not know is that I had the same owner as a woman called Thusnelda who told me that her husband was called Arminius by the Romans and that her son is called Thumelicus. Was she your mother?"*

Thumelicus said, *"Yes, she was! She always looked after me, even though Romans constantly raped her, and some of them sodomised her. Her owner at the time was Titus Flavius Comptomius, and his wife was called Octavia. She was as harmful to my mother as Titus was and raped her using a dildo! I heard that my mother killed both of those Roman pigs when they were raping her at the same time! It is a pity that both of them have been killed by my mother because if they were still alive, I would find a way of hunting them both down and killing them!"*

Early in the morning, the guard returned to the cell occupied by Thumelicus, and he took away Frida. He said, *"Thumelicus, consume your breakfast and prepare for your coming fight!* Thumelicus ate his breakfast of oat-porridge and figs, and then he prepared himself for the coming battle. He dressed himself and made sure that he had on his chain-mail armour over his left shoulder, broad leather belt, and one greave. His weapon was the gladius, which was supplemented with his heavy Roman shield. His trainer and mentor, Priscus, arrived.

Thumelicus – First Contest

At the mid-morning time, a guard appeared at the door of the cell housing Thumelicus and spoke to him. He said, *"Thumelicus, it is time for you to entertain the Roman senators in the arena. You have been matched with a retiarius we call Olaf and that Gaul does not like Germanic boys one little bit, so expect a hard fight!"* Having said that, he escorted Thumelicus into the arena.

Thumelicus walked straight into the arena, just like both his mother and father before him; he was totally unafraid and looked forward to the contest. There were no cheers to spur him on, just total silence as he was being appraised by the crowd watching as well as the group of Roman Senators. Suddenly, there was a lot of wild cheering and applause for Olaf's benefit. He was now entering the arena. Both gladiators now addressed the crowd with the standard form of address, *"Hail Caesar, we who are about to die, salute you!"*

Thumelicus saw a retiarius who was only wearing a cloth tunic and did not have a helmet. His right arm was protected by a thick layer of linen which was held in place by leather strapping. In his right hand, Olaf was holding a net with which he always tried to entangle his opponents before dispatching them with the trident he was holding in his left hand.

He called out the Thumelicus, *"Hey young Germanic boy, today; you will die by my hand, prepare to meet your doom!"* With that said, he rushed forward while he deployed his net towards Thumelicus. Who simply jumped backwards and upwards while side-stepping at the same time. That caused the net deployed by Olaf to miss him completely. He was moving like a cat, and again, he jumped, which enabled him to strike his gladius into the back of Olaf's neck. Olaf fell to the ground and was lying prone, helpless to defend himself.

Thumelicus now looked up at the dais where the Roman Senators were seated. The eldest Senator held out his right hand and then turned it so that his thumb was pointing at the ground. That was the signal for Thumelicus to despatch his opponent into the after-life. He thrust his gladius forward, resulting in Olaf's spinal cord being severed just below his head, which killed him.

Priscus rose from his seat and called out, *"Very well done, Thumelicus! You have beaten a champion gladiator who Tiberius ordered to kill you! You have done my Gladiator Academy proud! Hail to Thumelicus, who is a champion gladiator at the age of eleven years! Long live Thumelicus, my champion gladiator!"* Thumelicus was amazed at how the watching crowd now completely changed sides and began calling out, *"Hail Thumelicus, the boy gladiator champion!"*

The guard whom he knew by sight and whose name was Lucius now escorted Thumelicus back to his cell. After a short time, Priscus came to him and started speaking. He said, *"Thumelicus, your training and your natural ability are such that your next contest in a year from now shall be at the Colosseum in Rome as you are good enough for that now. At the moment, I do not know who you shall be facing, but it will be someone from outside of my Gladiator Academy, just like today's contest!"*

Priscus now said, *"My boy, you have done very well, and I have made a lot of money because of your performance! As a victorious gladiator, you are entitled to have the woman of your choice to spend the night with you. You can choose from any of the slaves, and perhaps even some Roman women may like to be fucked by you. Is there anyone whom you fancy and can name right now?"*

Thumelicus said, *"Priscus, I want the young woman you provided me with last night. Her name is Frida."* Priscus said, *"Done! Now Thumelicus, I want to discuss your coming event at the Colosseum with you! You shall have to build up your strength, but we have a year to do so before you perform at the Colosseum, so we shall prepare you with constant fighting drills and strengthening exercises! So far, you have had one fight to the death, which you have won. You need to win at least one more so that the Roman crowds will call your name. When that has been achieved, I will start to portray you as what you are: a formidable warrior who is the son of the dreaded Arminius, the Destroyer of three Roman Legions! That is what I shall be putting on the notices about your next fight in a year from now!*

A year appeared to pass very quickly, and the routine for Thumelcus was to rise early, and in the training yard, he firstly struck at the piece of timber attached to a chain very hard. That always caused the piece of timber he had hit with his rudus to swing to a point behind him. He saw that happening, and because of his attention and his cat-like movements, he was able to quickly and gracefully turn with such speed that he was again facing the timber from in front of it.

He next performed his push-ups. Priscus was happy the Thumelicus could now perform one hundred and thirty of these exercises without breathing hard or stopping. Next, Thumelicus was given an opponent who was older than himself, and both of them were using wooden weapons. In the case of Thumelicus, he was using his very heavy rudus because it was helping to strengthen further his arms! Toward the middle of the day, Thumelicus was given a new opponent armed with a net and a wooden trident. He was a retiarius.

Thumelicus welcomed this constant practice against the dangerous retiarius because Priscus had told him that he would continue to be matched with that class of Gladiator in all likelihood. As always, his light-footed and graceful moments gave him a significant advantage over his opponents, even though he was aged eleven years. Priscus went to Thumelicus and spoke to him.

He said, *"My boy, I am so thrilled with your progress. It has been a year since your last fight, and you shall again be fighting in two days from now, at the Colosseum in Rome! You shall be taken to your new quarters under the Colosseum tonight. I am coming with you to make sure that no-one will interfere with you in any way."*

He continued with, *"I have been told that the Emperor Tiberius has ordered that you must die in the arena because he is concerned that you could unite the tribes of Germania and Gaul behind you and then wipe out Rome! As I have told you from the beginning, you must now win the crowds at these games if you wish to survive, for Tiberius wants you to die!"*

Thumelicus – the Second Contest

That having been said, the man and the boy finally arrived at the Colosseum and entered the areas where gladiators were housed in cells on the eve of combat. Priscus said, *"The retiarius whom you will face in the morning is a Gallic warrior, and he is quite capable, or so I am told. Tonight, you shall again be provided with a woman, but she will not be Frida because she is still in Ravenna. I will organise the sort of woman you may want. So, tell me, do you want another slave girl, or would you like to fuck a high-born Roman bitch?"* Thumelicus replied, *"I really would have liked to be with Frida, but if that is not possible, then I may as well fuck one of those high-class Roman women!"*

Priscus said, *"Consider it to be done, my boy, you will have your high-born Roman woman within two hours from now, and you shall have her all night! Even though both water and wine is being provided with your evening meal, do not consume wine at all tonight so that your movements will be completely unaffected when your combat starts in the morning! How I wish that I could get the Emperor Tiberius to attend the contest! So far, it appears that he does not like to attend the games! I am now leaving with my scribe to take bets as to the outcome of your fight tomorrow!"*

Having said that, Priscus and his scribe left. Priscus's writer had the duty of recording the bets. So, both Priscus and he went to the Forum, the inns and brothels where they knew that many people would be present who were willing and able to bet on the outcome of the games. The aim of Priscus was to engage people in conversation so that he could steer them towards the fun and betting for or against Thumelicus.

To achieve that, he appealed to the patriotic nature of Romans by saying, *"There shall be a fight between Thumelicus, the son of Arminius and a Gallic warrior! Thumelicus is now eleven years old, and he is very big as well. He moves like a cat! The fight between Thumelicus, the son of the destroyers of three Roman legions and the older Gallic warrior, shall take place at the Colosseum tomorrow at mid-morning!*

I am happy to take any bets against Thumelicus, the son of the traitor Arminius! There is no limit on how much you can bet against Thumelicus! I am taking bets now; this is my scribe who will record the details of the bets and the people making them!" That was immediately followed by members of the Roman public pushing forward to get their bets on, with many of them saying, *"Give me a bet of fifty sestertii against the son of Arminius!"*. *In contrast,* some others said, *"I bet one thousand sestertii against Thumelicus!"* Priscus was happy that the money was flowing in, and he knew that he now had to move quickly to provide Thumelicus with the woman he had promised him for the night.

He went to his Roman friend, Markus, and found that he had left for Egypt; he spoke to Markus's wife. Her name was Loretta, and Priscus knew that she was a woman of loose morals. He said to Loretta, *"I have a young gladiator who needs you tonight! Please come with me to the gladiator's quarters at the Colosseum and spend the night with him!"* Loretta said, *"How old is he, Priscus?"*

Priscus replied, *"He shall soon be twelve, and he has already killed his first opponent in the arena. His opponent was aged 21 years! He has already had his first woman, and she told me that he was excellent, sexually speaking!"* Loretta said, *"A young boy! Oh goody! I will be able to teach him to do what I like, and he will be able to fuck me many times during the night! How wonderful!"*

And so, Priscus led Loretta to the cell holding Thumelicus and then he introduced Loretta to Thumelicus. He said, *"Thumelicus, this is the high-born Roman woman I was telling you about. Her name is Loretta. I am sure that she will give you a good time! Just do not ride her all night long because you need to get some sleep!"* Loretta said, *"Priscus, I want you to provide us with a large washbowl of water and some towels!"* Priscus immediately supplied these and gave them to

Loretta. He said, *"Here is the washbowl of water and the towels that you have asked for. Is there anything else you need?"* He then left the couple alone.

No sooner had he gone than Loretta spoke to Thumelicus. She said, *"I am so glad to finally have a boy! A boy can give it to me a lot more than a mature man can! Iam undressing in front of you. I want you to also undress, and then I will teach you how to make love to a woman in such a way as to have her moaning with pleasure and to be asking for more. I am going to tell you what I want you to do and how to do it. Remember that it takes a woman longer to get worked up sexually than it takes for a man to become aroused sexually! I will teach you how to get it right!"*

Having said that, she removed her clothes and let them fall upon the floor of the cell. Thumelicus was instantly aroused by the sight of her fine slim body. She went to him and gently placed his head into her hands and guided it to her left breast. She said, *"I am now teaching you how to sexually aroused a woman. I want you to suck the nipples on both of my tits very gently! While you are doing that, insert your index finger into my vagina and slowly but gently perform your finger's up and down motion while it is in my vagina so that you are gently finger-fucking me while you suck my nipples."* Thumelicus did as he was instructed, and Loretta was happy.

A short time later, Loretta said, *"Thumelicus, my lover, please bring that washbowl of water over here as well as the towels."* Thumelicus did as she requested, and she proceeded to wash his penis and dry it without saying anything. She said, *"Lover, now come over here and wash the outside of my genitals."* That was done, and she said, *"come with me."* That resulted in both of them going towards the bed.

She said, *"Lie down on the bed, my love. I will squat over your face and then lower myself down until my vulva is touching your lips. When that happens, I want you to pull apart the vulva folds gently until you can see my clitoris. When you see it, place your lips around it and start to suck my clitoris gently! When you do that the right way, it will result in me gasping for sex, and I will then lean forward and place your prick into my mouth, and I will give you a very good time.*

After we have both suck-fucked each other for a while and we are both completely aroused, I will take your prick out of my mouth. After that, I shall bend over. That is your signal to come to me and fuck me from behind me. I want you to use long and slow strokes of your penis inside my vagina! I want you to fuck me slowly and thoroughly. Do you think that you can do what I want?" Thumelicus said, *"That I most surely can and will do!"*

Thumelicus placed himself flat on his back upon the bed, and Loretta went to where his head was. She lowered herself until her vulva was very close to the lips of Thumelicus, who located her clitoris and began to suck it gently. He had only been doing that for several minutes when Loretta leaned forward and placed his penis into her mouth, and she started sucking his prick. After a short time spent ding that, she took his penis out of her mouth, and she spoke to him.

She said, *"I think that may do us for suck-fucking each other for now. I am getting out of the bed, and I will bend right over. I want you to insert your prick into my vagina from behind me. I will guide your penis into my vagina, and then I want you to fuck me very slowly and completely! I want your penis inside of me now! Give me a good root, now, please!"*

During the curse of the night, they made love several more times, resulting in both of them falling into a deep sleep. The Next thing they knew was being awakened by the Roman guard. That resulted in both of them getting dressed and Loretta leaving. Soon afterwards, Thumelicus won his second contest.

Thumelicus the Third Contest

Thumelicus was eating his porridge breakfast when Priscus came in to see him. Priscus said, *"My boy, it is good to see you looking so well and formidable! You are now thirteen years old, and already, the Roman crowds at the games are beginning to call your name when the games start. That is good because it is an indication that you are winning the crowds1 It also means that Tiberius will have to show up sooner or later. After all, he is currently your greatest enemy!*

Today, your opponent is another Gallic warrior; the main difference between him and your previous opponent lies in his name being Gorontoafix. He is strong, and he uses a battle-axe in his contests. He usually rushes forward, making sweeping strokes at the head and neck of his enemies. He will also try to kill you by making a sweeping circular attack towards your head and own towards your feet! Now then, my boy, have you taken my advice and not consumed too much wine last night?"

Thumelicus answered, *"Priscus, you do not have to worry about me having had too much wine last night. The woman called Loretta, with whom you supplied me last night kept me busy, and she would not let me drink any wine for fear that it could upset my sexual performances. It was all I could do to satisfy her sexual demands, so drinking was out of the question! Therefore, I am completely free of the effects of wine!"* Priscus said, *"That is very good to hear me, boy, because you will be fighting Gorontoafiix in about a quarter of a day from now. How do you feel about fighting someone armed with a battle-axe instead of the usual net trident?"*

Thumelicus said, *"There should be no problem, my movements are unrestricted, and I feel great! In fact, I am looking forward to the contest!"* That made Priscus smile. He said, *"That is my boy! Make sure that you go and get him! Once you have him at a disadvantage, make sure that you look up at the dais so that you can see the signal of whether or not to spare the life of your opponent!"*

The next two hours passed more slowly because Thumelicus was left alone in his cell. He found having nothing to do was boring, so he went to sleep. The guard attending him awakened him and told him to prepare for his coming fight. He rubbed resin onto his hands to stop them from becoming moist and slippery. He put chain-mail armour over his right arm and shoulder only and obtained his gladius, making sure that it was free of defects. That having been done, he put on his greave, obtained his heavy Roman shield, and walked out into the arena.

As he walked into the arena, some crowd members recognised him and began to call out. They were yelling, *"Hail Thumelicus, the brave and mighty! Long live Thumelicus! May Thumelicus be the victor again!"* As he advanced further into the arena, the crowd taking up the roar in support of him became deafening. The crowd was yelling, *"Hail Thumelicus, defeat the Gaul called Gorontoafix!"* He then saw Gorontoafix coming out of the entrance to the arena opposite him. He saw that his opponent was unusually tall and that he had the strong features of the Gallic people. He noticed that Gorontoafix was moving slowly and deliberately. He now wondered about the speed of movement that his opponent had.

The trumpets sounded, signalling the start of the contest. After the announcer finished introducing the contestants to the crowd, a repeating chant came from it. The crowd was calling, chanting. It was saying, *"Hail Thumelicus, the wonder boy and son of Arminius the Mighty! Kill Gorontoafix the Gaul!"* Priscus also heard the chanting of the crowd, and it pleased him.

He was thinking, *"Better and better! The crowd is becoming very involved, and Thumelicus now has won the crowd, which openly supports him! I am sure that Thumelicus shall win. The only problem is that Tiberius does not appear to be here. That means that I must post more notices on the walls of all public places, including the Forum!"* both of the gladiators now looked up at the dias and shouted, *"Hail Caesar! We who are about to die salute you!"*

It was now that the contest began in earnest. Goronntoafix ran at Thummelicus with his battle-axe raised above his head. Thumelicus used his cat-like reflexes to jump out of the way and then jump back in close behind his enemy. As his opponent was running past him, he struck out with his gladius and succeeded in stabbing the Gaul in the small of his back in the kidney region. The speed at which Thumelicus won this victory at first stunned the crowd, which expected a much longer fight. The next reaction of the crowd was the chant of *"Thumelicus! Thumelicus, hail Thumelicus the mighty! Hail Thumelicus, son of Arminius, the destroyer of three legions! Death to the Gaul who cannot fight!"*

Thumelicus looked toward the dais. Although Tiberius was not present, a Roman general was, and he held out his right hand and suddenly turned his hand so that his right thumb was pointing at the floor of the arena. Thumelicus now obeyed the signal from the Roman general and the will of the crowd. He destroyed his opponent by sharply drawing his gladius across the throat of the Gaul. That resulted in the crowd getting to its feet and delivering standing applause. The crowd began to shout, *"Thumelicus, Thumelicus, Hail to you, Thumelicus."*

Meanwhile, Priscus heard the chanting, and he was happy that his gladiator had once again won his contest. To Priscus, the result was what he wanted because he knew that word of the ability of Thumelicus would now be sure to reach Tiberius. Now that Thumelicus was approaching his thirteenth birthday, Priscus thought that it was high time to publicise the next fight involving Thumelicus, which he had scheduled for five months from that time. Priscus put up many posters about the next fight on as many buildings, walls and bridges as he could find. He also paid twenty people to do the same things all over Rome and its surrounding villages.

After spending the next few weeks training Thumelicus and making sure that he was at full strength, Priscus was seen going all over Rome putting up more posters promoting the coming fight between *"Thumelicus – the mighty, the son of Arminius the god-like warrior who destroyed three Roman Legions and an as-yet-unnamed opponent.* The news of the proposed match spread like wildfire throughout Rome and reached the ears of Tiberius himself.

When he was told of this, Tiberius stated, *"So, the son of Arminius called Thumelicus is a very capable gladiator who moves with both speed and grace. His next appearance at the Colosseum should be a major event because many Romans openly favour him over other gladiators. In fact, Thumelicus is so popular that if he loses a fight, the crowd will demand that I give him the thumbs-up, and he will not die from my signal!*

Son of Arminius, Thumelicus is very dangerous because, if he is left alone, he could quickly unite the tribes of both Gaul and Germania into an unstoppable force that will crush Rome! He is so great a threat to the existence ofRome that he must be removed from this life, and we must also erase his memory as well! The last time Rome faced a threat as great as Thumelicus and his father, it was from Hannibal and Carthage! That cost Rome very dearly!

In order to save Rome, I shall see to it that the son ofArminius dies in the arena by fair means or foul ones if necessary! Even if I have to order, that he is forced to have drugs that will slow down his performance, enabling his opponent to kill him more easily! The only way to remove the deeds of Arminius and his legacy to the Germanic people is for his son to die as a gladiator.

The Germans consider that courage and honour of their warriors is all-important, so they may well accept the death of Thumelicus in combat as a gladiator! They have no way of knowing that Romans are unfairly stacking up the odds against their hero! The Gauls and Germanic warriors' presence in both Germania and Gaul is too great for us to take any chances!

I have been informed that Thumelicus is aged between thirteen and fourteen years! I want him dead; you hear me; I said that Thumelicus must die at his next contest at the Colosseum! He usually fights as a sector, and his usual choice of weapons is the gladius! As it is normal for the sector to be matched with a retiarius (Net Man), I want you to find me someone who is very good at throwing nets and who has both a lot of skill at arms and who does not have any mercy towards his enemies!

Matching Thumelicus with his Victor

The optio of the Praetorian Guard who was standing close to Tiberius spoke. He said, *"Sir, I know a fisherman who catches his fish using casting nets. He uses the nets to catch garfish and other species in the estuaries and bays. He also, at times, performs as a gladiator in order to supplement his income! When he performs as a gladiator, he performs as a retiarius. His name is Sextus Aemilius. Would you like me to organise him to be bought before you?"* Tiberius answered, *"Yes, optio, that is something I shall welcome, the possibility of finally removing the threat to Rome coming from Thumelicus. Find this man and bring him to me! He could well become the saviour of Rome!"*

Sextus Aemilius was found and bought before Emporer Tiberius. He walked into the room where Tiberius was seated, and using a clear, loud voice, he spoke. He said, *"Mighty Tiberius, my Emperor, I am here as ordered by you! What is it that you want me to do?"* Tiberius said, *"Sextus Aemilius, Rome is in great danger, and I think that only you can save Rome from impending disaster!*

Have you heard of the fourteen-year-old gladiator called Thumelicus?" Sextus said, *"Yes, my emperor, I have heard that he is the favourite of the crowds at the Colosseum now. If that is the case, you risk a possible uprising if you signal me to kill him after he has been fighting me! You can be sure that the crowd will want him to live! Still, there is a way for him to die without you being seen by the public to have had any part in it.*

I could just throw my net over him and immediately kill him because I shall be in fear of my life because of his ability! That should be accepted by the crowds, and Rome will be safe as a result! Now then, my emperor, I am not about to risk my life against a young gladiator of the ability of Thumelicus unless I get an enormous reward!

Tiberius said, *"Yes, of course, you must be adequately compensated for your great service to Rome of ridding the city from its greatest threat for a long time! When you kill him, you will end the worst threat to Rome, and that will also be the end of the legacy of Arminius!*

When you kill Thumelicus for me, your reward shall be a grant of four hundred acres in the Tuscany region.

I shall have a large villa built for you, and you will be provided with a labour force of fifty-eight men and thirteen women. As well, I have already instructed the treasury to give you ten thousand gold pieces as your fee for ridding the empire of Thumelicus! Now go and collect your money from the Treasury building! I have given you both an escort and transport to take the money to where you currently live. Does that satisfy you?" Sextus Aemilius said, *"Yes, my emperor, it does! I shall kill Thumelicus for you when we meet in the arena!"*

The Final Contest

Thumelicus was resting in his cell under the Colosseum. He was fully prepared for the contest that was about to take place. The guard, responsible for him, came to the cell and opened it. He said, *"Thumelicus, it is time for you to walk into the arena. Today, you are fighting a very good retiarius called Sextus Aemilius. He is not a slave; he is a free man and a Roman citizen. When he is not fighting in the arena, he is a fisherman who uses casting nets to catch his fish. Now come with me; I am escorting you into the arena!"*

Thumellicus and his guard moved into the arena. As they were doing so, they could see Sextus and his escort coming into the arena from the opposite side. Then the trumpets sounded. They were announcing that the contest was beginning. By now, both gladiators were in the centre of the Colosseum's arena. Both gladiators now preformed the salute to the Emporer of Rome. They both said, *"Hail Caesar! We who are about to die salute you!"*

Again, the trumpets sounded, this time signalling the gladiators to begin fighting. Thumelicus knew that he had to stay out of the way of the net of Sextus. As Sextus threw his net, Thuellicus was able to jump out of the way of it due to his amazing cat-like agility. Again, Sextus threw his net at Thumelicus, who jumped sideways and upwards, avoiding the net and getting into the position where he could stab Sextus in the back with his gladius. Having inflicted several stab wounds into the upper body of Sextus, Thumelicus was about to deliver a killing blow when Tiberius stopped the fight. The announcer called out to the crowd. *"Ladies and Gentlemen, there shall be a short break in proceedings while Emperor Tiberius speaks with both of the gladiators! These games will resume shortly!"*

The crowd began to chant, *"Thumelicus, Hail Thumelicus, the great warrior! Death to Sextus Aemilius the retiarius!"* While the crowd was chanting, both of the gladiators were returned to their cells. Tiberius spoke to several members of his Praetorian Guard.

He said, *"Decanus, take your seven other Roman soldiers and go to the cell of Thumelicus. You are to force-feed a large amount of this drug-laced wine into his mouth when you get there! Make sure that he gets a lot of it into his stomach! Unless we tip the scales in favour of Sextus in this way, Thumelicus will win the contest, and I cannot have that! I want the Germanic boy to be dead! Do you hear me? I said that I want Thumelicus to die, but he must die in the arena!"*

Soon after that had been carried out, the decanus in charge of the reported directly to Tiberius that the operation had been carried out successfully. Thumelicus was ready to face his doom. Upon hearing that, Tiberius said, *"Excellent! Bring Thumelicus back into the arena and do the same with Sextus. Then the contest shall resume, and we shall see Thumelicus die!"* The contest was resumed, and at first sight, it appeared that everything was the same as before, with Thumelicus easily avoiding the net of Sextus.

Then, the graceful movements of Thumelicus slowed and began to appear sluggish. Sextus again flung his net towards Thumelicus, who became caught up in it. Sextus rushed toward Thumelicus, who was still caught up in the net. As Sextus approached the net, Thumelicus managed to free his right arm and strike Sextus on the shoulder with his gladius. Sextus was severely wounded, but he suddenly thrust his trident forward into the upper torso of Thumelicus.

That bought joy to Tiberius, who now ordered the announcer to speak. He said, *"Ladies and Gentlemen, Emporer Tiberius has ordered that there shall be a month of games and worship of Jupiter and Mars! I both thank and congratulate the winner of the contest, Sextus Aemilius! Rome has been saved from a great peril!"*

After the Final Contest

Tiberius was happy that the major threat to Rome had finally been removed. He now felt vindicated for ordering the abandonment of all things Roman in Germania. For the Germanic people, things continued much as they had before the Romans left their country. Although the Germans retained some Roman rules and regulations, most of them were replaced with new laws which respected the Germanic outlook and way of life.

The former trade with Romans was replaced with vigorous trading between the Germanic tribes and their Gallic neighbours.

Centuries later, a confederation of Salii, Sicambri, Usipetes and Tencherti became established, and these were joined by the Alemanni, Chauci, Amsivarii, Cherusci, Chamavi, Bructeri and Chatti under one banner called Franks. Over time, that tribe became dominant in Germania and Gaul. They overran Gaul in 275 A.D. and eventually had the warrior king Charlemagne as their leader. Under his leadership and that of his father before him, the Franks took on and defeated other Germanic tribes and converted them to Christianity at the point of a sword!

Soon after the Germanic tribes had been converted to Christianity, there was an influx of officials from the early Roman Catholic Church. They bought with them the ideas of the southern European nations of how to deal with women. Until that time, the Germanic and Nordic woman's status was one of equality with her male counterpart. The church officials bringing their ideas of how women must be treated and combining that with the new Christian religion meant that the complete equality between the men and women of Germania and the Nordic countries was gone within two generations after Christianity had been introduced.

By the time of the Middle Ages, the full equality status had gone and, as had the husband's ancient Germanic tradition supplying his wife with a dowry. As well, the ancient Germanic practice of not allowing the private ownership of land was replaced by centralised ownership of land by the lords who became established under the incoming feudal systems.

Ende.

Bibliography

Greenwood, T., 1836 *The first book of the history of the Germans: Barbaric period,* Longman, Rees & Co., London.

Josephus, F., T., 78 A.D. *The Jewish wars: The wars of the Jews against the Romans: Book 2,* Publisher unknown

Wells, C., M., 1972 *The German policy of Augustus; an examination of archaeological evidence,* Oxford Clarindon Press.

CPSIA information can be obtained
at www.ICGtesting.com
Printed in the USA
BVHW041309141221
624031BV00014B/531

9 780648 821953